THE SCHOLAR AS HUMAN

THE SCHOLAR
AS HUMAN

RESEARCH AND TEACHING
FOR PUBLIC IMPACT

EDITED BY ANNA SIMS BARTEL
AND DEBRA A. CASTILLO

CORNELL UNIVERSITY PRESS
Ithaca and London

The publication of this book has been made possible in part by a grant from the Andrew W. Mellon Foundation.

Funding to make this book available open access was provided by Cornell University's Office of Engagement Initiatives.

Chapter 9: Copyright © 2018, originally published as "Making Law" by Gerald Torres, chapter 15 in *ResponsAbility: Law and Governance for Living Well with the Earth*, ed. Betsan Martin, Linda Te Aho, and Maria Humphries-Kil. Reproduced with permission of Taylor and Francis, a division of Informa plc.

First published 2021 by Cornell University Press

Library of Congress Cataloging-in-Publication Data

Names: Castillo, Debra A., editor. | Bartel, Anna Sims, 1973– editor.
Title: The scholar as human : research and teaching for public impact / edited by Anna Sims Bartel and Debra A. Castillo.
Description: Ithaca [New York] : Cornell University Press, 2020. | Includes bibliographical references. |
Identifiers: LCCN 2020011148 (print) | LCCN 2020011149 (ebook) | ISBN 9781501750618 (paperback) | ISBN 9781501750625 (epub) | ISBN 9781501750632 (pdf)
Subjects: LCSH: Community and college—United States. | Learning and scholarship—Social aspects—United States. | Humanities—Philosophy. | Education, Higher—Aims and objectives—United States. | United States—Intellectual life—21st century.
Classification: LCC LC238 .S36 2020 (print) | LCC LC238 (ebook) | DDC 378.1/03—dc23
LC record available at https://lccn.loc.gov/2020011148
LC ebook record available at https://lccn.loc.gov/2020011149

Contents

THE SCHOLAR AS HUMAN

Introduction

ANNA SIMS BARTEL AND DEBRA A. CASTILLO

There are two great and immiscible tides affecting faculty life in the early twenty-first century: publicness and specialization. The publicness tide would sweep faculty work toward ever-greater public engagement and purpose, while the forces of academic specialization drive faculty toward more rarefied, often particularized, often short-lived, and "productivity"-oriented ways of knowing and doing. While the strength of each tide varies by institution and even by discipline, most faculty are likely to encounter some variant of both of them. And in these encounters, they may find profound questions of vocation and identity that are both crucial to address and foreign to most academic environments. Thus, many faculty are left to find their own way on these seas, perhaps carried along by funding mandates or institutional mission shifts, without opportunity for deep, rigorous reflection on their own sense of purpose and its action on and within their scholarship.

This book tells two kinds of stories. One is the set of stories each scholar brings, connecting their personal and professional lives in new ways, so generating valuable insights about their own integrative processes as well as important articulations of what the academic professions might do to better encourage such integration. The other, larger, story is that of the communal matrix in which these integrative stories grew—an experiment in co-creating new spaces of connection that might support the kinds of deep integration we seek.

During the academic year 2016–17, the Mellon Diversity Seminar at Cornell University performed an experiment. We acknowledged from the start that our scholarly lives may be formed by our identity but that we often miss the chance to explore *how*—what that formation looks like if we create space for such reflection, if we develop a microculture of larger human purpose that explicitly embraces our scholarship as an instrument of our work in the world. In the process of this seminar, we explored what happens to us, to our work, to our sense of connection to one another, our departments, our institution, our disciplines. And most importantly, the seminar made space for us to explore these questions together, on the theory that a community of practice, a learning community, meeting weekly over an academic year, can constitute a Sargasso Sea, shaped by but not swept up in these tides of faculty culture.

The coeditors, Anna Sims Bartel and Debra Castillo, share a profound commitment to advancing the public work of academics, and their collaboration allows them to develop both of these kinds of stories. As a named chair in comparative literature, director of the Latino/a Studies Program (LSP), and (in 2016–17) director of the Mellon Diversity Seminar, Castillo's leadership in and with communities has led to the creation of the LSP as an "engaged department," with meaningful curricular pathways in which students learn the public purpose and practice of their discipline by working alongside community colleagues. She also reaches across institutional barriers to promote research and teaching on critical social issues, most lately centering on migration studies. She is an active mentor and partner for other faculty with public interests and an advocate for institutional change to promote them. Bartel, on the other hand, chose not to pursue the tenure track and has built a career as academic, activist, and administrator, making higher education more useful in the world. She does this through coalition-building, strategic intervention, and network-weaving, recognizing that shifting cultures and practices toward public engagement sounds very nice but is in fact the work of a movement, not an individual. Deeply rooted in the multidisciplinary field of service-learning and community engagement, she is one of few colleagues (and even fewer staff members) at Cornell with serious and specific scholarly contributions to public humanities as well. And, of course, she brings the valuable capacities of the professional administrator, implementor, and strategist, enabling us to "herd the cats" of this enterprise more effectively together. Most of all, this collaboration embodies one of the central principles it champions: there are many ways of knowing and doing, and the hard work of the world demands them all.

This book, then, tells these stories. One is the set of stories each scholar brings, exploring a disconnect or connecting their personal and professional lives in new ways. The other, larger, story is that of the matrix in which these stories grow, of an experiment that took place in 2016–17, co-creating new spaces of connection that might support the kinds of deep integration we seek. We find both of these stories essential to the public work of academics in the world as they help us conceptually and practically push past the binary ways of thinking that have limited us for too long (faculty/administrator, campus/community, academic/human). We tell the story of our experiment in the way that academics feel most comfortable telling our stories: as reflections of our scholarship, embracing advocacy, theory, research, and teaching. In this way, this book performs its purpose: instead of merely talking about how humanists might deepen their scholarship through more rigorous engagement with their own humanity, it demonstrates it in each chapter as each author unpacks his or her scholarly work to display its (and their) public and human commitments. In these ways, we see that scholarly rigor is enhanced by the story that undergirds it, that gives it tensile strength.

The year in which this seminar took place, 2016–17, was marked by the election of Donald Trump. The historical moment gives a specificity to some of the analyses in this book (as, for example, Sara Warner's discussion of the Bad and Nasty collective) but is in no way limited to Trumpism or the election results of that November. Instead, we are tracing a larger question: what is the role of humanities in supporting critical thinking today, in a world marked by changing climate, rampant inequality, and powerful autocratic tow in some of the world's largest democracies (Trump, Narendra Modi in India, and Jair Bolsonaro in Brazil)? We are working as well in the context of a theoretical turn in the humanities, largely fueled by feminist, people of color, and queer interventions, away from the much-critiqued strictures of deconstruction and toward a constellation of theoretical approaches that take affect, emotion, lived experience, and the human as their starting point.

This book may be of use to those concerned with the "heart of higher education" (see chapter 1); those invested in supporting whole, healthy, and productive faculty lives; those committed to nurturing positive workplace and academic cultures; those interested in evolving as "sentipensante" beings; and those exploring with us the relationships between scholarly generativity and multidimensional meaning-making.[1] We depend on but do not explicitly undertake the debates about forms of knowledge; our work rests in multiple ways and sources of knowing and a sense of rigor that is integrative of those diverse forms and voices. The experiment related here is an affordable one worthy of replication, with the understanding that its highly organic, emergent nature will generate other results in other places. And, in a most personal way, the essays shared here can offer guidance and example to other faculty adrift in the tides.

The Cornell Context

"Public engagement [has been] an enduring priority at Cornell since its founding," said David J. Skorton, then Cornell president, in October 2014, announcing the Engaged Cornell initiative, the largest financial commitment to date in the country supporting collaborative learning with local, regional, national, and international non-university partners. Cornell University is New York State's land grant institution; in this sense, it is like Michigan State and Texas A&M, whose mission was framed in the 1862 Morrill Act that provided grants of land to states to finance the establishment of colleges specializing in "agriculture and the mechanic arts." The rise of modern science was becoming clear, as were its multiple real and potential benefits, and legislators wanted to ensure those benefits would accrue to public, not only private stakeholders—to all of us, in other words. Land grant universities were to be the engines of public progress, bringing the benefits of research to the state through extension. This mission marched well with founder Ezra Cornell's famous assertion that this is a university where *"any person* can find instruction in *any study*, . . . mastering all the practical questions of life with success and honor."

In an era when the humanities constituted the sign and substance of an education, such a privileging of "practical questions" made perfect sense. But over time, the original theory of the university—as defined by Ezra Cornell and modeled in the 1862 land grant legislation—was left behind by new academic cultures, which increasingly rewarded theory over practice and narrowly specialized scholarship over work accessible to a broader public. By the late twentieth century, with the waning years of deconstructive thought still framing the way we did cultural studies, we could well have asked ourselves: Where is the human in humanities? The public in publication? As the humanities became less central to student learning and as their hyper-specialization eroded their public accessibility, we seem to have forgotten the essential practicality of humanistic study and practice. This book offers insights from those who remember.

In 2006, during a time marked by the slow decline of Anglo-European High Theory, a key group of scholars at Cornell were asked to think about this question of practical knowledge, first in a symposium, then in the book *Do the Humanities Have to Be Useful?*, edited by G. Peter Lepage, Carolyn (Biddy) Martin, and Mohsen Mostafavi. Behind this project was the prolonged so-called "crisis in the humanities" that Paul Jay and Gerald Graff characterize as the "Fear of Being Useful" (2012) and Mohsen Mostafavi in his brief preface characterizes as an anxiety around communicating the value and importance of the humanities, which we knew would have an impact on continued funding for our fields. William Keith more harshly adds that by and large this was a climate in which scholars "spend a good deal of time on critique of various kinds of oppression and injustice in society and culture, but they do so from a professional setting that is itself riddled with contradictory motives and interests," especially an interest in credentialing and career building. Thus, the question posed in the title of the earlier book presupposed a context in which the humanities were presumed to be useless, at least as far as popular media had it—or at least not immediately useful for practical purposes, hence subject to budget cuts. There was a fundamental contradiction that underlay much of this anxiety. While professionally we were rewarded for our research, within the university our work was understood to be useful insofar as we taught languages or critical analysis or added unquantifiable cultural capital for our students.

For many years, scholars at Cornell as elsewhere have largely defined their work within institutional exchanges that inhabit this contradictory space, and our extension into public life was limited to the subset of humanists who wrote op-ed pieces for newspapers or feature articles for *Huffington Post*, served as expert witnesses, provided a quote for the press, or—in unusual cases like that of the late Edward Said—became a familiar face on television. Yet these outliers only confirmed our core understanding of our roles as academics: to increase knowledge in our field through our research and to share that knowledge with our students in the classroom. Beyond concern with the bottom line, the 2006 book challenged us to remember a larger public purpose for our work and to imagine how scholars might reflect on our roles: as Mostafavi wrote, "to find relevant ways in which the humanities could engage with audiences outside the academy." Now, over ten years later—when, according to a recent Stanford study, the majority of US college students cannot discriminate between fact and fake news—many of us are still in the process of thinking about how "knowledge with a public purpose" impacts our individual research and pedagogical practices.

In this post-fact, post-profound-budget-cut climate, humanists are more than ever questioning the last hundred years of increasing specialization that walled off humanists inside the academy, transposed public issues like relationship and representation into theoretical jargon, and turned the arts and performance into increasingly professional careers. The question is no longer, or not only, whether the humanities have to be useful where the context is explaining to our administrations why our budgets should not be cut. We want to know *how* the humanities are useful and how they can be more so. We are urgently concerned with the role of the university in these changing times, and while that means addressing the institutional structures that award scholarly legitimacy to only a subset of research work, we are also concerned about our roles as scholars, citizens, and human beings in these settings. While once we might have been content (rightly or wrongly) to trust that our democracy could manage itself without significant support from us, we are now living in constitutional crisis. For many of us, a sense of civic calling is shifting the perennial argument about the publicness of our work, and we have few skills and few spaces for those negotiations. The Mellon Diversity Seminar became such a space, and the essays that it produced perform these negotiations.

For a number of us, such publicness is our life's work. Our engagements are nested in interdisciplinary collaboration with colleagues in far-flung fields. Here at Cornell, for instance, the synergies around environmental studies, climate change, mass incarceration, migration, digital humanities, food systems, and neuropsychology are important examples of research clusters in which humanists are making signal contributions. Other colleagues are invested in citizen humanities and its deep ties to both historiography and activism, or they are pursuing community collaboration on research projects in the humanities and performance in the arts. One among us is a law professor, living always at the borders between academic life and practiced power in the world. But all of us want to speak more clearly to and through the public purposes of our disciplines, and we continue to work together to find ways to do that.

The Seminar Itself

Over the course of the year, we met over salads and sandwiches every Wednesday for a luxurious three hours of passionate and engaged discussion. We began with the 2006 book as a way to ground our questioning. We immediately found that we needed to restate the question that book posed about usefulness. Instead of asking whether the humanities have to be useful, we were asking: How are the humanities currently collaborating with and supporting communities outside or alongside those defined by our professional practice? What are the literacies we need to cultivate, celebrate, and share, and where do those come from? How and by whom are meanings created and policed? What constitutes knowledge, and who has access to it? How do competing politics and public philosophies shape and inform our identities, purposes, and practices as scholars? How does engagement expand the topics and scope of inquiry and learning in our work? What kinds of conversations among the physical sciences, social sciences, and the humanities are necessary or enabled by these projects? In short, how do we conceptualize and practice a more human humanities? How do we as individuals, as professionals, as members of disciplines, institutions, departments, and local communities, navigate these questions, and with whom?

We knew that while our book needed to be one of the ways we would engage with these questions, it would not be the only product of the seminar nor its only public face. We also set up a complementary web page for the book, including short videos and public-facing previews of the chapters in this volume. We gave ourselves the following guidelines (derived from a Liberating Structures exercise we used to design our contributions):

- Our purpose is to be human, to expose the messiness of the humanities that doesn't require a consistent message.
- We have no overt agenda; let stories speak for self.
- Communicate passion verbally.
- Humanities is what we love; we love humans: the things they make, the things they do.
- Embracing love of humanities without town-gown divide is a radical gesture.

As we built community during our lunches, we also built new ways to collaborate with each other and our many communities. Accordingly, we supported the Bad and Nasty initiative (see chapter 8); participated in Freedom Interrupted, the Witness Project, and other arts projects in the community; and contributed to the discussion about the controversial *American Spolia* exhibit on Cornell campus. We organized a humanities "exploratorium" during Ithaca's biannual Streets Alive celebration in early May (features included Riché Richardson's Rosa Parks and Martin Luther King quilts and cards; Edward Baptist's runaway slave interactive web project; A. T. Miller's racial empathy booth; Debra Castillo's *New York Times* found poetry project; Caitlin Kane's coordination of a performance "trailer" from the play *She Persists*; and Ella Diaz's graduation photo booth).

We devised our own syllabus, together, attending to key books and articles that make the stakes of this conversation clearer, at institutional, disciplinary, and individual levels. A number of scholars have gravitated toward, and organized around, key national groups like Imagining America, or have celebrated the work coming from the Critical University Studies series published by Johns Hopkins University Press. We read and discussed selections from *Oral History and Digital Humanities: Voice, Access, and Engagement* (2014), *The Humanities and Public Life* (2014), and *Spreadable Media: Creating Value and Meaning in a Networked Culture* (2013). We looked at well-received monographs like Lani Guinier's *The Tyranny of the Meritocracy* and Steven Tepper's *Engaging Art: The Next Generation of America's Cultural Life* (2007). We asked ourselves about issues raised by David Cooper in *Learning in the Plural: Essays on the Humanities and Public Life* (2014), which uses examples from his work at Michigan State University, and Doris Sommer in her book *The Work of Art in the World* (2013), focusing on Harvard's programs in Latin America. The best of these works bring both theory and practice to the conversation, understanding that our impoverishment (intellectual, political, and ultimately fiscal) as a field can be traced to their divorce.

Some weeks found us passionately debating topics like trigger warnings, the liberal bias in academia, citizen science, democratizing higher education, academic career pathways of women of color, or the place of activism in our institutions. We had a provocative and deeply confidential discussion on "things we can't talk about." We shared personal and professional experiences in many formats, and for many of us the most important breakthrough came after weeks of meeting together, when Caitlin Kane facilitated a story circle for us.[2] And, in the winter term, our "course content" consisted of reading and commenting on each other's draft contributions to this volume.

While the 2016–17 seminar encouraged and supported long conversations over a period of time, it is not the only such initiative. Many of the members of this Mellon seminar are also core participants in courses and projects supported by Cornell's Office of Engagement Initiatives, including its Faculty Fellows learning communities in engaged learning and engaged scholarship, which Bartel leads. Many of us are collaborating on the Rural Humanities initiative funded by the Mellon foundation in 2018 to take advantage of our rural Central New York location in the service of active dialogue with our rural communities and local landscapes in mutually beneficial research, teaching, and engaged practice. This substantial internal and external support is not always available across the board to other colleges and universities. However, academic administrations everywhere can indicate their support for such reinvigoration of the humanities through naming and promoting applied and public humanities projects in ways that signal institutional support in all the ways such support is usually validated in academia. Convenings like ours (as seminars, gatherings of cohorts, story circles, book clubs, brown bag luncheon series, or cocktail hours) are possible everywhere—this kind of work is a matter of will rather than of resources.

Some Notes on Tone and Content

This volume shares the stories of our own work and its relationship to what matters; it hints at the backstory of the experiment that gave us the space, time, and support to weave these stories in the first place. We recognize that dialogue across difference is a core responsibility of the humanities but one we rarely practice; we feel keen disappointment that our insights regarding race, gender, class, religion, and intersectionality seem unavailable to mainstream America. We understand that conversations about patriotism, assault, solidarity, theology, and terror are all conversations with the humanities, and we fear that we have been mostly absent from those, at least in public. This book is a way to challenge those traditions of reticence, to lift up the engaged scholarship and teaching we do, and to model and negotiate what public work in and with the humanities looks like.

Importantly, not every story in here is a tale of "classic" community engagement—we take seriously the scope of public scholarship as work on public issues, for public purposes, with public partners, and / or creating public goods. Similarly, not every piece takes a colloquial tone; in some of our most powerful discussions, we negotiated critical issues of academicspeak and found important new terrain. As a result, some authors go further than others in the project of reframing their academic literacies for other publics. The resulting tone across chapters feels uneven because it *is* uneven, not just in this book but also in life. There is no standard of what a scholar should look like, nor a human, nor certainly a scholar as human. What feels uneven here is the diversity of forms of representation of self and scholarship, which all offer some kind of bridgework between academic and human domains but which mostly serve to remind us that these domains are not in fact separate. Those of us who think they are (the Platonic binary is strong with us), may expect a certain kind of presentation on either side of that "divide," and that is part of the problem.

What we try to do here is not force everyone's writing through the same garlic press of "public" or "human" tone but ask instead what forms and flavors emerge when diverse scholar-humans respond to the same invitation. We had a lively conversation, in fact, about precisely this issue in the seminar and found that the women of color in particular were adamant about their right to speak in the languages of the academy (which, after all, they had been forced to adopt to earn their positions and the scholarly respect they command)—without risking the assumption that talking like an academic means you are deracinated, less human. Many of us recognize that the move to "rehumanize" academic language can be seen as yet another power play by the white ruling class (reinforced by the dominance and normativity of and in historically white institutions): those who first created the pressures toward esoteric language as a mechanism of exclusion now see fit, on certain occasions and perhaps for very good reasons, to change the rules again. Resistance can mean refusal of the new rules just as it can mean refusal of the old—which is how many scholar-practitioners who use only plain speech view their commitments and how we invite you to view even the most "academic" of contributions in this volume. "You need soft eyes," as the teacher in *The Wire* reminds us. There are many ways to do public work, and, just as we all hope for generous, multi-tongued writing, we also hope for generous, multifocal reading.

This volume includes chapters by fifteen Cornellians from a wide range of fields and is divided into four sections: "Humanizing Scholars," "Engaging Artifacts," "Considering Resistance," and "Using Humanity/ies."

Humanizing Scholars

Anna Sims Bartel opens by the book by addressing the challenges and necessity of organizing for public humanities work on campus. While we usually reserve the term "community" for the non-university residents of a town, we don't get faculty engaged in public scholarship without on-campus organizing as well. Bartel traces some of the common challenges of supporting public humanities as a form of professional practice and offers mechanisms for overcoming them. Cornell provides a particularly fertile ground for such analysis in this moment, with deep currents of energy from multiple sources, advancing engaged scholarship in and around the curriculum in every college. She traces the frameworks of civic agency, civic happiness, civic professionalism, and civic loneliness as ways of understanding and legitimizing the intellectual and vocational pursuits that drive us, and as she explores networks as paradigms that can help us shift our institutions toward more welcoming and supportive practices.

The section continues with essays by Shawn McDaniel and A. T. Miller. The authors start from the premise that knowledge—as an abstract category with very real implications—is at the heart of what we do (in terms of meaning, of relationship, of care, as well as in terms of centrality and circulatory significance). Public scholarship invites us as scholars to think through what we do, how we do it, and what the stakes are, and these chapters offer differing views of what that might look like in a classroom, in public, across a life.

McDaniel is interested in thinking about how we as scholars experience, grapple with, and negotiate incessant epistemological crises as an inherent cornerstone of what we as humanists do. Acutely self-reflective, critical, and hyperaware, our research and pedagogy contextualize and problematize the diverse ways in which we as humans make meaning, connect, communicate, and engage. He discusses his experiences in diverse terrains that speak to some of the current epistemological and ontological divides we are experiencing, such as the rupture between conservative and liberal, rural and urban, and Ivy League and public. He offers examples from growing up in rural Oklahoma, teaching in the CUNY system, and being at Cornell.

A. T. Miller focuses on the theme of "presence" in terms of witnessing and being human to one another. It is a discussion, with some poetry, about why live theater still has a profound place, why actually going to the exhibit matters, why being in the classroom at the same time with each other is important, why going to Standing Rock or Seneca Lake or Washington DC on January 20 means something, why we are drawn to stand at historic sites, and why we talk about the novel after we read it or smile or roll our eyes at the poet after the reading. In our efforts to humanize scholarship, we carry always these twinned gifts of our histories and our presence.

Engaging Artifacts

The second section, "Engaging Artifacts," includes essays by Matthew Velasco, José Ragas, and Riché Richardson. Current events (e.g., legislative cuts to education; diminished protections from predatory lenders and for-profit institutions; continued closures of HBCUs) underscore a deep challenge to our institutions and to the most vulnerable members of the population that we serve. More and more we come to understand the relationship between North and South, and Northeast and Southwest, as fundamentally colonial. Colonial relations intersect and overlap with divisions of region. How our institutions adapt will determine where the possibility of safety, resistance, and reconstruction lie, and how we provide the space and the model for that adaptation is critical. It will also present deep challenges to civil society and the movements that transform it. Material objects are also the occasion for storytelling and for reflection on these complicated human relationships. In each chapter of this section, scholars' engagement with artifacts (ancient bones; ID cards; art quilts) serves as the mechanism of engagement with their publics or the invitation to engage.

Bioarchaeologist Matthew Velasco shares a devotion to work that tries to perform or communicate the embodied experiences of others, to access different subjectivities and alterities that are often silenced by time or by design, and to communicate the unimaginable realities of what it means to be human in different times and places—all through studying the bones of ancient peoples. Such a practice of imagining is a humanistic discipline in grave need of amplification and adoption. For Velasco, returning to the same place, day in and day out, injected his own temporal rhythm into the landscape.

José Ragas's contribution to this book explores the fervor to apply identification technology, in his case in post-authoritarian Peru, as an alternative way to study the contentious relationship between identification technology and "techno-invisible populations." The artifact of identification papers both constitutes the human and renders the human searchable, in ways that have profound implications for the lives of humans and the work of humanists.

Riché Richardson's narrative piece begins with a reflection on the black body, its conflation with slavery and labor and its framing as other, outside of history, intellectually inferior and incapable of producing higher arts. She explores questions of the human in relation to blackness, a problematic that continues to be engaged even now through the discourses related to social and political movements such as Black Lives Matter and #SayHerName. She tells stories of sharing some of her quilt art work on key historical figures in public contexts, acknowledging how this work has expanded the public audience for her work, allowing her to actualize teaching projects and to support other initiatives in public spaces in some instances, in ways that reflect her longstanding commitments to making a difference through activism and community service and outreach, commitments we think of collectively as forms of public scholarship.

Considering Resistance

Following directly from Richardson's contribution, the next grouping of texts (including chapters by Christine Henseler, Sara Warner, Gerald Torres, and Ella Diaz) attempts to articulate modes of political engagement that are conscious of oppressive systems and intentional about using the humanities to help us respond. These chapters are here not because of ideological position or evangelical fervor but because they demonstrate with clarity and precision what it can mean to be a sentient human-ist in the era of declining democracy and changing climate. The forms of resistance they offer (intellectual, legal, theatrical, and educational) constitute careful considerations of their place in their disciplines and the place of their disciplines in the larger society they study. This will startle some readers, no doubt, as the academy has come to privilege "objectivity" and "neutrality" as key qualities of academics (see Peters's afterword). But many humanists would argue, with Archbishop Desmond Tutu, that neutrality serves the side of the oppressor and that the greatest good must be considered carefully and enacted with courage. Each of these contributors understands the ethical and political dimensions of their work through lenses of rigorous analysis, but they refuse to stop there, also engaging economic, communal, cultural, and lived experiences in performing the work of humanities in the world.

Opening this section, Henseler's "Finding Humanity" focuses on the unheard voices of the Millennial generation and examines the interconnection between their social values and their understanding of the social impact of the arts and humanities. She talks about a recent teaching experiment that took her students out of the traditional classroom into a professional space, in which they were asked to energize the next generation with stories of changemakers, and then edit, typeset, and publish their book, *Generation Now: Millennials Call for Social Change*. This experiment not only invited students to claim their own agency and voice but also to grapple expressly with the relationship between what they study, who they are, and how they hope to live in the world as it is and perhaps as it should be.

The more obvious academic space in which we expect to engage with questions of justice and power is the Law School, and indeed Gerald Torres's piece does just that. He takes on the critical contemporary question of the domain of law in a constitutional democracy, looking at Black Lives Matter, Standing Rock, and immigrant rights activism. His chapter frames the challenges facing not just at-risk individuals but also, crucially, what he calls at-risk institutions.

Sara Warner writes about Bad and Nasty (aka Bad Hombres and Nasty Women), a loose-knit national coalition of academics, artists, media makers, web geeks, designers, writers, rebels, and concerned citizens who, shocked and appalled by the results of the 2016 presidential election, began to plot a grassroots guerrilla theater action for February 20, 2017, called Not My Presidents' Day. What began as a small collective of friends soon swelled to more than nineteen hundred members who staged upward of sixty protest events across the country and around the globe. In performances of democracy that reverberated with the Women's Marches, airport protests against the Muslim travel ban, spirited town halls on the Affordable Care Act, and rallies to denounce immigration raids, members of the Bad and Nasty collective staged ingeniously inventive "patriot acts" to oppose the discriminatory policies of the Trump administration. Patriot acts are spectacles of civic engagement and civil disobedience that dramatize participants' desire for a more just and inclusive society. As a scholar of theater for social change, Warner's integrative and historical vision offers useful insight into this form of political engagement.

Equally intent on analysis of popular culture, Ella Diaz asks us probing questions about how we understand internet memes, both as a by-product of visual practices and as a development coming from theatrical traditions. How does one begin to explain to anyone other than a humanities scholar, let alone people born at the turn of the century, the significance of cultural and visual studies in their everyday lives? What is the impact of the images that surround us, that we stare at on smartphones and other screens, occasionally looking up to make sure we are not hit by cars or collide with other people moving through the *real* world? What is the power of an image combined with simple text, so recognizable that it is merely skimmed yet remains impossibly loaded with meaning? These are core questions of cultural studies and, we may agree, foundational capacities for understanding the world, let alone navigating or resisting it. If higher education is indeed education for civic life, then the academic practices of unpacking cultural texts are critical tools for engagement.

Using Humanity/ies

The final section of the book includes contributions by Caitlin Kane, Bobby J. Smith II, and Debra Castillo and Carolina Osorio Gil. Political scientists, sociologists, and movement scholars often overlook the role of the arts, poetry, history, and performance, as well as cultural studies in the broadest sense, in community organizing and social justice work. As the preceding section offers ways to consider political resistance to injustice, this section offers examples of scholarly and human engagement for social justice, through collaborative action as well as through the gathering and analysis of stories.

Caitlin Kane looks at documentary theater, coming back to a production of Emily Mann's *Greensboro: A Requiem* that she did with an ensemble of Chicago Public School students in the summer of 2015. She is particularly interested in the intergenerational and intercultural exchanges that became the core of that experience for all of them and in the ways in which the members of the Beloved Community Center, their chief collaborator, modeled collective resistance and modes of deeply engaged public intellectualism for both her students and herself.

Bobby Smith turns our attention to food justice, arguing that in contrast to most studies of food justice that center in food deserts in urban or rural spaces like Detroit, Michigan, or Grafton County, New Hampshire, little is known about how the movement is realized in communities with more vibrant food scenes. In Ithaca, New York, local, healthy, and organically grown foods are a way of life and offered through a number of outlets such as farmers' markets, community-supported agriculture, grocery stores, and restaurants, but low-income people and people of color still struggle to access it. Using food justice as lens, Smith interprets the story of a community farm in Tompkins County, New York, to explore how a farm uses food justice as a way to counter issues of race, class, and food in Ithaca.

Debra Castillo and Carolina Osorio Gil, in their coauthored chapter, use the small arts and educational organization CULTURA Ithaca as a case study, like Bobby Smith uses the community farm, also looking at the challenges of organizing in communities characterized by small numbers, heterogeneity, and a high degree of transience. CULTURA as an organization is now associated in many people's minds with providing support for homeless individuals, victims of domestic violence, undocumented and documented low-wage workers, migrant farmworkers, and runaway teens, and helping families with young children gain access to much-needed services including food stamps, emergency housing, health care, health insurance, and financial assistance. However, its roots are in the arts. The experience of CULTURA tells us that the most powerful tool for building bridges across diverse participants is the personal narrative. When people have the opportunity to hear each other's stories, whether through theatrically staged productions, shared cooking, gardening together, decorating an altar, or informal conversations, they are more quickly and more successfully able to work together toward a common goal.

The book concludes with an afterword by Scott Peters, former codirector of Imagining America and professor of development sociology, in which he makes a case for the prophetic roles, visions, and voices of public scholars. He opens with a description of "a particular way of understanding how trustworthy knowledge and theory are discovered, produced, and developed—a way that's usually described as being 'scientific,' 'disinterested,' and 'objective.' In dogmatic versions of this way of knowing, we are required to bracket or dismiss our . . . standpoints and worldviews, our beliefs and values . . . our humanity." He further argues that "dogmatic advocates of this way of knowing have succeeded in establishing . . . a norm in the academy that encourages—even celebrates—a sharp separation of the identities of *scholar* and *human*." That separation is what we are seeking to undo, by "taking up the task of (re)connecting and (re)integrating our identities as scholar *and* human." Peters offers a close reading of a historical treatise addressing exactly these questions in the 1930s; then, as now, there was interest in making sure that teaching and research could better serve students and their world by being "co-ordinated with human needs." Peters has discovered and examined "a hidden history in the land grant system of the embodiment of the scholar-as-human aspiration that is closely (and always everywhere, imperfectly) aligned with the prophetic project of building and sustaining a democratic way of life." What we did in our seminar, what we invite others to consider doing, is to bring together and lift up the prophetic stories, to "learn from and with the prophets who are already among us." Such stories "don't just offer visions of what can and should one day be. They also offer critiques of what is. And they illuminate paths for moving from what is to what can and should be."

Notes

1. "Sentipensante": Laura I. Rendon, *Sentipensante (Sensing/Thinking) Pedagogy: Educating for Wholeness, Social Justice, and Liberation* (Sterling, VA: Stylus, 2009).

2. Story circles are a method of sharing stories among participants, with specific guidelines to facilitate honesty, courage, and vulnerability. They are also a long-time staple of deliberative democracy and key in community organizing, as people can hear the perspectives of others and see patterns without intervention. Roadside Theater has articulated formal guidelines and a usage statement about story circles.

PART I

Humanizing Scholars

As the epigraph to his important 2009 Kettering publication *Civic Agency and the Cult of the Expert*, Harry Boyte quotes Elizabeth Coleman, then president of Bennington College: "Over the past century the expert has dethroned the educated generalist to become the role model of intellectual accomplishment. While expertise has had its moments, the price of its dominance is enormous. . . . Questions such as 'What kind of a world are we making?' 'What kind should we be making?' and 'What kind can we be making?' move off the table."

These questions are inherently human questions, concerned with the well-being of ourselves, our families, our society, our planet. They are questions of most extraordinary urgency today, questions that many of us are struggling to relegitimize in the scholarly contexts of academia.

This work of re-legitimation is complex: it involves shifting minds from entrenched positions; transforming institutional systems from historical traditions; transplanting networks of substance where we once grew hierarchies of prestige. In short, it is the work of humanizing the academy.

Whether or not we buy the arguments of nostalgia—which certainly have strong roots in the origins of US higher education—we can all agree that right now the conventional divorce of values, desire, and love from domains of rigorous scholarship is causing trouble. "Neutrality" now means complicity with the fall of democracy and the rise of the oceans. A form of scholarship in which, for example, the interests of users are not engaged in design of a public space, or in which arguments about racial history are divorced from their lived consequences for the bodies of living people, is newly visibly problematic. The dimensions of human experience are more essential than ever in this era of rampant inequality and risk, and if the engines of higher education can't engage them, we consign ourselves to irrelevance.

Relevance, then, and usefulness and meaningful engagement with the world begin at the level of the individual scholar. We all know people whose research was turned by a sense of urgency or importance, and we all know people who were subject to reprimand because of it. The research on this topic is compelling. But what does it mean for us, humanists with public interests, at the only university that is both Ivy League and land grant?

We began by exploring these questions in unfamiliar languages: what does it mean to "live divided no more?"—to be a human scholar, a scholarly human, someone whose intellectual work is aligned with their civic and soul work? We had many answers, explored here: it means engaging our histories in open and public ways; claiming our histories and identities and values; using words like "love" and "care"; committing to integrity. But it also means network-weaving, relationship-cultivation, and tending to one another as humans as well as colleagues. For us, it meant sandwiches together. It meant, not infrequently, tears. It meant checking in on job searches, on family health, on disappointments and frustrations as well as joys. In these chapters, we explore these foundational questions and model some of our engagements with them.

CHAPTER 1

Humans as Scholars, Scholars as Humans

ANNA SIMS BARTEL

> The thing being made in a university is humanity . . .
> Underlying the idea of a university—the bringing
> together, the combining into one, of all the disciplines—
> is the idea that good work and good citizenship are the
> inevitable by-products of the making of a good—that is,
> a fully developed—human being.
>
> —Wendell Berry
>
> How can higher education become a more multidi-
> mensional enterprise, one that draws on the full range
> of human capacities for knowing, teaching, and learn-
> ing; that bridges the gaps between the disciplines; that
> forges stronger links between knowing the world and
> living creatively in it, in solitude and community?
>
> —Parker J. Palmer, Arthur Zajonc, and Megan Scribner

Anna Sims Bartel's dissertation advisor once said to her father-in-law, "Anna's problem is that she is part activist, part administrator, and part academic." He replied, as she would have: "Exactly. But why is that a problem?" As someone passionate about the work of story in the world, Anna earned her PhD in comparative literature at Cornell and has put it to work trying to make higher education ever more useful in the world. She does this through faculty roles, consulting, and public humanities initiatives as well the development of community-engagement centers at several institutions of higher education in cold, white places (upstate New York, Maine, and Iowa). Currently Anna serves as associate director for community-engaged curricula and practice in Cornell's Office of Engagement Initiatives, where she works on advancing faculty growth and network development in engaged scholarship, teaching, and research. Her life's work is to transform higher education toward greater public engagement and usefulness, through structural, systemic, cultural and relational change. Anna's current research interests are broad and include social change and transformation; cli-fi; the US agrarian novel; and, of course, civic engagement. Her most accessible publication ("Why Public Policy Needs the Humanities, and How") appeared in 2015 in the Maine Policy Review, *and her recent work focuses on "demo-cratically engaged assessment." She works at and builds out the intersections of social innovation and civic engagement and networked models of faculty development. Anna enjoys the things that support chronic hope: the chaos of her young family; being in, on, or near moving water; the smell of dirt and the good things that grow in it.*

Her chapter here aims to provide intellectual framing for this project as a whole: as a reflective practice, a faculty development opportunity, a community-building moment, an institutional transformation initiative. She lays out discrete ways of thinking about civic professionalism, civic agency, public happiness, and civic loneliness, weaving them together into an argument for transforming our institutions and practices of scholarship.

I used to do an exercise with my students, as an introduction to the role of universities in US culture. I asked them to close their eyes and picture a college professor, then, keeping their eyes closed, to describe the professor. I wrote on the board what they envisioned: an older man, white, wearing a cardigan with elbow patches or a bow tie or both, who has a drinking prob-lem and may or may not be sleeping with students. He is probably lonely and divorced. His work is abstruse and of interest to few people besides himself. Then I asked them to open their eyes and describe the college professor in front of them: also white but female, just thirty, with purple cat's-eye glasses and short, spiky, blondish hair. Also: with a husband, two dogs, and commitments to various local boards. The class was on concepts of work as service, and it involved each student partnering with a non-profit for a semester-long internship to explore how they might connect the issues they were passionate about with paid work to sustain them more richly in life. And every Tuesday night we would gather to discuss the read-ings: theology, feminist theory, educational philosophy, sociology of work, poems, and stories. In short, we were using interdisciplinary humanities to learn reflection, deliberation, and ethical engagement with the world, understanding our work choices as a core component of our human being. That's higher education too.

These questions of the relevance of higher education and its faculty have new urgency in the face of rising tuition costs and declining public support for higher education (fiscal and otherwise), even more urgency in light of the assorted catastrophes we are facing in the world. Higher education has produced faculty who live divided lives (Boyte and Fretz; O'Meara; Palmer; Snyder-Hall), and reconnecting the pieces—reason and emotion, theory and practice, public and private—seems essential if we are to move on productively. These are not new ideas. The 2007 Heart of Higher Education conference and its 2018 follow-up (both from Parker Palmer's work) created important national forums for these discussions; the Democratic Engagement White Paper from Saltmarsh, Hartley, and Clayton laid out a case for the civic component of this; Sandmann and others have offered insights into how we can "create academic homes" for public and engaged scholars. The Fetzer Institute, the Kettering Foundation, the National Science Foundation, the Association of American Colleges and Universities, Imagining America, Campus Compact, and a wide variety of other national organizations have supported inquiry into these same themes. All of us are asking questions: How can we make engaged scholarship, or in our case engaged humanities, more relevant and better understood? How can we imagine a new reality, one in which more faculty are engaged, curious, and connecting their public aspirations and professional work in productive ways? And, most importantly, how can we actually shift faculty and institutional cultures to invite and enable such healthy, whole engagement as norm rather than exception?

The Mellon Diversity Seminar at Cornell University sought to do just that. We recognize that change is more than individual, that learning communities can support individual change even as they shift expectations and understandings for the group as a whole. We believe that the kinds of shifts necessary are cultural and institutional, professional and personal, perhaps even spiritual for some. Our interests are diverse and perform in many ways the kinds of connections we seek to lift up. In exploring our theme of "Scholars as Humans: Enacting the Liberal Arts in Public," we addressed issues including identity (conceptually, but also literally, as one studies focuses on governmental ID processes); slavery and its living legacies; the role of theater in promoting social change; social movements and "demosprudence"; the radical pedagogies of a Brooklynite Latino goat farmer; local collaborations with Latino/a communities; the ethics and practices of trust in rural Peruvian archaeological digs; the experiential impacts of physically visiting Underground Railroad sites; youth-driven collaborative urban theater; naming and talking about the things we cannot talk about; and, of course, the larger questions of the role of the humanities in public life and in our lives. We talked and ate; we each designed and led at least one session; we shared and responded to one another's writing.

Our project was designed as it was—a small, year-long weekly seminar, with lunch—partly because the format is comfortable for academic humanists and partly because the structure of a learning community, a community of practice, a community of transformation, is also comfortable. Our process stood in contrast to conventional methods of institutional change-promotion: counting on "aggregation of individual changes," thinking "in terms of scale and speed," and staying focused primarily on "top leaders" and "problem-solving." Instead we chose to emphasize structure and process, relationship, and "getting the questions right" (Block, 74–75). We recognize the dialectical relationship between individual and communal transformation, and we understand that we seek both. We further understand the tension and interdependence between what Adrianna Kezar, in her book *How Colleges Change*, calls "first-order changes" (those dealing with relatively straightforward shifts, say in pedagogical technology or dissemination strategies) and "second-order changes" (deeper shifts in values, attitudes, or culture). The breadth of institutional change we imagine will require both, and there is much energy at Cornell already being put toward first-order changes, particularly through Engaged Cornell and the Center for Teaching Innovation. Our seminar, then, can be described as working toward second-order change, building networks and communities that we hope and believe will lead to lasting systemic shifts in our work as scholars and humans.

As a staff member with Cornell's Office of Engagement Initiatives, which stewards Engaged Cornell ("advancing Cornell's mission through community-engaged discovery and learning"), I work at the intersections of higher education and public life, supporting faculty who seek to engage with their communities in learning how to do that better. Some do it for enhanced student motivation and learning; some do it out of their own sense of identity and commitment to the world; some do it for a sense of professional contribution, as a way to live out the public purpose of their discipline (Saltmarsh). And while I can and do provide support and deliberative exploration across these arenas of pedagogical, civic, and vocational concern, individual or first-order change is rarely enough if it's counter-cultural. Culture change, or deep second-order change, is what we're after ultimately. Faculty learn best from their peers both in terms of technical or practice dimensions and in terms of courage and conviction, so the creation of peer learning communities is a vital component of what I do. We see these communities as networks of engagement and support, enablers and encouragers of the brave and curious work of building community across difference. In such communities, as we saw in our Mellon seminar, people come to trust one another and one another's shared commitment to public purpose, and the community becomes a space of refuge, exploration, and transformation.

Peter Block says that *"community . . .* is about the experience of belonging . . . to belong is to be related to and a part of something." But he also offers a second meaning: "to belong to a community is to act as a creator and co-owner of that community. What I consider mine I will build and nurture. The work, then, is to seek in our communities a wider and deeper sense of emotional ownership; it means fostering among all of a community's citizens a sense of ownership and accountability" (Block, xii). In higher education, this means supporting a transformation from "the isolation and self-interest within our communities into connectedness and caring for the whole" (1). Even caring, as a concept, engaging heart and body as well as mind, flies in the face of our cognition-oriented, technocratic cultures of institution. Since Plato, academe has been relegated to provinces above the neck, when processes of knowing in fact depend heavily on passion, affect, and psychological comfort. These reconnections, fundamentally, are the challenging, hopeful, essential work of community engagement within higher education, and it is what our seminar was designed to nurture.

Building Community and Achieving Cultural Change

Change efforts can be sorted in many ways, by exploring the depth or nature of a goal as well as its process and ethics. A key consideration in their success or failure often stems from their engagement of multiple stakeholders, or, conversely, the extent to which they appear to be a top-down mandate. Although many high-level articulations of the shift to an engaged campus or an engaged faculty presume a sweeping change, some sort of lock-step progress involving "nothing less than a radical reordering of the nature of faculty work from the individual to the collective, from the personal to the social" (Plater, 158), the reality is that such an approach may be counterproductive, at least if faculty see it coming. The cultures of academic freedom that mark higher education and differentiate it from most other professions assume that our collective is made up of our individual contributions and that we should trust one another to be wise and brilliant and to offer contributions that will in some way enrich us all. Moreover, "higher education institutions, as social institutions, are supposed to be long-standing and support an enduring mission" (Kezar, 62). Even change efforts that are about reorienting "toward a founding mission" (as in the case of Engaged Cornell and similar initiatives elsewhere) may find themselves run aground on disagreements over the merit of the mission and its drift over time.

Two strong alternatives present themselves: organizing, as in social movements, and network weaving. We find them symbiotic and use network theory for its apparent rigor and data-driven-ness (using the master's tools, so to speak). Contemporary network theory suggests that different others in relationship can achieve valuable change more efficiently together than they could separately, and often in unpredictable ways; positive change that serves us all is more often, some theorists and practitioners claim, the result of vibrant, generative social networks than of well-executed administrative plans (Wheatley and Frieze). Plus, as the logic of human behavior would dictate (and as my own experience bears out), faculty tend to fear the loss of their freedom, especially to agendas they did not design. Their perennial tension with administration makes engagement by fiat, by appeal to institutional mission, untenable and unwise as a standalone approach.

What we seek to do, then, as we make our path toward the commonly desired end of academics with a public purpose, in hopes that "we might become a healthy people in a healthy land" (Berry 2002), is to incite in each faculty member engagement with his or her core purposes and fullest humanity. This is not unlike the Courage and Renewal work of Parker Palmer in that it is grounded in relationships of safety and bravery; we connect those text-driven reflective approaches with Liberating Structures that surface wisdom from many voices, to create heart-forward spaces of rest, introspection, deep listening, rigorous critique, and endless possibility. In such communities and in the relational work of network weaving (ideally conjoined in long-term learning communities like our Mellon Diversity Seminar or the Engaged Faculty Fellows cohorts I lead), we find the seeds of both enhanced individual engagement with the world and potential collaboration toward ever greater impact. "On the one hand, a campus must find ways for the work of individual scholars to fit into a collective purpose and, on the other, find a worthy purpose for its collective work" (Plater). Such alignment builds community even as it honors the basic human motives and propensities of each of us: to desire a fuller understanding of our own gifts and inclinations, to fear the loss of what we value, to be of use.

Why This Is Hard

Universities are difficult places because they have inherited a range of purposes, both implicit and explicit, including generating new knowledge, protecting and transmitting particular knowledges and cultures, training leaders, contributing to the public good, and advancing technological and economic progress, both broadly and in our home communities. Even at Cornell, where we have a specific contractual and historical public purpose, we have struggled to adhere to it in the face of rising pressures toward external funding, ranking systems, and disciplinary norms. Engaged Cornell's framing documents declare its intent to "reorient the university toward its founding mission of knowledge with a public purpose." Many faculty would contend that the knowledge they pursue and create is all about public purpose, but they also face enormous pressures to not waste time exploring those, even if public purpose is the force that gives our work meaning. Scholarly work is technical, quantifiable, our reward system seems to imply, rather than relational, and what matters is the sharpness and volume of what we can do *in* our field rather than the usefulness of what we can do *with* our field. Humans want to be useful, and our scholarship is often, for many of us, a way to "be of use."[1] So how did we come to this? How did we come to a place and a time where it is not only humorless but downright important to claim, as we do, that scholars are humans? Of course, we are! But by guiding our work away from its core social purposes, by devaluing more diverse ways of knowing and being, our institutions seem designed to make us less so.

Through promotion and tenure pressures, faculty are often channeled away from larger public interests and practices and toward the hyperspecialized, profoundly narrow, often theoretical interests of the disciplines (Ellison and Eatman). There are several reasons for this: one is inertia, which at this point represents a serious force in the academic mainstream; another is how "excellence" is defined; but another is that our power derives from our inscrutability. As Maria Regina Kecht reminds us in *Pedagogy Is Politics*, to demystify our work, to articulate it clearly, is to hand over the reins of power. Our value lies in the inaccessibility of our knowledges, in our doing what no one else can do, and perhaps what no one but our peers can understand well enough to properly critique.

This seminar is about healing these rifts between mainstream academic culture and the interests of humans, both individual and societal. In it, faculty from various disciplines explain and explore the intersections of their scholarly interests with their human lives and identities. We are aware that our own histories drive and shape our pursuits with force and specificity, and we are often aware of the sacrifice involved in stripping our scholarship of those personal dimensions. *It is relevant!* something in us shouts, *that I come to this work through my particular life, and for it to be my work, then, I need to offer it to readers through my particular lens.* But the academy has only so much tolerance for "other" voices, for approaches that are not recognizably "scientific," say, or for "soft" topics like children or justice or love. In technocratic cultures that make little or no space for the multiple dimensions of scholars as humans, that reward publication over impact, and that define the profession as narrowly research-driven, the fullness of a scholar's humanity suffers. And, we would argue, humanity as a whole suffers too. What we want to ask here is what does academic work look like if we do not insist that it be cored like that? What might it look like whole?

The question itself poses serious challenges, especially to those more senior faculty who have successfully built a career that engages more of themselves. We have among us several rock stars, in law, history, and African-American studies, for example, and in each case they have been able to cultivate both theory and practice of disciplinary engagement for rewarding and rewardable teaching and research. These are unusual cases, and we seek to learn from them, both to guide better future work in ourselves and our colleagues and to understand more richly how academic work can serve public life. There are twin aspects of this project: making space for and celebrating the scholar as human, but also lifting up the work that such human-scholars do. Their work is engaged with the world, it learns from the world. It seeks to "give back" but not in oversimplified ways: we believe in the complex equation positing both that we are better scholars when we engage in the world and that perhaps, in being better scholars, or at least by being present with our particular tool kits, we can make a better world. In short, we are performing and exploring the public humanities.

Why a Public Humanities Community Is Necessary

Our seminar met on November 9, 2016, the day after Donald Trump was elected president of the United States. We were traumatized, disbelieving, despairing; the hard work the world so obviously needs seemed not only halted but driven back. Facing climate change, nuclear threat, constitutional crisis, loss of health care, deportation of loved ones and students, egregious denigration of most vulnerable social groups, we were all asking what else we could do, how our work mattered in the world. Some of us had already designed our work to align with our sense of greater purpose in the world. And all of us needed to revisit these questions and to imagine what a deeper integrity might look like.

We agree: the humanities are of greater importance than ever before. The forces that threaten us now include popular cultural metanarratives that are profoundly damaging; disrespect for truth and inquiry; the devastation of journalism, a public-humanistic mainstay; ethical and constitutional dilemmas our nation has never seen; rampant, hateful discrimination; revival and reverence of Nazism; and actual torch-bearing professions of hatred. We are witnessing (and no doubt participating in) stark contrasts between "us" and "them," including a failure of empathetic connectivity or awareness that our roles might be reversed.

The humanities are where we learn such empathy, where we practice the skill of walking around in others' shoes, as Martha Nussbaum's classic *Cultivating Humanity* illustrates. But our fields do more than that. They are the home turf of ethics, of history, of concepts of war and peace and religion and otherness. They teach us, as Paulo Freire points out, that reading the word is reading the world, and, as Peter Brooks points out, that both activities must be pursued with rigorous training and good faith. We can practice, with texts, attending to specifics, to details, reading with integrity and courage, and we can hope to live out those commitments to clarity and generosity in our work with actual humans. In texts, we can practice not-knowing, or knowing too much; we can practice suspending disbelief and embracing impossible conflicts; we can enter into the possibility that we are wrong, without the fear of lived consequences, the possibility of failure.

And even beyond the methodological gifts of the arts and humanities, there is the simple fact that what we are most grappling with right now are fundamentally human questions. Questions about terrorism, nuclear holocaust, faith, identity, difference, patriotism, justice, belonging, and fear. Questions about how to make decisions together, how to love others, how to channel the marvelous energies of the human toward some kind of fair and durable future. These topics are, of course, ancient human questions, but they are also cropping up in the current poetic resistance to the forty-fifth US presidency. "Writers are responding to this turbulent moment in the country's history with a tsunami of poems that address issues like immigration, global warming, the Syrian refugee crisis, institutionalized racism, equal rights for transgender people, Islamophobia and health care. . . . The recent resurgence of protest poems reflects a new strain of contemporary American poetry, one that is deeply engaged with public policy and the latest executive orders coming from the White House" (Alter). At the 2017 March for Science, Jane Hirschfield presented a new poem titled "On the Fifth Day," which begins as shown below; she went on to found Poets for Science (https://poetsforscience.org/about).

On the fifth day
the scientists who studied the rivers
were forbidden to speak
or to study the rivers.[2]

We need poetry because it exposes the fiercest problems with disjuncture, contrast, and brevity, and because it is pithy and portable and might be set to music. We need the poem because it can lure or jolt us awake, because we don't even have to want to go there, but there we are. What if Adrienne Rich is right, in "In Those Years" and we really are standing alone and tiny on the barren shore, amid the rags of fog, still saying "I" while the great dark birds of history scream and plunge around us? What if our only solace or salvation is in the "we"—but we have forgotten it? Is that how we have ended up cold and alienated, suspicious enough that even when actual crime rates drop and drop, we cannot stop feeling less and less safe?

We also need the novel because it gives us many voices, many eyes to see through. Most of all, it gives us a chance to be what Jonathan Culler calls "omniscient readers," understanding from a variety of perspectives in ways that human experience doesn't quite allow. The rise of the novel parallels the rise of the city-state, theorists argue, which makes sense because we can't really understand something as complex as a concentrated society without the conceptual tool of the novel. For concrete social change work on particular issues, novels are indispensable. Cli-fi, or climate fiction, has proven a powerful tool in understanding not only the science of climate change but also the ways in which humans can shape their own systems and choices in the face of what is coming. Communities with dynamic local food system efforts can find agrarian novels necessary companions, because despite our intellectual grasp of the issues at hand, most of us cannot readily occupy an affective or emotional space different from our own. In *The Grapes of Wrath*, for example, we consider the Joads to be living in poverty—but then they are moved off their land and we come to understand how rich they were before. We can wonder at the drive and resourcefulness they show, but also at the inhumanity of the system, the economic "monster" that justifies their eviction, even the tractor that can tear up the earth and then stand zombie-dead in the barn. We can rage, sick in our souls, at the piles of oranges ripe on the ground, that are doused in kerosene and burned in front of starving families, lest corporate profits be diminished by someone eating an orange they didn't buy. The novel makes clear the systems that drive our world, in their absurdity and injustice, but it can also offer alternatives. Ruth Ozeki's novel *All over Creation* provides systemic counterpoints in its band of guerrilla gardeners, planting fruit trees in the medians in LA; its anti-chemical activists doing pop-up theater in grocery stores; its populist heirloom seed purveyor, crippled by Alzheimer's, being rescued by young rabble rousers who use the internet to literally farm out that sacred work through an actual agricultural world wide web.

My own past work with the Maine Humanities Council provides several useful examples, including those above. In a term-length seminar called "Feeding the Human Animal: Visions of Thriving and Surviving," I led open discussion at our local public library on selected US agrarian novels. "What is the point of reading novels?" my introductory materials asked. "To better understand the world, of course. To see ourselves in different lights, in different places, in different relationships. To imagine other ways of being and to try out other ways of seeing. The process of living, then, demands the novel. And the process of living wisely and well, in ways that feed us and sustain the world we depend upon, demands the agrarian novel." Together, in a town whose food policy council was making waves nationally, in a region where collaborations between aging white farmers and young refugee farmers were crafting new models of cultural and environmental sustainability, we discussed the meaning of agriculture, of caring for land, and of the systems of inquiry, respect, and commitment that it demands. After the Mellon seminar, Gerald Torres and I taught a short version of that seminar to Cornell law students, as a kind of precursor to a two-semester sequence he pioneered on law and policy of food systems. Our novel-based seminar was necessary, he felt, so that students moving into the study of law and policy knew what they were talking about.

In a different Maine Humanities Council program, called "Choosing Civility," we undertook a text-based, civic reflection process titled "Imagining the Communities We Want to Live In." We used Adrienne Rich's "In Those Years" to explore the gap between "I" and "we" as we worked to envision together the communities we aspire to be. The slip and slide between poetic interpretation ("the dark birds of history felt like warplanes to me, they terrify me" said one participant), the affective experience of the reader ("I feel so alone since moving here, I don't even know my neighbors"), and the complex, vulnerable work of negotiating how to live with different others ("the most moving thing I've seen lately was the neighbors keeping the walkway shoveled for the one guy who is in a wheelchair") is necessary and generative movement, provoked by nothing so well as a good bit of art, explored in company. One participant commented at the end of the discussion that this had been great, that he had expected us to spend two hours discussing *Bowling Alone*, but this was new, using unexpected tools to think about the same old problems in a valuable new way.

And in a third program, called "Let's Talk Local," we codesigned a participatory process that would move us outside of problem-solving altogether. I did this with two communities, both choosing a tension that they wanted to explore and creating or finding "texts" that would help ground the discussion.

In Lewiston, Maine, a largely white, Franco-American, Roman Catholic, depressed postindustrial mill town that had seen vast in-migration of Somali refugees, the group settled on "The Changing Face of Home." And rather than choose a poem or story, they wanted individuals to share their own stories, live, in the style of the nonprofit storytelling group the Moth. And the emphasis was not on cracking the nut of how to live together but on listening carefully to better understand one another. One story came from a young Somali man who had spent most of his life in a refugee camp; he spoke about family and friends as his sense of home, mobile yet solid. One story came from a white woman in her fifties, a long-time administrative assistant at Bates College, who was raised in Lewiston by Franco-American parents and who never learned English until she started first grade at the public school. There were others, including an Iranian immigrant who had been in Lewiston thirty years and was responsible for vast contributions in the nonprofit world. In facilitated civic reflection later, people came to understand that the issue is not about "foreign" versus "native" (no, none of the displaced peoples of the Wabenaki tribes spoke at this event, and no, not many of the historical white residents recognized the irony of using the term "native") but about our capacity to live a sense of home that feels like home to us. We recognized our own innate sense of the world as it should be, and we dug further into the world as it is, coming to understand the smallness and specificity of our personal desires in the context of our larger human needs for thriving and surviving.

This practice of seeing the world as it is and working toward the world as it should be is not only the province of Saul Alinsky and broad-based community organizing. It is also, I'd argue, the province of public humanists. We hold up the great mirror and invite ourselves to see, but we also hold out possibilities, describe the adventures we might choose. We negotiate ethics; we imagine utopias and dystopias; we historicize the "commons" and "common good" and "commonwealth" as ways of understanding the consequences of our choices. "Our obsession with dystopia," says Afrofuturist adrienne marie brown, "is our realization of what we've already set in motion" (Mar-Abe). To understand what we've set in motion, to do what we do, then, is to attend carefully to the world ("attending" in the way that Dean Hernandez, in Kirsten Greenidge's play *Baltimore* uses it, as paying attention, showing up, being present) and to do so with care. As Mary Oliver learned from her lifelong love, "Attention without feeling . . . is only a report. An openness—an empathy—was necessary if the attention was to matter" (Popova).

As academics, we are asked too often to "report," which we can feel is insufficient, but when reward structures are pegged to certain kinds of performances, the options seem limited. "Plato's general theory of learning and knowledge—which argued for the great superiority of elegant 'pure theory' and 'pure science' compared to 'inferior' real world practice—and his elitist theory of governance are deeply embedded in the culture and structure of American colleges and universities" (Benson, Harkavy, and Puckett). Bringing together new learning about the yoked roles of affect and cognition in student learning and the importance of ethical judgment and intuition in wise work, Laura Rendón developed the term "sentipensante," sensing and feeling together. She offers a powerful alternative to strictly cognitive approaches; she seeks to develop a vision "based on wholeness and consonance, respecting the harmonious rhythm between the outer experience of intellectualism and rational analysis and the inner dimension of insight, emotion, and awareness" (Rendón, 2). She acknowledges that these ways of knowing are often considered "too controversial to discuss publicly in higher education" but contends that we must dream this alternative vision into being, for the sake of our students, if not ourselves.

Part of the point of the humanities is precisely to dream up alternatives, to imagine ourselves into better worlds rather than keep us stuck in a problem-solving, putting-out-fires mentality. As Martín Espada's poem "Imagine the Angels of Bread" demonstrates, sometimes we have to move right out of the domain of fixing things and into whole other possibilities:

> this is the year that the hands
> pulling tomatoes from the vine
> uproot the deed to the earth that sprouts the vine,
> the hands canning tomatoes
> are named in the will
> that owns the bedlam of the cannery;
>
> .   .   .   .
>
> If the abolition of slave-manacles
> began as a vision of hands without manacles,
> then this is the year;
> if the shutdown of extermination camps
> began as imagination of a land
> without barbed wire or the crematorium,
> then this is the year;[3]

As Alice Mar-Abe writes in her article "Ferguson Is the Future," "Despite all my grand aspirations to help craft a better future and a better country, I had never taken the time to envision it, to imagine how the average citizen would live in a utopic America. Instead, I usually approach social justice from a highly realistic, fact-based standpoint: what's the problem and how do we fix it? Yet I inevitably hit a wall when I return to the deeper societal inequalities that no policy could possibly touch. And that's where radical imagination comes in: we have to dream new worlds into existence before we can ever hope for them to materialize."

Those of us who are public scholars in the arts and humanities are trying, it seems to me, to do all of these things: to see the world as it is, to work toward the world as it should be, to dream new worlds into existence, to persist in the possibility of hope. Which is why it is so unutterably vital that we bring our full humanity to our work—a project we can do only and best in the company of others.

Weaving Faculty Networks for Change

It is worth noting that our embrace of public humanities and scholars as humans is not necessarily an obvious choice. For us, the logic of it is sound: it represents a capacious worldview that understands my liberation as bound up in yours, but it is also clear from critical university studies that what "counts" in scholarship is closely aligned with what "counts" in scholars. Restrictions on my scholarship end up being restrictions on how I can be, who I can be, as a scholar. It is our contention and our experience that being our fullest selves, most interested in the well-being of the world, brings out our most powerful scholarship, and not only because it capitalizes on our passion. When we engage in the world as humanists, we can come to see our field as not only an object of study but also as a tool for addressing complex problems. At bottom, that is what concerns us here: How can the arts and humanities, practices of creating and interpreting human culture, contribute more powerfully to the public good? And how can we, as would-be contributors, find our ways more easily to the forms of engagement that we desire?

These two questions invite distinct but inextricably linked responses, one about the inner lives and satisfactions of faculty and one about their outer engagements as public humanists, which might embrace everything from genteel delivery of speeches at the county historical society and forceful op-eds to participatory after-school projects with urban kids. Our work can show up as scholarship on public issues, for public purposes, with public partners, creating public goods. All of these are significant, and all demand a fluency and wholeness in identity that enables us to care, to listen, and to create something of public value. And, most importantly, all of that depends on us, as public scholars, as the contact points between the practice of academic humanities and the worlds in which they matter. If we lack the conviction or the space or the role with which to take up this work, we won't.

The work, then, of creating spaces in which faculty can explore and inquire with a sense of trust and generosity, becomes paramount. Such spaces are necessary for the careful integrative work of designing scholarship that feeds the multiple aspects of self, that serves both the system and the soul. Such concepts of wholeness, integrity, and "living divided no more" have various manifestations today—William Sullivan's notions of "civic professionalism," KerryAnn O'Meara's research into faculty "civic agency," Claire Snyder-Hall's work with "civic aspirations" and "civic happiness," and Wendy Willis's work on "civic loneliness." The UCLA Higher Education Research Institute found significant evidence of spirituality as a force in the lives of faculty, and KerryAnn O'Meara's work on faculty growth and civic agency also points to a greater need for such integrative work. Furthermore, Carol Colbeck's research has demonstrated that faculty who engage in public scholarship find the "three-legged stool" of teaching, research, and service to be more hindrance than help, as it asks them to divide work that is fundamentally integrative into artificial categories. The whole (often civic, often spiritual) power of their work is invisible when it is carved into pieces to fit the mold. The "hidden wholeness" that Parker Palmer describes is a well-known avenue for reintroducing these questions of meaning to faculty culture, but the academy rarely feels like a welcoming space for such quasi- or even outright spiritual work. Our experiment was to see if we could design a space that was more welcoming, and to see what, once we did, it might produce.

Civic professionalism is a concept William M. Sullivan lays out in *Work and Integrity: The Crisis and Promise of Professionalism in America*. He unpacks the origins of the professions (medicine, law, and clergy in particular), with attention to the question of public purpose—and the corollary "hunger for something which is often missing or suppressed in work . . . a sense of engagement, through one's work, with shared purposes which give point and value to individual effort. These purposes—dignity, justice, fellowship—make possible a civil and meaningful public realm. They are the promise of professionalism" (Sullivan, 16). Our seminar worked to explore what is missing, to voice such hungers as were there, and to lift up the purposes of dignity, justice, and fellowship as meaningful bases of our work. But it was not easy: "The everyday practices of higher education work against the collaborative practices that are the heart of engaged scholarship, service-learning, and reciprocal, fluid, respectful partnerships with communities. The way faculty members are educated and rewarded encourages working in isolation or primarily with colleagues within their own academic disciplines, and seeing their own knowledge as qualitatively superior to other forms of knowledge and knowledge-making" (Boyte and Fretz). Our group was made up of engaged scholars with civic tendencies, people working on issues that have relevance in the "real world." But even so, it was counter-cultural to spend time digging into questions of public purpose rather than parsing arguments, and it seemed to take some time to unearth and validate the civic aspects of our professional lives without feeling vaguely threatened by the process.

That sense of hovering threat, of knowing that an important way of being and working is discouraged (at least in pre-tenure years) contributes deeply to faculty unhappiness. KerryAnn O'Meara's work on faculty civic agency with the Kettering Foundation explored this through interviews with "faculty who are deeply frustrated with narrow conceptions of what counts as scholarship and seek to connect their professional work with deeply held civic aspirations." Faculty civic agency, as she uses it, describes the drive and strategy though which faculty engage with publics even against the currents of culture and rewards. Such agency is also important well beyond faculty development or job satisfaction, she notes, because faculty are "a key strategic agent of change in efforts to strengthen the democratic mission of higher education" (O'Meara, Terosky, and Neumann 2). A key further benefit of O'Meara's framework for our thinking here is its emphasis less on barriers than on possibilities. She cites Marshall Ganz: "A structural bias in social movement studies seems to have made it more productive for scholars to identify the constraining conditions that make certain outcomes more probable than to focus on enabling conditions that make many outcomes possible. Agency, however, is more about grasping at possibility than conforming to probability" (Ganz, 511). While our seminar saw its share of complaint about structural obstacles to change, we were also committed to being something more than critics and to imagining together the possibilities we might cocreate (here in the academy as well as in and with larger publics).

And the purpose of all this, after all, is to create cultural conditions in which it is possible for faculty to live out a sense of civic agency as a civic professional—toward the end of improving the world, of course, but also for a deeper sense of "civic happiness." Claire Snyder-Hall, also through work with Kettering, unpacks this notion, derived from Hannah Arendt.

She identifies civic happiness as akin to Aristotelian "eudaimonia," a happiness larger than one's private experience, that "relates to feelings produced through interaction with others, specifically the sense of fulfillment human beings experience when they work with others on projects that have public relevance" (Snyder-Hall, 9). Her own interview-based research (which intentionally builds on O'Meara's) centered on questions of faculty fulfillment, albeit with a smallish group of respondents, but, she says, "While my small, nonrepresentative sample limits the generalizability of the study, a very strong set of common themes and similar experiences emerged out of the interview data. What I found was astounding: all those interviewed felt positive and energized by their civic engagement, found that it helped them do their academic jobs better, and experienced increased levels of connection with others and meaningfulness in their work" (Snyder-Hall, 3). So those civic professionals who approach their work with public purpose and use civic agency in creative ways achieve civic happiness. And everyone else?

"Civic loneliness" is the alternative to the kind of beloved community we seek to build. Wendy Willis, executive director of the Deliberative Democracy Coalition, writes, "Apparently, loneliness is the new sitting, which for a few months was the new smoking. According to recent reports, social isolation and loneliness increases mortality at the same rate as 15 cigarettes a day." But her analysis is serious. She says: "The war correspondent Sebastian Junger in his book *Tribe*, argues that returning soldiers suffer at least as much from the transition out of a purposeful highly connected society as they do from exposure to combat. In other words, reentry into the individualism and disconnection of American civilian society is nearly as traumatizing as war itself." She reminds us that nearly half of Americans report being lonely, and the number who report they have no close friends has tripled since 1985. She argues, with Hannah Arendt, that loneliness "is existential and is a pre-condition not just to tyranny but to totalitarianism." The remedies she locates in civic deliberation and engagement: "People around us are literally dying for lack of connection and purpose. And the work of democracy is dripping with both connection and purpose." But we have to do it differently, she says:

> All too often, I find myself falling into the traps set by efficiency and goal-orientation. I find myself "cutting to the chase" so that communities I am working with can make some decisions and get on with it. I find myself saying things like, "I want to respect your time." But what if I were to respect something in addition to their time? What if I were to center those healing values of connection and individual purpose in

my own work? What if—alongside hard-nosed public decision-making and rational deliberation—we also considered people's needs to connect with one another in less goal-driven but meaningful conversation around things that matter to them?

This is the very point of our seminar, to create a shared sense of meaning and purpose and a space for relationships that can live those out.

What Emerged in and from This Seminar?

As we know from systems theory and from close studies of substantial change: "The world doesn't change one person at a time. It changes as networks of relationships form among people who discover they share a common cause and vision of what's possible" (Wheatley and Frieze, 2006). And mechanisms of change are different from what our institutions have trained us to expect: "When separate, local efforts connect with each other as networks, then strengthen as *communities of practice*, suddenly and surprisingly a new system emerges at a greater level of scale. *This system of influence* possesses qualities and capacities that were unknown in the individuals. It isn't that they were hidden; they simply don't exist until the system emerges" (emphasis in original). This "emergence" is why we build networks, in hopes that connecting individual efforts will yield something greater and more organic to the network than what we might conceive of ourselves. "In nature, change never happens as a result of top-down, pre-conceived strategic plans, or from the mandate of any single individual or boss. Change begins as local actions spring up simultaneously in many different areas. If these changes remain disconnected, nothing happens beyond each locale. However, when they become connected, local actions can emerge as a powerful system with influence at a more global or comprehensive level" (Wheatley and Frieze, 2006). If the academy is to change, it will be because of the networks that advance such change and the emergent qualities they generate. But deliberately investing in emergence is countercultural now and hearkens back to an agrarian ethic of ancient wisdom and trust. Nannie Rawley, in Barbara Kingsolver's *Prodigal Summer*, keeps a back meadow fallow for wild apple trees to seed in. She is always looking for the next great accidental cross, and so she devotes that land to the possibility of the emergent unknown fruit rather than plant a predictable cash crop.

A nonfictional example of emergence in practice: in April 2017, Philadelphia-based artist Pepón Osorio completed a two-year residency at Cornell University with the Cornell Council on the Arts. It was a challenge for the council to place its faith in his practice, which is fundamentally emergent: he enters into relationships, listens, attends, and sees what comes of it—a very different practice than many that foreground outcomes-oriented planfulness and intention. His exhibit, based on his relationship with an African American family in downtown Ithaca and staged in Rand Hall, was a hand-built, upside-down house, showing videos of the family in relationship to one another, dancing or neck-deep in water. There was also a second part of the installation: a beautiful, long, polished dining table that he made by hand and set in a nook, separated by screens. There he participated in a series of hosted conversations, over food prepared by local chefs. Our diverse experiences as parents, transplants, climate change activists, history buffs, and trailing spouses informed our readings of the piece and shaped our conversation together in powerful ways. Some people saw the lottery tickets that papered the upside-down house as markers of chronic hope; others saw them as signs of a systemic oppression that takes people's investment in a dream and puts it toward state systems that by and large don't serve them. Some people saw the sandbags underneath the house as keeping the floodwaters away from the house; but the water was already in the house, so perhaps they were keeping the rest of society safe from this rising water. Our ways of knowing and being, brought together around a congenial table, could inform each other, creating emergent learning and insight.

Because of the ways in which it challenges Western and institutional forms of thinking, emergence is rarely something we seek to achieve. When we plan, we plan strategically, with logic models and theories of change that advance particular desired outcomes through particular tactics and inputs. To approach the work of change instead through a network-weaving strategy that places faith in its member "nodes" and in what might emerge from their interaction is a tough sell. Everything in our cultures (corporate and scientific, as well as academic) is geared now toward cause and effect, quantifiable interventions with knowable outcomes. The humanities teach us that the world is more complex (indeed, emergence is the very essence of what seminar-style learning has depended on all these years), yet it can be hard for us to make time in our productivity-oriented culture for the relationships that will yield emergence. Just as Pepón Osorio's process shows us, inquiry, relationship, and commitment can be immensely fruitful, but it is an act of faith to undertake them without predictable outcomes and concrete aspirations. Already, from this seminar, we have seen certain planned outcomes: this book project; an associated website; participation in a community street fair. And we have seen a range of other outcomes that emerged without plan:

- Over the course of the term, we witnessed a gentling of comments, a growth of supportiveness, and a courage of sharing new writing, new approaches, often with "risky" personal connections and stories that had not been publicly shared before.
- Several scholars found new connectivity between their histories and identities and their scholarly commitments; several others reinforced them or dug to new levels (including me—identifying my own alienating "third culture" upbringing as a source of my deep attraction to community was a result of deep reflection in this seminar).
- Several scholars found new or renewed interest in direct community engagement—one attended the two-day Community-Engaged Learning and Teaching Institute; one joined the Engaged Faculty Fellowship Program upon his return from sabbatical and is working with colleagues to create a new minor in Public History; one served as a fellow in the same program and has also received grant funding to develop a course using community-based research and community-based theatrical production to explore the impacts of climate change in our region; a third became a Faculty Fellow in Engaged Scholarship as a way of moving her scholarly work more intentionally toward public impact.
- New collaborations emerged: two colleagues are developing new scholarship on "civic humanities," and two others developed a new course for law students on US agrarian novels, intended as a fuller-story, more engaging way to understand law and policy of food systems (the topic of another community-engaged course developed). Furthermore, several of these colleagues are involved in a new Mellon-funded initiative from the Society for the Humanities, on rural humanities.
- New systems of support emerged as well: one faculty member made important decisions regarding a tenure and promotion process in deliberation with the group, responding to critical moments in our nation's history with a deepening commitment to students.

The point of emergence, of course, is that it is unpredictable and often takes a while. Perhaps more importantly, it takes attention to the network: "Emergence has a life-cycle. It begins with networks, shifts to intentional communities of practice and evolves into powerful systems capable of global influence" (Wheatley and Freize). Our task, having built a network, is to sustain an intentional community of practice. And to better understand the long-term shifts our collaborations engender, we intend to use Ripple Effects Mapping (Kollock et al.), a long-term impact assessment practice, to better understand the "ripple effects" caused by this seminar, including those that are now unforeseeable.

Conclusion

What the humanities provide the world is essential: an understanding of love, of relationship, of war, of diplomacy, of terror, religion, heartache, discrimination. It is the home turf of ethics, of culture, of all our ways of understanding one another in our fullness and creativity. Scientific methods have led us to imagine that what is most important or most true can be fixed, stripped away from all the rest, like Vitamin C tablets as a substitute for a whole, fragrant orange. Academic humanists are subject to these pressures to reduce and distill, to compete, to work from the head up instead of the heart out, to live in deference to the iron grip of Plato's cold, dead hand (Benson, Harkavy, and Puckett). But such pressures make the least of us: they compromise our public scholarship, curtail our civic happiness, and impede our civic professionalism. Adjunctification and the postdoc circuit can create "a culture of perennial homelessness" (Roebuck), which further prevents relationship and rooting. The division of teaching from research from service further fractures people's sense of their "public scholarship . . . as an inseparable whole" (Colbeck and Wharton-Michael) when what we hope to develop are whole scholars, whole humans, who live their work with integrity. To give us back a sense of hope, home, and wholeness, we need to nurture regular learning communities, communities of practice, wherein we can imagine together the work we want to do and support one another in doing it.

Notes

1. Marge Piercy's poem "To Be of Use" is often cited in such conversations, both around scholarship and around social justice.

2. Quoted from Jane Hirshfield, "On the Fifth Day," *The Washington Post*, April 14, 2017, https://www.washingtonpost.com/posteverything/wp/2017/04/14/on-the-fifth-day/.

3. Quoted from Martín Espada, "Imagine the Angels of Bread," *Imagine the Angels of Bread* (New York: W. W. Norton, 1997).

Works Cited

Alter, Alexandra. "American Poets, Refusing to Go Gentle, Rage against the Right." *New York Times*, April 21, 2017.

Benson, Lee, Ira Harkavy, and John Puckett, John. "Democratic Transformation through University-Assisted Community Schools." *"To Serve a Larger Purpose":*

Engagement for Democracy and the Transformation of Higher Education, edited by John Saltmarsh and Matthew Hartley, Temple University Press, 2011.

Berry, Wendell. "The Agrarian Standard." *Orion Magazine*, July 1, 2002. https://ori onmagazine.org/article/the-agrarian-standard.

Berry, Wendell. "The Loss of the University." *Home Economics*, North Point Press, 1987.

Block, Peter. *Community: The Structure of Belonging.* Berrett-Koehler Publishers, 2008.

Boyte, Harry C., Eric Fretz. "Civic Professionalism." *Journal of Higher Education Outreach and Engagement*, vol. 14, no. 2, 2010, p. 67.

Brooks, Peter. "Introduction." *The Humanities and Public Life*, edited by Peter Brooks with Hilary Jewett, Fordham University Press, 2014.

Colbeck, Carol, and Wharton-Michael, Patty. "Individual and Organizational Influences on Faculty Members' Engagement in Public Scholarship." *New Directions for Teaching and Learning*, no. 105, Spring 2006, 17–26.

Ellison, Julie, and Eatman, Timothy K. *Scholarship in Public: Knowledge Creation and Tenure Policy in the Engaged University.* Imagining America: Artists and Scholars in Public Life, Tenure-Team Initiative on Public Scholarship, 2008.

Espada, Martín. "Imagine the Angels of Bread." *Imagine the Angels of Bread*, W. W. Norton, 1997.

Ganz, Marshall. "Leading Change: Leadership, Organization and Social Movements." *The Handbook of Leadership and Practice,* edited by N. Nohira and R. Khurana, Harvard Business School Press, 2010, pp. 509–50.

Kezar, Adrianna. *How Colleges Change: Understanding, Leading, and Enacting Change.* Taylor & Francis, 2014.

Kollock, Debra Hansen, Lynette Flage, Scott Chazdon, Nathan Paine, and Lori Higgins. "Ripple Effect Mapping: A 'Radiant' Way to Capture Program Impacts." *Journal of Extension*, vol. 50, no. 5, October 2012. https://www.joe.org/joe/2012october/tt6.php.

Mar-Abe, Alice. "Ferguson Is the Future." *Nassau Weekly*, October 11, 2015. http://www.nassauweekly.com/ferguson-is-the-future.

Nussbaum, Martha C. *Cultivating Humanity: A Classical Defense of Reform in Liberal Education.* Harvard University Press, 1997.

O'Meara, KerryAnn. *Because I Can: Exploring Faculty Civic Agency.* Kettering Foundation Working Paper 2012–1. Charles F. Kettering Foundation, 2012. https://www.kettering.org/sites/default/files/product-downloads/OMeara-KFWP2012–01-FINAL.pdf

O'Meara, KerryAnn, Terosky, Aimee Lapointe, and Neumann, Anna. *Faculty Careers and Work Lives: A Professional Growth Perspective.* ASHE Higher Education Report, vol. 34, no. 3. 2008. Jossey-Bass, 2008.

Palmer, Parker J. *A Hidden Wholeness: The Journey toward an Undivided Life.* Jossey-Bass, 2004.

Palmer, Parker J., Arthur Zajonc, and Megan Scribner. *The Heart of Higher Education: A Call to Renewal: Transforming the Academy through Collegial Conversations.* Jossey-Bass, 2010.

Plater, William M. "Habits of Living: Engaging the Campus as Citizen One Scholar at a Time." *Colleges and Universities as Citizens*, edited by Robert G. Bringle, Richard Games, and Edward Malloy, Allyn & Bacon, 1999, pp. 141–72.

Popova, Maria. "Mary Oliver on What Attention Really Means and Her Moving Elegy for Her Soulmate." *BrainPickings*. 2015. https://www.brainpickings.org/2015/01/20/mary-oliver-molly-malone-cook-our-world.

Rendón, Laura I. *Sentipensante (Sensing/Thinking) Pedagogy: Educating for Wholeness, Social Justice and Liberation*. Stylus, 2009.

Roebuck, Kristin. Discussion in seminar, spring 2017.

Saltmarsh, J. "Creating New Knowledge: A Pathway to Civic Engagement." Presented at Bates College. 2007.

Saltmarsh, John, Matthew Hartley, and Patti Clayton. *Democratic Engagement White Paper*. New England Resource Center for Higher Education, 2009. https://repository.upenn.edu/gse_pubs/274.

Sandmann, L., J. Saltmarsh, and K. O'Meara. "An Integrated Model for Advancing the Scholarship of Engagement: Creating Academic Homes for the Engaged Scholar." *Journal of Higher Education Outreach and Engagement* 12, no. 1 (2008): 47–64.

Snyder-Hall, Claire. *Civic Aspirations: Why Some Higher Education Faculty Are Reconnecting their Professional and Public Lives*. Kettering Foundation, 2015. https://www.kettering.org/sites/default/files/product-downloads/Civic%20Aspirations.pdf.

Sullivan, William M. *Work and Integrity: The Crisis and Promise of Professionalism in America*. HarperCollins, 1995.

Wheatley, Margaret J., and Frieze, Deborah. "Using Emergence to Take Social Innovations to Scale." *Margaret J. Wheatley: Writings*. 2006. http://www.margaretwheatley.com/articles/emergence.htm.

Willis, Wendy. "On Civic Loneliness." Deliberative Democracy Consortium. 2017. http://deliberative-democracy.net/2017/06/24/on-civic-loneliness.

Chapter 2

To Be, or To Become?

On Reading and Recognition

Shawn McDaniel

Shawn McDaniel is an assistant professor in Cornell's Department of Romance Studies. The day after Shawn was born, his crib was placed in the Queen's Kitchen, his grandparents' diner in rural Oklahoma, where he would spend most of his early life. Alongside his mother, he grew up serving coffee and chicken fried steaks to wheat farmers, cattle ranchers, and oil field workers. Shawn left the southern plains and made his way to Nova Scotia, where he pursued a degree in Celtic studies and became a fluent speaker, singer, and folklorist of Scottish Gaelic. Since then, he has traveled extensively, learned several languages, and earned a few degrees along the way. Shawn researches and teaches Cuban literary and cultural studies and continues to find a sense of self and home with his partner and dog in and between New York, Nova Scotia, and Oklahoma.

Shawn's chapter tells these and other stories as way of unpacking the humanness that undergirds and drives his scholarship. He details his discovery, while teaching continental theory to urban community college students, of a core principle underlying public scholarship: that intellectual work is not the sole property of the credentialed elite. He writes, "They had lived in various ways what was theorized by preeminent critical thinkers." For him, that point illustrated "a crucial cornerstone of the humanities: the willingness to see humanness in other people, to see ourselves in others, and resist being beholden to presumptions, projections, and paranoia." With dexterous, humorous prose, he is able to demystify his home state of Oklahoma *and offer specific insights into the value of attention to particulars that shape who we are. In the face of "the immense diversity and fraught trajectory of the human condition," Shawn explores "how the idea of personality can serve as a capacious concept for exploring subjective processes of becoming."*

Like many of my classmates, I worked as an adjunct in New York City while pursuing a PhD. After years of teaching all levels of Spanish language during the day, usually at two colleges, and completing my graduate studies at night, a wonderful opportunity fell into my lap. For the first time, I would be able to design various upper-level intensive writing courses, taught in English, aimed at juniors and seniors. I was ecstatic to be able to teach a different kind of class in another language. After carefully crafting a syllabus for Imagining the Americas, a course that used critical theory and cultural studies to examine such diverse issues as democracy, citizenship, borders, gender, race, sexuality, and linguistic normativity, I enthusiastically walked through the readings and assignments with the director who had hired me. He seemed impressed by the work I had invested but cautioned me bluntly, "You know, our students aren't readers."

Momentarily deflated but ultimately undeterred by such a perplexing statement, I got the green light to proceed. A week or so later, while discussing my new course with a colleague, she echoed the director's skepticism, stating unequivocally, "Our students aren't writers." My reaction to this two-pronged negation was incredulity followed by confusion. I wondered, *Well, if they aren't readers and they aren't writers, then what* are *they?* I figured that those disqualifying statements were most likely related to the frustrations that any educator has felt when their students don't do the readings, or just aren't that into the class. Or that maybe those generalizing dismissals were fed by the realities of lack of resources and heavy teaching loads at a public university, and that my colleagues were, in their way, trying to protect me from becoming too invested, trying to lower my expectations for a course trajectory that they considered too difficult for "our students" to handle.

So I entered class the first day with the aforementioned admonishments lingering in my mind, and quickly decided that I would teach that class like I would any other. Nearly all of my twenty-seven students were either immigrants or children of immigrants, from countries like the Dominican Republic, Jamaica, Eritrea, Pakistan, Guyana, the Philippines, Syria, and Ghana. Most had a job, if not two. Some had children. Some lived long commutes from campus. Many endured personal, family, and financial hardships. It quickly sunk in that "our students"—enunciated not with pride and partiality—only reinforced stereotypes of pathologized mentalities and inadequacies of urban youth of color and immigrants. I wondered if "our students" were underperforming, undeserving, or perhaps underestimated.

Or maybe I really had been too ambitious. After all, critical theory is no cakewalk. We were on the verge of jumping into challenging texts by Marx, Gramsci, Derrida, Foucault, Stuart Hall, Audre Lorde, Judith Butler, Slavoj Žižek, among other heavy hitters. Big ideas were in store for us, and my first-day nerves, which were exacerbated by my colleagues' input and the fact that it was the first time I had ever taught this class, had me fretting whether I had bitten off more than I could chew.

The class remains one of the most gratifying teaching experiences of my career. Each class was filled with dynamic discussions, productive silences, and gratifying takeaways. It didn't take long for me to realize that the students already comprehended the rather complex concepts we were exploring in class but did not share the same critical lexicon to talk about it that I had. And not only were students reading, they also wrote insightful essays that beautifully blended the academic rigor of close reading and secondary research with moving personal testimonials that spoke to, among other things, the trials of being targeted by "stop and frisk" police tactics, later ruled unconstitutional but ever looming on a not-so-distant horizon. "Our students" understood Foucault's analysis of carceral and social surveillance, since their neighborhoods and routes to campus were littered with NYPD mobile surveillance towers. "You never know if anybody's actually in there behind the tinted glass, but you assume someone always is," remarked one student. "And I think that's the point."

It turns out that the assumption that "our students" neither read nor wrote well—even about issues so central to their lives—was a fallacy. They had lived in various ways what was theorized by preeminent critical thinkers. Moreover, once they had read the texts, discussed them in class, and written about them, they were empowered to point out the nuances that some of those philosophical heavies overlooked, abstracted, or miscalculated. They were quite adept and sophisticated readers in an experiential sense. They were no strangers to the myriad ways in which language, national origin, race, and class have real-world consequences. And far too many knew all too well the realities of displacement due to war, genocide, climate change, or gentrification. "Our students" didn't require critical theory to understand themselves and the ideological forces and sociohistorical factors at play in their lives. The class merely gave them a new expressive vocabulary.

Please don't misunderstand this anecdote as yet another Hollywoodesque narrative of the outsider believing in and subsequently changing the lives of inner city youth. Nor do I intend to reproduce the cliché—as legitimate as it may be—that in seeking to teach I was taught something. If anything, this episode illustrates a crucial cornerstone of the humanities: the willingness to see humanness in other people, to see ourselves in others, and resist being beholden to presumptions, projections, and paranoia. Surely within being there is room for becoming.

Rurality

Growing up in rural Oklahoma, I wasn't much of a reader myself. "Boys can't sit still and read like girls can," so I was told at an early age. The fact that I'm now a university literature professor is, for me, ironic to say the least, given that I was a rather average student. Northwest Oklahoma (not the panhandle but up that way) is flat and sparsely dotted with small canyons, creeks, and plateaus of red dirt, clay, or mud, depending on the conditions. Mostly dry and warm, always windy, Tornado Alley delivers powerful, illuminating thunderstorms in an impossibly expansive sky. There, in my small Bible Belt hometown, many farm wheat or raise cattle (or both) or work in the oil fields. Both sides of my family opted for the latter, and for generations landmen, roughnecks, oil refinery workers, and rig shop component suppliers in my family have traversed sunny, dusty backroads in an area that thrives or declines by the price of oil and natural gas.

When I left the state for college, I was taken aback by the frequent mystification of Oklahoma. In both foreign and domestic locations, most people I have encountered don't really know where it is and what is there and have never been there. Much to my surprise, people seemed fascinated to meet me because I was from Oklahoma, a state that I considered remarkably inconsequential while growing up. Many would say, "I've never met anybody from Oklahoma." Most sang, with varying degrees of accuracy, the title song of Rodgers and Hammerstein's musical. Others inquired if we all rode horses. And a select few talked about how they would love to run through our vast cornfields (perhaps they were thinking of Iowa). Oklahoma seems like a mysterious place to a surprising number of people.

Conspicuously concealed in the middle of the country, Oklahoman cultural geography is a blend of southern and western. Not Southwestern, mind you. And never, ever midwestern (as most people I've met seem to think). An ambiguous spot on the map until designated Indian Territory in the nineteenth century, the state juggles two identities: Native America (as our license plates read until recently) and the Sooner State, referencing those settlers who jumped the gun to stake their claims to the choicest plots in various land runs (events which we reenacted in grade school). My town came to be thanks to the Cherokee Strip Land Run of 1893, the last and largest of the land runs in the state, that displaced the already relocated Cherokee tribe. A farming town settled largely by Mennonites, my hometown borders Cheyenne-Arapaho territory in the south and the home of the oldest rattlesnake hunt in the state in the east. And looming on the northern horizon lie the Gloss Mountains, a small range of unusually large, red-earth buttes and mesas with glistening gypsum caps jutting out from an otherwise flat, expansive landscape.

Here my grandparents owned and operated a diner and worked it hard, 6:00 a.m. to 10:00 p.m. every day for three decades. I started waiting tables when I was a "little squirt," about seven years old. The Queen's Kitchen was the center of our world. Our hair and clothes constantly reeked of fried food, our hands of bleach water from wiping off tables with thin white rags soaked in a pickle bucket. Coming up in the Queen's, as we called it, you knew everyone's name, around what time they'd come in, and what they were eating. We were known for our chicken fried steak: a cut of tenderized cube steak pounded thin, coated in crushed oyster cracker crumbs, cooked in Crisco on the flattop. Grandma's chicken fried steak hung over the sides (all the sides) of an oblong plate, with mashed potatoes, white gravy, and corn—in ascending order—on top. Our daily interactions with large swaths of the fixed and transient populace gave us a unique vantage point of the community and a pivotal role in it.

Personality

Now that I find myself working at Cornell University (in the "Irish League," as my grandma once proudly proclaimed), I think back to my rural roots and my urban public teaching chops. During our year-long Mellon Seminar at the Society for the Humanities, I couldn't help but reflect on the incongruity between my Okie upbringing on the dusty plains and my cushy gig at an elite university on a hill. One feels distant, the other unfamiliar, yet their convergence constitutes the pillars of my past and present. I know that my students have similar feelings about leaving home and setting up shop somewhere else. As they navigate new experiences, come to terms with changes in perspective, they become other iterations of themselves. They are at a university to equip themselves with the skills to continue learning, questioning, and changing. Therefore, imagining ourselves and others, by default, in terms of constancy and comprehensibility can leave little room for recognizing the multiple ways that we exist and persist in the world.

As a scholar of Latin American and Latinx literary and cultural studies, my research and pedagogy explore how the human (as a construct, quality, and category) continues to be sized up, ascribed, negated, negotiated, and reimagined in various terrains. From Christopher Columbus's disqualifying documentation of indigenous populations, to the highly racialized core of the civilization or barbarism debate in the nineteenth century, and through the advent of new disciplines and technologies that scrutinized, quantified, and categorized the human in new, dehumanizing ways, the common thread is an attempt to pinpoint what constitutes a person, and which "deviations" reduce a person's status as such. As my colleagues' contributions in this volume attest, the history and actuality of these and other gestures are of vital importance to understanding the immense diversity and fraught trajectory of the human condition. Despite the liberatory aim of theorizations of the individual, or subject, that permeate Western philosophical traditions, those very articulations come with their own baggage that keeps them from approximating their purported or perceived universalism. Given the vastness and slipperiness of these epistemological and ontological questions, and the limited purvey of this essay, I would like to think instead about how the idea of *personality* can serve as a capacious concept for exploring subjective processes of becoming.

Uruguayan essayist José Enrique Rodó's *Motivos de Proteo* (1909), translated and published in English as *The Motives of Proteus* in 1928, is one of the most effective and challenging books that I give my students to consider and interrogate the inner dimensions of the self. Inspired by the sea god in Greek mythology renowned for his shape-shifting abilities, Rodó's "book in perpetual becoming" consists of diverse and at times dense meditations on the human's capacity to mutate.[1] The book's catch phrase, "Reformarse es vivir" ["To renew oneself is to live"] (Rodó 1928, 2), orients the reader through the cultivating terrains of a *personality*, a word that appears 130 times in the text. In his attempt to facilitate a deeper understanding of human subjectivity, Rodó advocates not a static, sedentary sense of self but rather one that experiences distinct and sometimes simultaneous iterations informed by our respective convictions, opinions, hypocrisies, and hopes, but not beholden to them. According to Rodó, "Each one of us is, successively, not one, but many. And these successive personalities, which emerge one from another, usually present the strangest and most astonishing contrasts" (Rodó 1928, 2–3).[2] Citing the "dynamic character of our nature," Rodó challenges the idea that we can ever be "definitively and absolutely" constituted at any point in time (Rodó 1928, 5). Existence, then, constantly begets modification and self-development. And, furthermore, that process is ongoing and ideally unfettered:

> As long as we live our personality is on the anvil. As long as we live, there is nothing in us that is not likely to be retouched and comple- mented. Everything is revelation, everything is a lesson, in everything there is a hidden treasure and the sun of each day wrests from things a new flash of originality. And within us, as time passes by, there is a constant need for renewal, for acquiring new force and new light to guard oneself against unknown evils, to aim at riches not yet enjoyed, and, finally, to prepare our adaptation to conditions alien to our experi- ence. To satisfy this necessity and to utilize this treasure, it is necessary to keep the idea that we are in perpetual apprenticeship and in constant initiation, alive. It is fitting, from the intellectual standpoint, to take care that our interest does not wither nor vanish completely, nor our childish curiosity with the liveliness of its fresh and candid attention. Nor must we allow the stimulus which grows from the knowledge or our ignorance (since we are always ignorant) to fade, nor must we lose faith in the power which consecrated the lips of the teacher and which made holy the pages of the book, that faith founded no longer either in a single book nor in a single teacher, but dispersed and diffused wher- ever one must seek it. (Rodó 1928, 5–6)[3]

A complex mosaic constantly in flux, our personalities are inherently susceptible to swift moments of change and reversal:

> Indeed, how varied and complex we are! Has it never happened that you felt yourself different from your true self? Have you never discov- ered in your consciousness something unknown and strange? Has an act of yours never surprised you after you had done it, on realizing its inconsistency with your trusted past experience built upon a hundred previous actions in your life? Have you never found in yourself things which you did not expect and have you never failed to find those which you considered most assured and certain? (Rodó 1928, 46).[4]

When such moments of transition or rupture arise, as unpredictable and inevitable as they may be, we tend to promptly internalize, normalize, and firmly situate them on the shelf with other supposedly steadfast convictions, until perhaps they themselves are altered or replaced. How can complete- ness and consistency constitute foundational human attributes? Our innate susceptibility to variation, in ways large and small, positions *personality* as an implied, not denied, humanity, one already achieved yet ever evolving and elusive. If the human is too vast and abstract a concept to entertain, perhaps personality points us toward a shared specificity, albeit one far from monolithic and unvarying. In short, our personalities, just like the human, are fraught constructs constantly open to revision and multiplicity.

"Do Your Job"

I write this as Trumpism is in full swing. As the sociopolitical climate that appeals to, and normalizes, the most inhumane instincts among us continues to intensify, and the cornerstones of competence, credibility, and care dissolve to new depressing depths, Stanley Fish's deflationist motto, "Do your job," lingers in both an appealing and an appalling way. In *Save the World on Your Own Time* (2008), Fish argues that university professors cannot, and therefore should not, aim to shape students' "moral, civic, and creative capacities" (11). He rejects the idea that seeking to make students more conscious and informed will necessarily translate into more engaged citizens and, in short, more responsible or ethical human beings. On the one hand, I agree with Fish's skepticism that the objective of changing the world is a daunting one. I also concur that this seems to position professors as sacrosanct purveyors of ethical thought and behavior, which is to say the exact type of normative authority that we consistently question and many times undermine. I echo Fish's reticence to assign this task to academics, who themselves are, like any other human beings, complex, flawed people prone to mistakes and hypocrisies.

Yet, for Fish to aver that we as educators should do little more than acknowledge that there are two sides to every story, and that each issue has various competing modes of thought as to how to address or resolve them, converts us into little more than relayers of information. This analysis-over-advocacy paradigm overlooks an important caveat: that we spend our lives examining how individuals and collectivities have thought and acted, in both horrifying and uplifting ways, throughout history. Are we expected to scrutinize humanisms but remain distant from the humanness of the human? It is precisely this proximity that animates us to be dedicated mentors to our students, to equip them with productive analytical skills but also with a greater sense of themselves in relation to other people and places. We should be mindful to not, as Fish insists, propose ourselves as models for the transformation we seek to bring about in our students. In fact, one of the first things I tell my students is that they should question everything, including what I tell them. It's true that we can control what we do in the classroom and how we do it. But I must disagree with Fish when he stipulates that we are not responsible for the effects of our teaching. Why, then, do transformative moments happen so often in our profession? That is not to say that we hit a home run every at bat. But to bring about, in the measure that we can, a moment of recognition, clarity, appreciation, or purpose is a remarkable privilege and responsibility.

Recognition

One of the most pivotal roles that I can play involves locating particular skills that students have, of which they may be completely unaware. Sometimes our most unique assets are those we don't even realize exist. For example, up until a few years ago, I had no idea that I saw the world in a different way than most people, and I'm not just talking about another instance of Arthur Schopenhauer's frequently quoted idea of "taking the limits of [my] own vision for the limits of the world" (Schopenhauer, 40). Just as there are people with prosopagnosia (aka "face blindness"), a condition that makes it difficult if not impossible to recognize faces, even of the people most close to them, there are also so-called super recognizers, who can see a face once and recognize and remember it forever. My partner would often question why I greeted people throughout our neighborhood in Upper Manhattan, or how in the world I recognized a person on the subway in a different part of town that we had seen once months ago in another part of town. Perhaps I had crossed paths with folks around the way, exchanged a passing smile, nod, wave, or words at some point. Or perhaps my small town upbringing instilled in me a propensity to be overly familiar. When I discovered that I was a super recognizer, it dawned on me that I knew them (or who they were), but the vast majority didn't know me. This realization had a profound effect on me, as decades of awkward exchanges came roaring to my mind and clarified a part of my life that I never knew needed explaining. I was stunned to learn that it can take people two or more times of meeting somebody for them to recognize or remember that person. How could I possibly have known this?

Facilitating critical moments of recognition like these is something the humanities does particularly well. Given that we frequently dialogue and write in my courses, I have ample opportunity to gauge how students think, express themselves, and see the world. When I inform a student that their prose is creative and engaging, that their acutely analytic style could be more effective with affective touches, or vice versa, I am telling them something about how they read, interpret, and question, and, ultimately, something about themselves. Part of the humanness that I bring to my pedagogy means trying to enact a moment (or moments) in each of my students when things click, to recognize the potentiality of their own strengths in new ways, or perhaps for the first time.

Notes

1. "Un libro en perpetuo 'devenir'" (Rodó 1967, 309).

2. "Cada uno de nosotros es, sucesivamente, no uno, sino muchos. Y estas personalidades sucesivas, que emergen las unas de las otras, suelen ofrecer entre sí los más raros y asombrosos contrastes" (Rodó 1967, 309–10).

3. "Mientras vivimos está sobre el yunque nuestra personalidad. Mientras vivimos, nada hay en nosotros que no sufra retoque y complemento. Todo es revelación, todo es enseñanza, todo es tesoro oculto, en las cosas; y el sol de cada día arranca de ellas nuevo destello de originalidad. Y todo es, dentro de nosotros, según transcurre el tiempo, necesidad de renovarse, de adquirir fuerza y luz nuevas, de apercibirse contra males aún no sentidos, de tender a bienes aún no gozados; de preparar, en fin, nuestra adaptación a condiciones de que no sabe la experiencia. Para satisfacer esta necesidad y utilizar aquel tesoro, conviene mantener viva en nuestra alma la idea de que ella está en perpetuo aprendizaje e iniciación continua. Conviene, en lo intelectual, cuidar de que jamás se marchite y desvanezca por completo en nosotros, el interés, la curiosidad del niño, esa agilidad de la atención nueva y candorosa, y el estímulo que nace de saberse ignorante (ya que lo somos siempre), y un poco de aquella fe en la potestad que ungía los labios del maestro y consagraba las páginas del libro, no radicada ya en un solo libro, ni en un solo maestro, sino dispersa y difundida donde hay que buscarla" (Rodó 1967, 311–12).

4. "En verdad ¡cuán varios y complejos somos! ¿Nunca te ha pasado sentirte distinto de ti mismo? ¿No has tenido nunca para tu propia conciencia algo del desconocido y el extranjero? ¿Nunca un acto tuyo te ha sorprendido, después de realizado, con la contradicción de una experiencia que fiaban cien anteriores hechos de tu vida? ¿Nunca has hallado en ti cosas que no esperabas ni dejado de hallar aquellas que tenías por más firmes y seguras?" (Rodó 1967, 332).

Works Cited

Fish, Stanley. *Save the World on Your Own Time*. New York: Oxford University Press, 2008.

Rodó, José Enrique. *Obras completas*. Madrid: Aguilar, 1967.

——. *The Motives of Proteus*. Translated by Angel Flores. New York: Brentano's, 1928.

Schopenhauer, Arthur. *Studies in Pessimism*. Translated by T. Bailey Saunders. New York: Cosimo, 2007.

CHAPTER 3

Present

Humanity in the Humanities

A.T. MILLER

A.T. Miller grew up in a large, active, musical, creative, overeducated, and socially engaged family with many siblings and cousins, on the shores of two lakes in the Chicago region, one very large and one very small. Museums and libraries, outdoor adventures, and concerts and plays— both on stage and in the audience—were a constant part of his childhood. His father's family has a long Quaker heritage to which A.T. maintains a commitment, serving as an adult in the leadership of the Friends Committee on National Legislation. In the online companion site for this book, one can see in A.T.'s video contribution the top of a chair on which A.T. is sitting, a chair that belonged to his forebear of Ebeneezer Miller, brought from Connecticut, where Quakers were not welcome, to Salem, New Jersey, in the eighteenth century. The famous Quaker saying "Let us see what love can do" inspired one of the songs A.T. has written and sings with his husband, Craig Kukuk, in their folk duo, Bridgewater.

With much of his time devoted to interpreting and seeking to influence the world he encounters through poetry, religious philosophy, music, public action, and social justice teaching and cultural awareness, A.T.'s life is centered in the humanities. This didn't prevent him from being elected as a Bernie Sanders delegate to the Democratic National Convention in 2016, his first engagement in active electoral politics since the Rainbow Coalition of 1988.

A.T. has a long association with various African communities. In the video on the Scholar as Human website, one can see the prominent Tuareg necklace, a traveler's protection, that A.T received on a visit to Mali in West Africa. He was there twice, first for the engagement of his niece to a Malian doctor, and then for their wedding. In Malian engagements and weddings a maternal uncle plays a significant role, and A.T. was happy to do so. As a young person, A.T. had spent eight years on the opposite side of the continent in East Africa help- ing to establish a secondary school that now bears his name and devoting time over a number of additional years to working with the National Music Festivals of Kenya. Some from those communities called him "mukhwasi," meaning "in- law," and in later life it is interesting how his niece has made that distantly more literally true. Not wishing to objectify his African friends and work, his PhD study was devoted to African American cultural studies but informed by his experience of rural Africa as well as his commitments to a view of the North American continent that connects to justice and love.

The chapter that A.T. offers here plays with presence and poetry, shaping experiences of his courses and encounters as opportunities for being-with in powerful, reflective ways. These courses include an experiential course on the Underground Railroad in upstate New York, and another such course interact- ing with places and people exploring 150 years of Latinx, women's rights, and indigenous experience at Cornell and in Ithaca. In the presence of history and of each other, he argues, we come to know ourselves.

May I have your attention, please? I'd also like to give you mine. It's some- thing that we can do together, to be fully present to each other, as a gift, as mutual exchange, as food for thought, inspiration, and perhaps some level of relationship. We share stories and interpretations of our lives and worlds in ways that require one to be present. I actually need to go to the gallery, to attend the concert, to become part of the audience in the theaters of dance and drama, to visit the historic site, to actually read the whole book, to engage in the discussion, to share my ideas, to tell my story and to hear others, and to listen, to protest. My opinions and my analysis are informed by, shaped by, and depend on my presence. One of the pleasures of our semi- nar has been being with each other on Wednesdays, in the same room, and of bouncing our ideas off of one another, mixing the serious ideas with the humorous asides and the excited interruptions. Amid the rising tide of medi- ated messages and manipulative iconography designed to make us jump to hurried, uncritical conclusions at their bite, we still wish to get together and exchange ideas and to be witnesses to each other's making of meaning in the stories we tell about our lives, this world, ourselves.

At Cornell I have taught a new course in Africana studies, "The Under- ground Railroad Seminar," that gives the students and me an opportunity to explore regional heritage, discuss current incidents of human trafficking, and place in physical and geographic context some of the classic narratives of individuals who freed themselves and assisted others. Each week the seminar meets in a different location on campus or in Ithaca, with two longer off-campus trips during the course. One day early in the course we hike down the Cascadilla Gorge to downtown, following Cascadilla Creek, and talk about those who followed streams, who might have had to walk in them to hide their scent from tracking dogs, who might have walked such trails with children or elders without the benefit of our paved path. While I empha-size to the students that there is no evidence that any nineteenth-century fugitive walked this particular trail, we do walk to the sites in DeWitt Park where twice Frederick Douglass stood and spoke, once to jeers and once to acclaim. A remarkable thing happens on this outing. Despite the tremen-dously compelling nature of Douglass's narrative, which the students have just read, something about being on that spot matters to them. Something about that walk and talking of the people we speak of moves some to tears. We stand outside the Clinton House, a former hotel and current office building where Peter Webb, the only enslaved person in Tompkins County to purchase his own freedom, worked. Several students speak in somewhat incredulous tones—"Do you mean this building? Here?" We visit the building where he filed his freedom papers. We visit a storefront that was once the barber shop of George Johnson, who gave fugitives and refugees the kinds of makeovers that would assist them to remain unrecognized during their jour-ney onward to Canada or their ongoing stay in Ithaca. Several students have told me that in the following weeks they brought their roommates, and in one case mother, to stand on the same sites and hear the same stories. Often, when I share some of the details of the class, fellow faculty and staff members at Cornell ask me to take them to these sites. Perhaps you feel something of the same reading this now? I am happy to share being present in these places. It moves me as well, and in the course we try to figure out why. What is it about the combination of story and place that seems to make the story more real and the place more meaningful? Why does it mean so much to do it together?

But presence is also opportunity and connection. We visit St. James AME church, the oldest standing church building in Ithaca, on land purchased by Peter Webb for the purpose of building a permanent church. Harriet Tub-man worshipped here frequently, and the church was very active in assisting people who were fleeing the violent terror of the United States. One year the class was unexpectedly fed a meal there by a warm and gracious group, and we all noted that the tradition of hospitality that had founded this congrega-tion still grounded it. They invited us to come back any time and noted that they offered regular meals on particular days. A student unable to attend the day the group went became part of one of those events. Another year, the elder who met us to talk about the church mentioned that he had been born in Alabama. One of the questions toward the end of the presentation focused on him, as a student asked how he had ended up in Ithaca, New York, of all places, from Alabama. When he was sixteen, his father's involvement in a small civil rights movement gesture brought an immediate threat from the KKK, and the family left Alabama the next morning. In the elder's presence and in his life story, we all experienced an immediate understanding that a historic path to and through this town was still active, and the testimony to that was happening in class. In the university archives, we hold the real shackles, we see Olaudah Equiano's first edition, we view every issue of Douglass's *North Star,* we talk of George Washington Fields, the Cornell student whose narrative we also read, learning how his mother freed herself and her children by dashing to Union lines at night, hiding in the bushes in the battles of the Carolinas, suddenly losing heart at having somehow to cross a river with five small children. We think of Fields sitting in the classrooms of Old Stone Row, where we sit, a nontraditional older student in the 1870s. The presence, the place, the touch, the careful conservation and collection in order to show us again the precious and real documents in this place. We are separated by time, and they are long dead, but somehow this form of presence matters, it matters deeply. It matters that we in the class do this together.

Late in the semester we take a longer trip, to the Canadian border at Buffalo and Lewiston, where Harriet crossed with so many. She lived for a time in St. Catharines, Ontario, when life in the United States became too dangerous. So many New Yorkers were uprooted in those days. By then we would have watched *12 Years a Slave,* the astounding film depiction of Solomon Northup's twelve years kidnapped away from Saratoga Springs. We have passed through Rochester, where Linda Brent (Harriet Jacobs) had her tea room with her brother. We stood on that corner and looked at that building—which is also the same building where the *North Star* was printed. It is cold in Rochester late in fall semester. It is cold in Buffalo and in Lewiston. Yet this was the time of year, post-harvest, when fugitives were most likely to flee and, after hundreds of miles, to face that last obstacle, the river. It is a terrifying sight. The Niagara at these points is often the fastest flowing river in North America. One year, in Lewiston, as we huddled on the banks, some folks in a small boat were struggling to tie up. I asked the students, "Would you get in that boat?" We know there are those who swam. How many could not have made this final challenge after so many miles of walking and hiding? We think of the boats in the Mediterranean Sea. We think of the walk from Guatemala. We think. We stand as witnesses in the place, in the presence of the many thousands gone. It's a way that I've gotten to know upstate New York. Who would I have been then?

Toward New Destinations

Imagine worlds
Imagine suns
That germinate, that generate—
The generations

Imagine you and you again
Your many selves
Amid the one—
The congregation

Imagine earth
Its single moon of many moods
And guiding stars
Reflecting and producing light
Within the beauty of eternal night
The darker time of shining dreams
That wake us to inspire beyond the parch of day

The years,
 The seasons, days,
  The now.

Three sowers—many seeds
The rich dark earth
The prism's many-colored warmth of light
We plant the autumn crop
A winter wheat to meet the hunger
And years of blinding snow, the cold
Will break and melt will water shoots of early spring

We'll let the older things decay, but keep them near
To mix with what we've planted
In the loam that's all the richer
As we cultivate this home

And from those worlds
And from those suns
And from those selves
These seeds

The grow,
     The light,
          The we.
A.T. Miller, September 2011

I answered the phone one day in my office to learn that I was speaking to a colonel at West Point who invited me to speak to an important alumni diversity committee there and interact with their faculty. My first thought was, "Do they know what I look like?" I am a Quaker and an activist on the board of the Friends Committee on National Legislation, the largest peace lobby in Washington DC, and a gay man. When I shared the news that evening as I was seeking some clarity about whether to go or not, my husband told me that he had always wanted to see West Point, so I guessed we were going as a couple. As I discussed the visit with various officials at the United States Military Academy, the responsibilities grew to involve a two-day itinerary of events that included guest-teaching two classes and giving a keynote speech at a formal dinner, along with several hours' work with the diversity committee and a series of one-on-one and group faculty discussions. For the first time, the leader of the corps of cadets that academic year was a woman, and disparaging social media comment (via Yik Yak) was emerging during parade, a gross violation of discipline. The full acceptance of out LGBT cadets in the army and in the corps was just about one year old officially. There remained long-term racial and ethnic equity and representation issues in the corps and on the faculty. I was in both a very familiar and an extremely unfamiliar place. They wanted my expertise, but I also needed to offer them myself. It is one of the fundamentals of diversity practice to be all in and to share honestly and authentically.

In some ways, the uniformity of military discipline stripped several of the layers of social navigation I was used to in situations like this. There was a directness to getting to the problems that was refreshing, and a sincerity that was palpable. A week after my visit, one of the young male cadets in a class in which I guest-lectured sent me a paper he was doing on gender equity issues in the army. Ostensibly for comment, it was also clearly for affirmation. I had not been called "Sir" so many times in two days since serving as head of a rural high school in East Africa many years ago. The dinner was attended by a fair number of four-star generals, who were very cordial to my husband and me. They really are trained to kill, but they also really don't want to have to do so. Lee and Custer trained there, losers and losses. I learned a great deal from deciding to be present to several humanities classes and the constituents of an institution that gave me pause at the invitation, and as

I left, my hosts asked if they could print the poem I wrote for them in the West Point alumni magazine.

Taylor and Bradley, Sullivan and Pershing, Petraeus and Mattis all studied there. The opposite of the humanities is dehumanization, is inhumanity, so I'll stop. Here is the poem I shared that night.

West Point

Down from the mountains and out to the sea
In wide waters deep this current flows
Where stones stand strong
Becoming every grain of sand that shows
The many facets, blues and greens, yes gold, brown, red
That make the grey, the stately run
Of river and rock—
We are the river,
We are the rock—|
The river passage to and through a newer world

On higher ground we can survey
Perspectives on the seen, unseen, the parts we never knew
The backdrop scenery
Ensouled, envisioned, peopled
By the stars' early light
That dawn of knowing who we're with
With whom we are
The more that makes us units, all

We see the distant fields
The scenes of action of the mind
Reaction to the minds of those
Who see with other eyes that land
This earth, our homeland shared
And where forever rests

Led to and from the stone
Made stronger in the passing through and by
Where leading leads us to the many
You and I
Our many selves that make us true
And every part, yes every facet|
Every grain of sand within the flow|

Comes from the rock, brings down the heights
To common ground
The fields.

A.T. Miller, April 2014

A profound response to the violent struggle over apartheid was the truth and reconciliation commission designed and led by Archbishop Desmond Tutu. This was an incredibly daring and sweeping use of presence under circumstances of injustice that could never be made right, and a history of deep and lasting harm. Being able to tell the terrible stories and to speak about what was hidden and what was gotten away with in the presence of the perpetrators had remarkable effects. Personal burdens and personal transformation have a depth and importance within human understanding that is on a different plane from institutional and social justice but holistically is also a part of it as restorative justice. We can be witnesses and speak truth to power as we also diffuse power with truth. It all happens with presence, and it happened again with the desire of a committee that gives the Wallenberg Medal to engage and honor the presence of Desmond Tutu. It is another form of presence to attend the lectures and shake the hands of those who boldly write and speak. Even when we have known the message and known the words, we still desire that presence. I served on that committee, and at the reception before the prize was awarded noted that no one was actually talking beyond introductions with the archbishop, who is a lively and humorous person. So I spoke with him, and we touched on my class, and he agreed to speak to my students the next morning during a time of engaging and funny banter before the ceremony. To introduce him to my students, I wrote for him this poem:

Praise Poem for Archbishop Desmond Tutu

It's a little name you wear
A smile that's small
That fits your dancing soul
With room for both of us and yet another also
And points out where we're going—
Oh, take us with you, merry man.

The dream you had
For all of us
Came really true
And planted seeds of other dreams

In soil of clay and rock, both desert dry and fertile, too,
Inspiring songs from notes and bars, the prophet's voice—
The chorus grew.

And let us pause with love for ancestors,
The grandfathers whose dreams were never known,
But were the gold they buried in the mines
and never sold.

When hope is hard
A spirit speaks,
But needs a voice of steady pitch
And principles are paths that must be walked with strength,
Though where they lead, the walker only dares to know
By moving forward in the front of fear,
A bramble only faith can clear.

The life you've lived for all the ones whose lives were lost
In times where color killed, was read all over.
It's your humility that gives us pride
Your power in the stand the disempowered held.

Across the sea, in other worlds far south
Where spring is blooming, just as here the winter comes
What balance do we find in opposites?
It's only 'til they're reconciled, the tipping stops,
And that which would have sunk is steadied in a calming sea.

The struggle in the life to which we're born
Cannot be dodged, but also when the round is through
The fighter knows the count, and after ten
Must leave the vanquished on the mat,
But who can shake that bloody hand?

There are the saints who show us all
What is the victor/victim's wound that must be seen
To then be healed
And tears can cleanse the hardened heart that did the wrong,
But only in the light of truth,
The glaring white that finds its match
In sable darkness, comfort of forgiven crimes.

The little girl . . .
That youthful dream . . .

And grandma's hope . . .
The men . . ., the fists . . ., *awetu*!

How did you gather pieces all, each tragedy
And build a home, from shards, a glass
Reflecting on a world anew?

You were the one who went to school
And made your education free for all
And taught the ones we thought would never learn.

And so we build
We honor lives both lost and found
And give to those who gave, a prize.

Take wisdom from the dancing stars
The southern cross
A bishop's prayer.
Equality has many names
And glory comes when truth is told,
No gilding words, but boldly paid
In stories where we kiss the ring, we find the gold.

Inspired, the young embrace the old
Whose youth
Will live within our hearts
And ripen in a wider world of gratitude
For what will come.

A.T. Miller, October 2008

Karl Polanyi, the Austro-Hungarian socialist social theorist of the late nineteenth and early twentieth centuries, in his major work *The Great Transformation*, sees a level of natural resistance to the market and commodification in human life and society, while Stuart Hall sees a necessary resistance in *The Empire Strikes Back*, and Augusto Boal finds the dramatic and artistic method of engagement used by Olivio Dutra in Porto Alegre to make the people authentically present as participants in public affairs.

In the days after the 2016 US presidential election, my husband began telling many of our friends that we would be in Washington for the women's march the day after the January inauguration, and telling made it so. We rode "Harriet's Hometown Bus" from Auburn, New York, as the only two men among a determined and joyful fifty-four passengers. Our friend Sigrid, who could not go, called up two days before and told us she had two pussy hats for us to wear. She dropped off a third when she stopped by, for our bus captain, as it happened, who did not have time to get her own earlier. We presented ourselves in the hundreds of thousands to the seat of power, crowded, dancing, and decorated for the battle. It was and is a source of strength.

Last fall on campus an artist sought to show the measure of ethnic cleansing on our slope and in our town in *American Spolia* but failed to note that those he thought were gone had family here among us, on the lake that bears their name. He saw the faults of Washington's orders and DeWitt's survey and Sullivan's campaign, our fellow white men, but not the objects of the plan, the people, those present. Yes, that founding time was wrong, but it is not over, we are not erased in reality, even if in his rendering. He was told but found his own idea more compelling than the presence of the others. And there are other others who, very present in our work and days, but lack the documents that borders crossed, are under threat. We came, we come, we stay. Upon this beautiful and enduring land the great bear scratched with lakes, the many claims of those who occupy, and those they thought were gone, and those who are here but they wish were gone, all meet and are present. We struggle with the art, and we struggle with the policies, and we struggle with ideas, and we struggle to be here with each other. Still here.

Solidarity

We stand above Cayuga's waters
Here upon Cayuga's land
The people here who keep the beauty from so long ago—

Can we adopt the ancestors, can we with honor
Stand upon these heights that are not ours?
Come down, bend near, rock low
For sun and earth are loaned to us for these days here with you
And how injustice lingers, listen, notice, even now as you reclaim the shore,
With us, if we so dare to say, take us with you,
Oh bear us up, with knee and arm and shoulder square
We honor you, Cayuga, we.

All the deepest cracks within the earth, and
All the falls that run the rocks
The tumble and the splash
The violent rush, the diving tempting fear upon the bridge

Yes, all the cooling waters that reflect the day, the falls, the fall, the trees
The burning branches, cooling evenings there
The nights, the dropping droplets flow
To one, the lake, that bears us up
The boats, the float, the know—
We ride the depths upon the fracture filled,
The will to one, the cracking full,
No further fall, the all, the water's wide—
We wade, we drink, we live.

Alone we never sing
For it is not a song without a hearing one
In harmony the notes belong
And tune to one another, yes
Anticipate the time
Compose the power of our beauty
In d'Artagnan's mode
The one in all, the all, the one

And when we reach divide, no conquer then,
No long division comes because
We know the waters
Yes, we know the falls become the lake,
The chasm filled, we cross,
And of the French, as kin, say we / oui

A. T. Miller, October 2012

I felt a tickle on my hand from behind as I was walking on Park Avenue in New York City, turning to find Christopher and a hug of recognition—my student of thirty years ago! I was a graduate student and administrative fellow in an undergraduate college house where Chris was a resident. I had served as a character witness in his trial and dealt with all the press and the Penn administration when he was summarily suspended. Visiting his brother in Harlem during a drug raid, he was swept up and had his photo on the front page of the *New York Post* with the headline "Ivy League Crack Dealer." Every reporter I spoke with was an uphill climb of re-righting the story of the pre-written trope within their heads. He had no car, no flashy clothes. He was not trying to keep up with a fast Ivy crowd. Our college was the diversity college. His financial aid covered everything. He was a kind and considerate person. "Everyone we interview says that," said the doubting reporters—perhaps because it was true. I spoke at rallies and conferred with William

Kunstler, the top pro bono attorney, met with his mom, later cleaned out his room. The police case fell apart on the stand. The prosecutor had only one final argument: "No law-abiding citizen would be in a place like that!" In the press, on the stand, I was the flaky hippie academic. My New Jersey uncle saw me on the evening news. The apartment house where Christopher's brother lived condemned him just by being there. Christopher got twenty-five years. He served nineteen. I wrote and visited over those many years as he got religion. The Bible-laced letters were not my style, but the Bible was certainly not a bad focus in Green Haven. We never missed birthdays. After his release, my husband and I attended his wedding a few years back, and he got his accounting degree, and there on Park Avenue he told me of his son, another baby to become a proud black man. He recognized me walking down the street near his office. He loves me, and I love him over all these years. It is all a complex exchange between real people. There are stories we live, chance meetings, and stories we cannot stop, embedded in society.

The ACLU found my husband and me for the 2005 lawsuit in Michigan against the state's recent ban on health benefits for domestic partners because the ACLU needed couples with legal standing who would be willing to handle public scrutiny. Craig was connected to the state through my employment benefits at the University of Michigan, all four of our Michigan-based parents were supportive, and we met through church—how could we not agree to be the plaintiffs? We felt generous as they asked us, and we gave up our privacy. We won the first trial. The benefits allowed Craig, a mental health therapist, to serve the most vulnerable with group therapy after hospitalization, most likely for a suicide attempt. They were on disability, severely depressed, and their lives had not changed on discharge. Some paid five dollars a week for life-giving support. So much of nonprofit community support work is done by those on the benefits of others. Cutting off Craig would cut off forty people. It was a story we told, the truth, against the tide of tropes that saw our benefits as selfish, as if we were the ones who sued and not the ones the ACLU approached. Young gay professionals resented. The photographer came to our house for the article and for most of the shots wanted us to sit in separate chairs and at one point told us not to smile. The dimmed photo that ran large above the article made us look angry, like people who would sue. The state appealed, and we lost, and we lost again at the state supreme court. Through creative means, at the university, Craig became my "Other Qualified Adult" until even that was challenged.

Those present can be themselves and not summed up, not packaged, and not told, but ever telling and revealing more and more again. The humanities are a constant exchange in the search for meaning, for broader life, for the complexities of what cannot be easily understood or summarized, for the alternative view. We are not simple, we may have standing, but we have more when we are present, the humans at the gate, open to interpretation and able to speak.

At Home

Let us be uncomfortable together.
Let us depend upon surprises.

The unexpected is a place we hope to find most every day,
And by the way we get there—
Moving off the trodden path.
What difference makes is wisdom,
As knowledge brings the unfamiliar home.

The educated one is all unbounded and is never one,
Nor truly singular as through the curiosity the we flows in
And out to all the others who have come to know—
Above, below, in front of us,
We look behind the simple sign of who we are.

We raise a flag, but don't salute before another flag is raised
Devoted in our hours and days to signs and wonders
Semaphore that by interpretation tells us more
About our many selves.

Do come in,
Don't be our guest—
This house is theirs,
And yours.

A. T. Miller, October 2011

PART II

Engaging Artifacts

When Ed Baptist, a historian who participated in our seminar, shared some of his work on runaway slave ads, he brought some images of such ads and focused our attention on the small black figure of a runner. This icon appears in every print ad seeking the return of "property"—a tiny, eloquent image of freedom that bespeaks its opposite. What Ed impressed upon us was the physicality of the icon. In every print shop around the country, there was iron type for every letter and punctuation mark as well as sorts—special characters—including the sort of a runaway. Boys, Ed told us, were often typesetting assistants, and so he painted for us a picture of a wood-floored printing office, where the news and advertisements were set and where a twelve-year-old assistant picked up this sort of a human being fleeing slavery and set it in a composing stick. What did such assistants feel as they handled the sort? Did they realize they were participating in ending someone's hope for freedom? Encouraging violence? Advancing the dehumanization of an entire people?

Ed Baptist (a member of our seminar but not a contributor to this volume) is a key collaborator and founder of Freedom on the Move—an NEH-funded national archive of runaway slave ads. The fact of the archive itself emphasizes the importance of artifacts. The work of arts and humanities scholars is rooted in ideas, but it depends on artifacts—books, of course, and archives, but also textiles, ruins, signage, blueprints, exhibits, paintings, videos, websites, and much more. Artifacts proclaim not only information but belonging and context. Their embeddedness in communities, organizations, landscapes, and homes make them extraordinary opportunities for place-based and creative connection to others. In short, all artifacts are already bridges with the potential to link communities and scholars. Ed and his colleagues in Freedom on the Move write, "[We] use crowdsourcing to enable the general public to take part in creating the database. Though the data collected will be invaluable to academic researchers, we also see this as a collective public history project: the crowdsourcing platform will provide an opportunity for people in all areas of life to engage with the history of slavery in the US in a concrete and meaningful way, by excavating small details of enslaved peoples' lives, bit by bit."

Much of the work of humanizing scholarship seeks to demonstrate that kind of commitment to public benefit and participation, to treat artifacts and their home communities with the respect and collegiality that they deserve. To the surprise of many scholars, the hard work of demonstrating that respect is not a cost of doing business but an opening toward greater learning and deeper impact—again, this is a core lesson of community engagement, but it is shared here in the particular stories of individuals grappling with their own instinctual sense of right practice.

CHAPTER 4

Humans Remain

Engaging Communities and Embracing Tensions
in the Study of Ancient Human Skeletons

MATTHEW C. VELASCO

Matthew C. Velasco was born and raised in Southern California, the son of a first-generation Mexican father and immigrant Cuban mother. In high school, Matt dabbled in TV and film production. He even planned to go to film school, but his acceptance into Stanford University led to other paths. As a sophomore, he took courses in archaeology and human osteology, the scientific study of bones. During a lecture in Introduction to Archaeology, his professor showed the class an animated 3D model of Chavín de Huántar, a three-thousand-year-old ceremonial center in highland Peru. Matt was enthralled. The following summer he had the opportunity to participate in archaeological excavations at Chavín and explore firsthand the site's scenic landscape, monumental architecture, and labyrinthine passageways and crypts. In the words of Obi-Wan Kenobi, he had taken his first step into a larger world.

Since that formative experience in 2006, Matt has continually returned to Peru. As a graduate student at Vanderbilt University, he gained valuable field and laboratory experience on a number of other projects, and finally, in 2012, he directed his dissertation fieldwork at two cemetery sites in the Colca Valley of Peru. Proyecto Bioarqueológico Coporaque aimed to elucidate the biocultural history of the Collaguas ethnic group, which dwelled in the central Colca Valley during the era preceding and encompassing Inka imperial expansion in the fifteenth century. As a bioarchaeological anthropologist, Matt studies the skeletal remains of these ancient people to reconstruct how they lived and died; what their childhood was like; what they ate; whether they suffered from malnutrition, violence, or disease; how they were treated by others in life; and how they were remembered after death. Although his research focuses on the ancient dead, it is his engagement and relationship with the living community of Coporaque, the descendants of the Collaguas, that forms the focus of his contribution to this book—a retrospective on the tensions, negotiations, meanings, and possibilities surrounding the study of human skeletal remains in Peru.

An assistant professor in the Department of Anthropology at Cornell University, Matt lives in Brooktondale, New York, with his partner, Briana, a public interest lawyer; their dog, Jack, a black-and-white boxer mix who loves peanut butter; and their hyperactive cat, Tweet, who was adopted from the high-altitude environs of Coporaque.

Prologue: Mourning

The path strikes northwest from the village, stretching across the porous boundary between domestic and agrarian life in highland Peru.[1] It passes a series of small residences—rustic dwellings of stone and adobe—most arranged around central patios and many interspersed with open-air stables and coops of wood and wire. These homesteads are sparsely occupied at this hour of the morning, when most folks are off tending to their crops and canals. Still-frozen sheets sag the clotheslines crisscrossing the patios. Only the clamorous bray of an unseen donkey breaks the calm. Past the edge of the village, the cobbled-street-turned-dirt-path proceeds through a walled corridor, bordered on either side by harvested fields of maize and alfalfa. The aroma of manure and dried vegetation wafts over. Reaching the base of the mountain, the path narrows and curves southward to make its steady crawl up the slopes of Yuraq Qaqa.

At elevations surpassing eleven thousand feet, the sun spares no inch of exposed skin, but the air is cool and unpolluted, and the vista commanding. From the ascending path, the picturesque village of Coporaque lies completely in view. Just over a quarter-mile from end to end, the gridded streets of the colonial planned town quickly give way to an arresting landscape: the deeply cut Colca River valley and the snow-capped Huarancante to the east. Closer to us, grazing cattle and horses fleck a quilted patchwork of agricultural fields browned and yellowed under the austral sun. A lone laborer strides silently in the distance. Rising above her: the pre-Hispanic and early colonial settlement of San Antonio, the forerunner to the modern village. San Antonio sits on a natural promontory at the edge of a terraced amphitheater rimmed by Eucalyptus trees (see fig. 4.1). Remnants of some one hundred house structures are scattered upslope, westward and southward; even to a trained eye, they seem little more than gray shards amid the shrubs, tombstones to ancient domesticity.

Saddled with expensive archaeological equipment, I bend my eyes toward the ground and the path before us, leaving this highland scene behind me. Amid heavy breathing and heaving wind, few words are spoken. Even Enady, two years my junior and a native of Coporaque, occasionally stops to catch her breath. She and the other women from the village carry metal buckets, brushes, and trowels carefully wrapped in the embroidered shawls slung across their backs. The student volunteers from the United States and Peru fare little better as they march along to the beats of their respective headphones. Only Richard, born and raised in the even higher-altitude altiplano (high plateau) surrounding Lake Titicaca, speeds ahead, his compact yet stout frame swiftly scaling the mountainside. His purple-hooded figure soon vanishes from our collective view behind a jagged double outcrop of white rock, *yuraq qaqa* in Quechua.

In due time we too pass the white outcrop and arrive soon after at a weathered sign. It directs us upslope to a footpath that zigzags across half a dozen unfarmed terraces. About halfway up the switchbacks, I catch a glimpse of three stone structures emerging beyond the uppermost terrace bench.

FIGURE 4.1   View southeast along the path of Yuraq Qaqa, the white rock outcrop visible at the edge of the frame. This photo was taken on July 9, 2009, the first time the author visited the site. Photo by author.

They are merely the zenith of an elaborate complex of stone chambers built one against the other and camouflaged against the cliff face. Sun-bleached skulls sentineled at the openings of these buildings reveal their purpose (see fig. 4.2). Temporarily shadowed by the escarpment, we will rest here— at the final resting place of the men, women, and children of San Antonio.

The mausoleums of Yuraq Qaqa have stood for over half a millennium in one of the most seismically active regions of the world, the Colca Valley of southern Peru. They have not only endured earthquakes and volcanic eruptions but also destructive forces of a different sort, having escaped Spanish attempts to eradicate ancestral shrines and indigenous religious practices during the so-called "extirpation of idolatry" campaigns of the seventeenth and eighteenth centuries. Yet in the latter half of the twentieth century (and perhaps earlier), looters and collectors ransacked these accessible, above-ground tombs, seeking curiosities to keep for themselves or treasures to sell in the burgeoning black market of pre-Columbian antiquities. What once were scores of carefully prepared "mummy bundles"—bodies naturally desiccated, wrapped in textiles, and encased in a basket of woven grass—have been reduced to mostly disarticulated human skeletal remains, intermixed with fallen stones, torn textiles, and vegetal fibers (see fig. 4.3).

The looting of these tombs presents unique challenges to standard archaeological excavation. As the director of Proyecto Bioarqueológico Coporaque, I must decide how disassociated skeletal parts are to be documented,

FIGURE 4.2   The tombs of Yuraq Qaqa. Photo by author.

FIGURE 4.3   Commingled human remains at Yuraq Qaqa. This photo is taken from the "looter's entrance" at the northeast corner of the burial chamber. Photo by author.

bagged, and inventoried. Do spatially or anatomically associated parts merit separate registry in the field? Should they be point-plotted on a scaled map? How *many* skeletal parts in association constitute an "individual"? Making this decision would then require the spot's designation as a separate area of excavation, in order to document body position and screen the surrounding soil matrix for small artifacts (such as shell beads or copper pendants) that may have escaped a looter's grasp. These questions and their answers are not trivial for the archaeological excavator, who relies on clearly defined protocols for the systematic recovery and analysis of human skeletal remains from archaeological sites.

Yet, as an anthropologist fundamentally concerned with both the diversity and complexity of human experience, the reality that these skeletal parts were once living, breathing *humans* ruptures the routine of field research. I wonder: How many hundreds or thousands of people have grieved at the very spot where I now sit, thumbing through my field notebook? What path did they walk to reach this place of mourning? I imagine making the breathless hike to Yuraq Qaqa, my lungs swollen with sorrow, the landscape emptied and washed in tears.

For the people who lived here long ago, death must have also represented another kind of rupture. Would the passing of a community leader have placed political alliances in jeopardy? Might it have occasioned conflict? And what of the loss of a father or mother, sister or brother? Were close kin called on to prepare their body for burial, to fulfill their labor obligations, to tend to their herds and fields, or—to avenge their death? When they stood before the desiccated body of an ancestor, what did they *see*?

The chamber of bones calls me back to the present. *It is time to begin our work.*

Stories in Bone

The vignette that opens this chapter is a narrative retrospective of the experience of walking to Yuraq Qaqa and encountering the dead who dwell there. These pathways of contemplation were trodden innumerable times throughout the course of the archaeological research I directed in the Colca Valley from 2012 to 2015. The memories are distinctly my own yet illustrate, I believe, a common aspect of archaeological field research. Our experiences of *being* in other places, moving and thinking through the landscape and engaging with tangible (and sometimes morbid) remains of the past, inevitably shape the questions we ask and the interpretations we put forward to the scientific community and broader public. As a bioarchaeological anthropologist who studies ancient human skeletons, I will pore over the bodies of evidence from Yuraq Qaqa and document the age, sex, and social identities of the people buried there. Were they male or female?[2] Did they die young or live to old age? Why did some individuals adopt the practice of binding and reshaping the heads of their children, while others abstained? And how did this new way of signaling identity shape cooperation and conflict between peoples living in an era of unprecedented violence—the period before the Inka Empire rose to power in the fifteenth century? Scientific analysis of their bones and teeth will tell me if individuals who had different head shapes also had distinct life experiences, whether they were closely related to one another, whether they immigrated to the Colca Valley during their lifetime, whether they consumed a diverse array of foods or maintained a more restricted diet, and whether they suffered from chronic disease, nutritional stress, or physical violence.

By reading and translating the stories written in bone, bioarchaeologists possess a unique capacity for channeling the public's curiosity about the morbid into larger scientific and humanistic inquiries into the lives once led by these ancient bodies.[3] For any given historical and cultural context, a bioarchaeologist may ask how ancient humans not only adapted to their social, cultural, and physical environments but also how they actively transformed them. Other stories untold lie with the marginalized or forgotten "makers" of histories—the laborers, slaves, or chronically ill—whose physical remains testify to the ways social hierarchies and inequalities literally mold our bodies, penetrating to the bone.[4] Ultimately, the stories we tell, though deeply rooted in data, are just that—stories that seek to make meaning of verifiable but incomplete evidence to explain how societies change over time and how that change is rooted in individual human actions and behaviors. At a deeper level, our work seeks to communicate the embodied experiences of others—what it means to be human in different times and places.[5] The playwright's undertaking, as voiced by Suzanne Lori Parks, resonates, quite literally, with the tasks of the bioarchaeologist: "to . . . locate the ancestral burial ground, dig for bones, find bones, hear the bones sing, write it down."[6]

This humanistic pursuit, however earnest and well-intentioned, involves multiple, inherently imperfect acts of translation, beginning with the exchange between the researcher (me) and the nameless dead (humans/ specimens/data) whose stories I presume to tell. My colleagues will eventually encounter versions of these stories in scholarly publications and— through conversation, critique, and citation—establish their place within a field of knowledge. Through popular outlets and social media, these stories are translated for broader audiences, with the hope that they will engage the public imagination and contribute a bioarchaeological perspective to the most pressing issues facing humanity today, including climate change, sectarian violence, population displacement, and migration.[7] Often lost in the cacophony of academic and public discourse are the communities most directly impacted by archaeological research. As the descendants of the Collaguas, the pre-Hispanic peoples who built the tombs and were buried in them, the inhabitants of Coporaque have their own interests in and hopes for archaeological research that are, of course, not the same as my own nor evenly shared among themselves. This is, then, an unequal translation, where multiple languages (English, Spanish, Quechua, academese) are spoken but not with equal facility by all. As a North American, phenotypical white researcher with academic credentials and resources, I claim an authority to analyze and write about ancient peoples that is rarely accessible to my "non-academic" interlocutors.

When does our desire to make meaning of the dead collide with other meanings the bones may have for the living—stories that are *not* our own? Contentious debates over human remains have defined three decades of (bio-)archaeological research in the United States, where indigenous peoples' claims to ancestral bones are legally recognized, even as processes of repatriation have been unevenly realized. While imperfect analogs for the political discourses surrounding human remains in other countries, these struggles compel us to recognize that a scientific-humanistic perspective is only one of many ways of experiencing the materiality of bones.[8] Constructive engagement with descendant communities is made all the more difficult where ethical or legal guidelines concerning the excavation of human remains are nonexistent, as is the case in Peru. Cultural attitudes toward the dead also vary widely between communities in this Andean country. As Bethany Turner and Valerie Andrushko observe, these factors lead to "situational, dynamic, and sometimes unclear routes for ethical practices in excavating, storing, and analyzing human remains."[9] This is the story of one such route traveled.

This chapter explores the tensions, negotiations, meanings, and possibilities surrounding the study of human skeletal remains in foreign countries. I build on recent work that broadly outlines the ethical dimensions of bioarchaeological research by bringing into focus the community dynamics that underlie most archaeological research but rarely enter the published record.[10] My aim is not prescriptive but reflexive. In archaeology, community engagement is a lauded ideal and ethical obligation but one for which students are woefully undertrained and underfunded. In my own experience, community engagement was naively conceived of as prologue and coda to the *real* field experience of "doing bioarchaeology." I would seek permission from the community at the start of the project and then share the findings at the end. In this mind-set, I fell into many of the pitfalls of community archaeology.[11] Chief among these is the presumption that the benefits of archaeological research would inevitably overcome its disturbances. The process of working through the tensions of bioarchaeological research—the moments of vulnerability and serendipity, discord and tentative understanding—has long outlived the period of fieldwork.

Before recounting how these conversations unfolded (and continue to unfold), some background on the "official" discourses and regulations surrounding archaeological research in Peru is in order. In the next section I briefly describe the legal parameters of archaeological research in Peru, which might be unfamiliar to a North American audience, and ask how a nationalist discourse of cultural patrimony shapes the terms of engagement between foreign archaeologists and local communities. I then turn to local relationships with the dead and the archaeological past, showing how they come into conflict with state claims to ownership and scholarly claims to knowledge production. Rhetoric surrounding the removal of objects from gravesites reveals ritual and economic concerns that are ultimately inextricable from the colonial legacies that undergird field research by foreigners.

The next two sections of this chapter revisit the many meetings and chance encounters that shaped the course of my fieldwork. In the final section I return to Coporaque, literally and figuratively, exploring what remains with me and what remains there. While an epilogue to the chapter, it is prologue to a continued commitment to the people of Coporaque.

Who Owns the Past in Peru?

The regulations governing the excavation of human remains in Peru are quite distinct from those in place in the United States. US citizens may be familiar with the Native American Grave Protection and Repatriation Act (NAGPRA), which empowers *federally recognized* tribes to determine the final disposition of ancestral human remains and associated funerary objects discovered on federal or tribal territory or housed in federally funded museums and institutions.[12] While not without serious legal and logistical flaws, NAGPRA offers a measure of protection for Native American gravesites that for centuries were plowed through, plundered, pillaged, and profaned.[13] Even as this landmark legislation has transformed archaeological practice for the better, the desecration of Native American ancestral lands remains a highly contentious and continuous struggle. In 2016, illegal construction on Dakota sacred sites at Standing Rock destroyed ancient burial mounds.[14] These abuses are the outgrowth of centuries of colonial and extractive policies by the US government and US-backed corporations.

At least in theory, then, federal and state laws grant agency to Native American tribal groups over ancestral graves that are encountered by archaeological excavation or development activity. In Peru, however, no such laws or norms exist regarding the ethical excavation and curation of human skeletal remains.[15] The cultural patrimony of Peru, by definition, belongs to the nation—that is, to *all* Peruvians, regardless of indigenous or ethnic identification. To investigate sites of cultural patrimony, the archaeologist must submit a detailed project proposal to the Ministry of Culture in Lima. Research design and methods are vetted, including the number of units to be excavated, their location on the landscape, how archaeological material will be processed and labeled, et cetera. From a legal standpoint, permission from the community is a courtesy, as is its participation. No stage of the solicitation, authorization, or evaluation process for archaeological projects requires the formal consent of local government, let alone the informal consent of the local community.

By extension, archaeological materials of any kind discovered on communal or "private" lands fall under the jurisdiction of the state, as the custodian of national heritage. In Bolivia, Peru's neighbor to the east, excavated or privately held archaeological materials are also property of the state, but local communities exercise greater autonomy there over the process of archaeological research and management of archaeological collections and museums.[16] Either case is a sharp contrast to the United States, where private property and ownership are sacrosanct.[17] The Peruvian Ministry of Culture may grant temporary custodianship of collections to the investigator, but at the culmination of this determined period (typically within one year of completing the field project), the law requires that all excavated materials be submitted to and stored with the appropriate regional division of the ministry.

On June 14, 2012, the Ministry of Culture issued Resolución Directoral 374–2012 and legally authorized our project to conduct archaeological excavations in the district of Coporaque. It would be nearly two months until our excavations began in earnest. Indeed, the four pages of boilerplate clauses contained in this authorizing document were little more than a legitimate basis to *initiate* concrete discussions with those whose fields and canals run through the archaeological complex of San Antonio and Yuraq Qaqa.

Local Views on Removal of Bones and Objects

In Coporaque, local responses to state-authorized archaeological fieldwork and understandings of its purpose centered on the removal of bones and objects from archaeological sites, even if they did not challenge the legal status of cultural patrimony directly. Three intersecting themes are relevant for understanding how archaeological research, by its fundamentally extractive nature, justifiably breeds skepticism in small, rural communities of highland Peru. These are: (1) local conceptions of descendant-ancestor relationships with the pre-Columbian dead, (2) local stakes in the tourism economy and awareness of archaeological heritage as a profitable market, and (3) colonial appropriation and destruction of ancestral remains. Our archaeological intervention at the site—regardless of its intellectual justification, legal authorization, and best intentions—is entangled with a much longer history of economic modernization and object removal in the Colca Valley.

In the Andes, indigenous attitudes toward ancient human remains can vary considerably from community to community, ranging from affection to ambivalence. The ethos of ancestor-descendant relationships, which dominates discourse surrounding the repatriation of human remains in the United States, is not pervasive in the Peruvian context, if not altogether absent. Anthropologist Frank Salomon describes how rural communities living in the province east of Lima refer to the bones of ancestors as "the beautiful grandparents" (los hermosos abuelos). Yet the dead possess the force of both life-giving benevolence and capricious volatility: "If one disturbs a tomb, even accidentally, one ought to bring a gift (an animal, coca, liquor, etc.) to its offended tenant."[18] Among the K'ulta Aymara (Bolivia), bones found in ancient sepulchers are thought to represent peoples (known as "Supay-Chullpas") from a pre-Christian age of darkness, who took cover from the coming of the Solar-Christ in these east-facing tombs, only to be overtaken by the rising sun. Emphasizing a narrative of cosmological upheaval, the K'ulta negate a pre-Columbian heritage. "Although the Chullpas were not Christians, they were most assuredly not the ancestors of anyone in K'ulta," writes anthropologist Thomas Abercrombie.[19]

In Coporaque, local community members with whom I spoke did not negate a pre-Columbian past per se; the local tourism economy thrives off its recognition. Yet a similar ontological distance between communal identity and the identities of the dead (referred to by one community member as gentiles, or non-Christians) exists. There is nonetheless a recognition of the power of the dead, in general, and the efficacy of bones, in particular. I was warned that inhaling the dust and air of the tombs could cause sickness, even death. To avoid these dangers, local community members and our archaeological team made a "payment" (pago) to the earth, a series of ritual offerings seeking permission from the local mountains themselves to carry out our labor. These beliefs exist alongside more quintessentially "intellectual" interests in local history. There was a strong desire to know more about the antiquity of the tombs of Yuraq Qaqa, and whether or not the individuals buried in them were "Collagua" or "Inka." Yet the sentiment that human remains represent our ancestors was never—to my memory—invoked in public discussions concerning the objectives and impact of the project.[20]

Local stakes in a rapidly growing tourism economy bred both support and skepticism of the project. On one hand, the dozen or so individuals and families who participate in homestay tourism (turismo vivencial) and guided tours to the many "natural" and archaeological wonders of the Colca Valley were acutely aware of Yuraq Qaqa's attraction to nonlocals. Despite pervasive looting, few mausoleums in Peru so well-preserved still contain human skeletal remains. No official figures of visitors to Yuraq Qaqa exist (which is completely devoid of a formal site infrastructure, save the aforementioned weathered sign), but the Colca Valley as an autonomous region receives well over two hundred thousand tourists annually.[21] A scientific investigation of the tombs could offer local tour guides valuable knowledge about the site, rendering it official by printing and disseminating informational pamphlets. It could also provide the basis for soliciting future investment in the conservation of the site. By digitizing the location of each tomb and documenting which structures were at greatest risk of collapse, our project could literally put Yuraq Qaqa on the map and substantiate the need for additional funding to preserve standing architecture.

At the same time, there were anxieties that tomb excavation would irrevocably alter the character of the site. Arriving at Yuraq Qaqa, tourists are drawn to the east-facing opening of one of its largest tombs (fig 4.2). Here local townspeople have arranged sun-bleached skulls on a makeshift altar. Coins from around the world interspersed with dried coca leaves attest to the entanglement of local practices of veneration and international tourism. Would archaeological excavation leave the site emptied of its morbid wonders?

More than a matter of aesthetics, this concern emerges from a long colonial history involving the removal or destruction of local archaeological remains. Rumors of earlier episodes of foreign pillaging were retold in town hall meetings and personal conversation. These stories took on a sort of rhetorical vagueness that nevertheless communicated a real and pervasive grievance. "We've had bad experiences in the past," some would impart: An unnamed foreigner came to the village and absconded with intact mummies. Or mummies were taken (by whom?) to the neighboring village (when?) and placed in the safekeeping of the local school. Where are they now? Answers conflicted. When these stories were presented to imply that I too might leave with these invaluable objects and never return, I would playfully, if sardonically, ask if any of these persons had arrived with formal documents from the Ministry of Culture. If I were a thief, why would I present myself to the community and seek its support and participation in the excavation? Most acknowledged the logic of the argument; but, then, did authorization and transparency really change the inescapable fact of material extraction?

As oft repeated as the trope of the foreign thief was the decidedly less vague tale of Juanita, the Ice Maiden. In 1995, an international team of archaeologists led by Johan Reinhard discovered the frozen body of a young girl atop Mount Ampato, towering twenty thousand feet above the southern rim of the Colca Valley.[22] Recently exposed by glacial melt, Juanita had been selected centuries earlier for *capacocha*, an Inka ritual in which young children from noble families across the Empire, prized for their status and beauty, were sacrificed to the mountain. They were marched for days across the rugged Andean landscape, fed a special diet, and adorned in beautiful camelid fiber cloth and feathered headdresses. As their small bodies succumbed to the effects of sedatives, they were clubbed behind the head and buried with fine ceramics and small camelid figurines made of gold and silver. To be chosen for *capacocha* was a unique honor, one that startles our Western sensibilities.

To have chanced upon a *capacocha* of such excellent preservation was a marvelous find, one that captivated the archaeological community—but alienated another. Only days after her discovery, Juanita was transported from the district of Cabanaconde in the Colca Valley to the regional capital of Arequipa, located about five hours away by bus. Local villagers were never consulted by the archaeological team and only learned of Juanita's discovery from press coverage.[23] For decades, they have demanded her return, and they even constructed a museum that bears her name but to which she will never return. In an ironic twist of events, the Ministry of Culture denounced the regional authority for authorizing construction in an archaeological zone without properly consulting the central government.[24]

Juanita is now housed in a special climate-controlled chamber in the Museo Santuarios Andinos in Arequipa, operated by the Catholic University of Santa Maria. But her memory dwells in the minds of the people of the Colca Valley, a cautionary tale of archaeological patrimony exported for the benefit of archaeological, national, and global communities.

Mount Ampato is visible from Coporaque.

FIGURE 4.4   A cluster of residential buildings in Coporaque, including a *casa vivencial* in the foreground. In the upper third of the frame is a pre-Hispanic Collagua house, which has been incorporated into one of the larger tourist lodges in the village. Ampato is the snow-capped mountain in the center of the horizon. Photograph by Briana Beltran.

Many Meetings

I had visited Coporaque several times from 2009 to 2011, formally presented myself before local authorities, and sought and acquired a letter of support from the municipality to include in grant proposals—a testament that my interests and credentials were known, my face recognizable, and my project feasible. When I returned in 2012, I did not expect an unquestioning endorsement of our newly minted project, but I believed the validity of the archaeological research, its academic objectives, and its potential to deepen knowledge of local history would win the day. Moreover, the project offered distinct, if minor, economic benefits. To the community, it would cost nothing monetarily. The project would also employ three to four townspeople a week, providing a supplementary source of income for women, in particular, as men preferred higher-paying, if more backbreaking, jobs in construction and mining. Finally, we pledged to organize educational workshops that would invite local schoolchildren to engage hands-on with archaeological materials and formulate their own questions about the past.

I prepared my PowerPoints, printed handouts, and announced the first of many public meetings to provide information on the project and its goals. That the language of academic merit might not be the only logic through which to evaluate our objectives was easy to overlook for a young graduate student at the cusp of discovery. All my training had brought me to that point; I was there, ready to "engage" with the "community."

This mirage of idealism quickly dissolved into the political realities of small-town life in highland Peru. Those intimately involved in rural community tourism (*turismo rural comunitario*) stood to gain from a project that could increase the visibility of Coporaque and its cultural heritage. Local elected authorities, on the other hand, ran a risk of short-term political losses by endorsing a low-impact archaeological excavation amid other contentious debates related to land development and the expansion and financing of irrigation infrastructure. In theory they approved of the project, but they voiced concerns of being accused of profiting from the sale of archaeological materials—an idea somehow both ludicrous and reasonable, when considering the troubled history of object removal in the valley and the power of rumor in small communities. Still others living in what is predominantly an agricultural community expressed little outward concern for what I imagine must have seemed to them like a trivial pursuit; some may have even remained unaware of our purpose, if not our presence. The lessons here are ones well known to anthropologists who have long remarked on the illusion of a singular community.[25]

Yet the plurality of perspectives and priorities in Coporaque usually converged around one crucial point: the bones of Yuraq Qaqa and their associated objects were located on communal lands and therefore ought to fall under norms of communal decision-making. No one authority would grant us the elusive blessing I naively sought. When I visited the governor of the District of Coporaque—the representative of "the state" within the community—I was referred to the mayor of the District of Coporaque. The mayor, in turn, recommended that I discuss our objectives with the president of the Comisión de Regantes, the local water authority. After several false starts, local authorities asked that we bring our project before the leaders of nearly a dozen community entities. Approval (*aprobación*) could only come from consensus.

A meeting of authorities scheduled for 6:30 p.m., on Wednesday, August 8, 2012, would provide the appropriate venue for vetting these issues. I imagined that it would start with the usual formalities and then the floor would be turned over for a brief presentation on the project and its objectives (which, at this point, I had rehearsed well). I arrived early. Waiting in the nondescript reception area on the second floor of the municipal building, I greeted friends and associates as they slowly trickled in to the large office of the mayor, its furniture rearranged and supplemented to accommodate the crowd of twenty to thirty. Once inside, community members sat in rows of chairs parallel and perpendicular to the large windows overlooking the town plaza, now shrouded in darkness. The mayor sat behind a large desk facing the gathering, and I shifted in my chair a few meters to his left, alternatingly shuffling my notes and scanning the audience. Beneath one of the windows sat Juan, president of the community and the father of Enady. I imagined—hoped—she had told him of her involvement in our preliminary and exceedingly mundane task of clearing cactus and inventorying funerary chambers at the site, so that he might relay to others the nature, tempo, and seriousness of archaeological work.[26] (Or at least he could speak to the positive, if short-term, economic benefits of employing community members, I reasoned.) The young deputy mayor, Javier, sat farther back in the crowd, as if to minimize his position of authority. As an enthusiast of local history, who himself possessed an archaeological sensibility toward ancient places and things, I looked to him as the relatively progressive voice of a younger generation of community leaders. Among the few women present who held a position of authority was Rocio, the president of an association of families involved in rural community tourism and the co-owner and entrepreneur of the homestay (*casa vivencial*) where our team lived. My host mother knew me better than did anyone else in the room. Rocio had counseled me through the many meetings that had preceded this one. On this night, however, she looked concerned.

Unbeknown to me, just days before, the municipal mayor had sent a letter denouncing our project to the regional office of the Ministry of Culture. *This* meeting, I later learned, was to be a public repudiation of the project, on the grounds that archaeological materials should not be allowed to leave the district of Coporaque, even though the law ultimately required such a move. The mayor opened the meeting aggressively. Juanita's name was invoked. I was caught off-guard. My heart pounded. Was the mayor expressing a minority opinion or a general consensus reached in my absence? Even if others disagreed, would they risk their own standing to stake an equally firm opposition on behalf of a twentysomething researcher from the United States? What words could give voice to the potential benefits of archaeological research—the inestimable value of knowing what was once unknown? Not my own—nor those of any single community member. Instead they came from the most unanticipated of places.

Two days earlier, our crew chief, Diana (a student-archaeologist from Lima) and I had taken a short fifteen-minute trip to Chivay, the population and commercial center of the Colca Valley, by virtue of being the gateway though which all tourists must pass. I went to coordinate the purchase and transportation of furniture for our field laboratory, confident our project would soon be underway. Diana, meanwhile, sought pure chocolate that could be melted and mixed with caramel and nuts to make a Peruvian confection called *chocotejas*. (Such diversions are the small pleasures of fieldwork.) Her search took her to a small bodega owned by Fernando. Born and raised in Chivay, Fernando is also a sociologist by training, having spent years studying and teaching in France. Not only familiar with archaeology as an academic pursuit, he also actively participates in regional initiatives to preserve cultural heritage and promote tourism. Diana and Fernando struck up a conversation. He learned of our project and our upcoming presentation. A connection was made.

By this simple twist of fate, Fernando came to the meeting that night. Though not of Coporaque himself, he was well-respected and known by community members, having previously run for regional political office. He requested the floor after the tumultuous start. Without prompting, Fernando spoke beautifully and humbly on our behalf, imploring the community to take part in the investigation and preservation of the region's archaeological heritage, which faces threats from increased traffic and development. Having recently become a father, Fernando framed his plea as a question of legacy: what will we leave our children, and what will we teach them? He drew from his depth of experience in the social and political life of the Colca Valley to relay anecdotes of successful collaborations between other towns and archaeologists. He completely changed the tone of the meeting, the course of the project, and maybe my career.

By the end of the night, we had reached an agreement. Our *convenio* stipulated terms of our research within the municipality, established a system for the rotation of local workers in the project, and affirmed an "open door" policy in the temporary laboratory space offered by the municipality.[27] We would work during the municipality's hours of operation, so that interested community members could freely enter the laboratory, observe all that we were finding, and learn more about the kinds of conservation efforts underway to clean and protect the fragile ceramics, bones, and textiles that would be recovered from the tombs. In this way, the project could distinguish itself from past episodes of surreptitious removal and desecration of objects. The terms of this agreement would be formally presented at the annual *rimanakuy*.[28] This community-wide meeting would be held the coming Saturday, during which a broad range of issues affecting the community, municipality, school, parish, et cetera, are put forth and discussed.

The unfolding of these events lays bare the limits of scholarly "authority" and legal "authorization," foregrounding how all collaboration, in a sense, is "coauthored." Plainly put, Fernando was able to do what I never fully could; traverse the boundaries between local and foreign, merge an insider's perspective with an academic one, translate the opaque objectives of archaeological research into words that mattered and could be trusted. His short speech framed (and maybe even encouraged) supportive statements from Juan, Javier, Rocio, and others—even if they could not extinguish all doubt. "What will the people say?" one man asked rhetorically, "They'll say we sold the objects." In response, others spoke of a grand opportunity for the town to learn of its history and educate its youth. "We don't even know how old the tombs are." The tensions between these perspectives still linger in the community and in my own thoughts.

Tinkuy, or Coming Together

The sun was setting on September and soon our archaeological field season would enter its final month. Just days before, we had stumbled across an unexpected find. Reaching the base of one tomb, we found another one beneath it! Though partially collapsed, the earlier tomb contained the nearly intact mummy of a middle-aged male, encased in a cocoon-style basket made of vegetal fiber. This virtually complete skeleton, though stripped of its accoutrements, remained fully articulated and in a flexed, fetal position. His skull showed signs of healed blunt force trauma, but it was *not* artificially elongated in the style emblematic of the late pre-Hispanic Collaguas. In fact, none of the four crania in this unique context exhibited artificial reshaping, in contrast to other larger mortuary chambers where cranial modification was prevalent. This skeleton would provide vital clues for understanding the emergence of this peculiar tradition and its transformation across time.[29]

But to properly study Individual 1029.0001 and his life history would require that his remains be carefully excavated and conserved. To actually transport the skeleton down to our temporary laboratory in Coporaque posed another challenge. So Richard and another team member began work constructing and reinforcing a large cardboard box that could support the weight of the bundle. The MacGyvered box was lined with crumpled acid-free conservation-grade paper and makeshift plastic "airbags" to provide cushioning.

Concerns of the community weighed on my mind. Buried beneath layers of loose bone, brush, and semi-compact soil, this mummy bundle had probably never been seen by any living member of the community. To be sure, the sight of two young men slowly carrying a cardboard coffin along the gravel path from Yuraq Qaqa would attract attention. Recalling Juanita and the controversies surrounding her surreptitious removal, I gave Richard clear instructions: Take your time, but take no detours. Walk straight to the temporary lab in the municipal building. If anyone inquires as to its contents, let them know it contains fragile human remains from the site. Invite them to the lab where I can address any questions and, if necessary, open the now tightly sealed box.

Richard and his compatriot set off down the path to the village, while I wrapped up our day's work at the site. I followed about ten minutes behind. Passing through the double rock outcrop, I spotted them far below at the head of the trail. They had reached level ground. Just as they were starting down the walled corridor toward the village, they came to a halt. Five minutes passed, and still they lingered. *Why aren't they moving?*

In a raised field above them were several people harvesting alfalfa. One from their group ambled toward the walled edge of the elevated field, approaching Richard. *What are they saying to one another?* My mind raced to a dreaded conclusion. Richard had been stopped. *Have the community members demanded to see our authorization? Are they asking of my whereabouts? Wishing to inspect the box and its contents?* Anxious to extinguish a conflagration of rumors, I quickened my pace.

As I moved closer, I saw Richard's face, and my anxieties washed away. His thirst quenched, he returned a *q'ero* to the *señora* crouched at the field's edge. She refilled the wooden cup with a frothy beverage—*chicha*—a fermented corn beer brewed in the highland Andes since ancient times. It is a festive drink. Each town boasts its own recipe, and claims to brew the strongest or most flavorful *chicha* are often expressed with zeal. Shared from the same cup, it is also a drink charged with communal sentiment and ritual significance.

Richard gestured toward me, and I hurried to his side. The *señora* offered the cup to me. I recognized her as Julia, one of the local authorities who was present at the August meeting. I raised the cup in acknowledgement, in relief, in thanks. I let flow a torrent of *chicha* toward the ground, and it moistened the soil, an offering to the earth. I drank. We drank. A recognition of our mutual labor.

Epilogue: Remains

Looking back, it is these moments of transcendence that rise above the lingering tension. After the conclusion of our project in April 2015, I did not return to Coporaque until July 2017. Sometimes it feels like I never left. Walking its dirt paths, each footfall cracks with memories of the place and our time here, but whatever hopes I might have had to return to the past are shaken by the present. On the night of August 14, 2016, just as neighbors were getting ready for bed, and only a day after the annual *rimanakuy* and its accompanying festivities, a 5.3 earthquake struck the Colca Valley. In Coporaque, several houses, those made of adobe, were reduced to rubble. Of the floor plan of the *casa vivencial* where our team lived in 2012 and 2013, only Richard's room—and fortunately the family's living spaces—were unaffected. By the time of my return visit in 2017, most families had rebuilt their houses and cottages, some with support from the government, others at great personal expense and labor. As I moved from one *casa vivencial* to another to distribute an informational pamphlet on the key findings of my dissertation, I felt woefully lacking in anything useful. Results can build knowledge, but they can't build houses.[30]

Although these pressing needs came to the fore of my conversations with community members, the memories of bones remained. Perhaps the only question more common than "Where are the remains now?" was "When will they return?" Having maintained contact with some folks in the community, I was well aware that rumors of their disappearance and calls for their return persisted. In fact, the purpose of my trip was explicitly to address these concerns and inform the municipal government (and the community at large) of the current state of affairs—namely, that the archaeological materials remained in storage and under the protection and custodianship of the regional office of the Ministry of Culture in Arequipa but that their return could be solicited if and when the appropriate space was accommodated to serve as a museum. Asking the community to commit energies and funds to a new building project, at a time when their colonial church stands fissured and buttressed by wooden beams, was neither convenient nor ideal. It was made more difficult by the fact that, for many, the project and its purposes remain opaque. While passing out our flier to attendees of a community meeting, I was met by the confusion and shock of one woman: "Se han llevado las momias?" ("They have taken the mummies?"). Another man, startled, echoed her words. With the aid of another community member, I worked to calm their concerns by explaining the project and its history—and the many meetings that had made it possible. It was a stark reminder that the work of "engaging the community" is never complete.

But I am hopeful. Another kind of momentum is building. My return coincided with an official visit of representatives from the United Nations Educational, Scientific and Cultural Organization (UNESCO) who were evaluating a proposal to make the Colca Valley and neighboring valley of Andagua the first "Geopark" in Peru. UNESCO Geoparks is a global initiative that aims to promote and conserve the geographical and cultural heritage of a region by empowering local communities toward sustainable development. Many in the valley hope an enhanced international profile will bring more income, as some families diversify their economic strategies and increasingly turn to the tourism market. At the national level, slight revisions to the legal language governing cultural patrimony have opened the door to greater participation of local communities in the management and protection of cultural patrimony.[31] Locally, an initiative is underway to rehabilitate the cultural center in Coporaque into a vibrant hub for tourism and artistic production. How our archaeological research might connect to these present concerns is part of the ongoing conversation.

Five years after our trowels hit the dirt, the dust is settling. The path ahead is clearer. We have only fragments of the past, yet we know more now than we ever have about the ancient Collaguas and their way of life. After the skeletons have been inventoried, grant reports submitted, and dissertations filed, the work continues—so long as the bones remain outside of Coporaque, so long as humans remain committed to writing their story.

FIGURE 4.5 Coporaque, seen from the southern rim of the Colca Valley. The town lies nestled between the slopes of Yuraq Qaqa to the west and the mesa-like Pampa Finaya to the east. Photograph by Lauren Kohut.

Notes

1. I thank my colleagues in the 2016–17 Mellon Diversity Seminar for encouraging me to write this piece and to think critically about my own positionality as a scholar. Immeasurable thanks are also owed to Hayden Kantor and Alejandro Omidsalar, both of whom provided incisive comments on the chapter's content, structure, style, and prose; of course, I absolve them of all its lingering shortcomings. Finally, this chapter acknowledges the many people in Peru whose paths have crossed my own; many more remain unnamed. *A todos ellos quiero reiterar mi más profunda gratitud por la oportunidad de aprender de su hermosa cultura.*

2. Generally, bioarchaeologists use the terms "male" and "female" to describe individual sex inferred from the size and shape of bones. To interpret gender identity, skeletal sex should be analyzed in concert with skeletal changes that reflect habitual practices during life (e.g., repetitive, patterned labor), grave location and associated offerings that may suggest how an individual was perceived and treated by others, and/or other contextual information pertinent to the society being studied that sheds light on gender norms, such as the depiction of bodies in art and iconography.

3. Christopher M. Stojanowski and William N. Duncan, "Engaging Bodies in the Public Imagination: Bioarchaeology as Social Science, Science, and Humanities," *American Journal of Human Biology* 27, no. 1 (2015): 51–60.

4. Molly K. Zuckerman, Kelly R. Kamnikar, and Sarah A. Mathena, "Recovering the 'Body Politic': A Relational Ethics of Meaning for Bioarchaeology," *Cambridge Archaeological Journal* 24, no. 3 (2014): 513–22.

5. Bioarchaeologists have even explored explicitly narrative techniques for conveying the emotional experiences of ancient peoples and the daily rhythms of their lives. See, for example, Alexis T. Boutin, "Written in Stone, Written in Bone: The Osteobiography of a Bronze Age Craftsman from Alalakh," in *The Bioarchaeology of Individuals*, edited by Ann L. W. Stodder and Ann M. Palkovich (Gainesville: University Press of Florida, 2011), 193–214.

6. "Since history is a recorded or remembered event, theatre, for me, is the perfect place to 'make' history—that is, because so much of African-American history has been unrecorded, disremembered, washed out, one of my tasks as a playwright is to—through literature and the special strange relationship between theatre and real-life—locate the ancestral burial ground, dig for bones, find bones, hear the bones sing, write it down." Suzanne Lori Parks, "Possession," in *The America Play and Other Works* (New York: Theatre Communications Group, 1994), 4.

7. Stojanowski and Duncan, "Engaging Bodies in the Public Imagination."

8. Ann M. Kakaliouras, "An Anthropology of Repatriation: Contemporary Physical Anthropological and Native American Ontologies of Practice," *Current Anthropology* 53, suppl. 5 (2012): S210–21.

9. Bethany L. Turner and Valerie A. Andrushko, "Partnerships, Pitfalls, and Ethical Concerns in International Bioarchaeology," in *Social Bioarchaeology*, edited by Sabrina C. Agarwal and Bonnie A. Glencross (Chichester: Wiley-Blackwell, 2011), 44–67.

10. For a notable exception, see Pamela L. Geller and Miranda Stockett Suri, "Relationality, Corporeality and Bioarchaeology: Bodies qua Bodies, Bodies in Context," *Cambridge Archaeological Journal* 24, no. 3 (2014): 499–512. For a recent review of community-engaged bioarchaeology that provides recommendations for ethical research design, see Alexis T. Boutin et al., "Building a Better Bioarchaeology through Community Collaboration," *Bioarchaeology International* 1 (2017): 191–204.

11. In hindsight, I would characterize my approach to community engagement in Coporaque as an invitation to "participate," rather than truly "collaborate." For an overview of different modes of community and public engagement in archaeology, see Chip Colwell, "Collaborative Archaeologies and Descendant Communities," *Annual Review of Anthropology* 45 (2016): 113–27. For a critique of the rhetoric and practice of collaboration itself, see Marina J. La Salle, "Community Collaboration and Other Good Intentions," *Archaeologies: Journal of the World Archaeological Congress* 6 (2010): 401–22. La Salle's reflections on how good intentions conceal the reality of extraction might be used to critically frame the experiences I recount in this chapter.

12. For a general review of the law and its transformative effects on archaeological practice, see Jerome C. Rose, Thomas J. Green, and Victoria D. Green, "NAGPRA Is Forever: Osteology and the Repatriation of Skeletons," *Annual Review of Anthropology* 25 (1996): 81–103.

13. Perhaps the most contentious aspect of NAGPRA has been the establishment of "cultural affiliation" between living tribes and ancient skeletons, which, until recently, was the sine qua non of NAGPRA litigation (see Kakaliouras, "Anthropology of Repatriation"). However, there are other logistical and ethical challenges. For example, decades of irresponsible or shortsighted collecting and curation practices have resulted in the disassociation of skeletal remains from the objects with which

they were buried, making "original" funerary assemblages virtually unlocatable and the repatriation process itself literally disjointed. NAGPRA does not require that federally funded institutions coordinate with one another to restore original contexts, and private collections fall entirely outside of the scope of the law. See Margaret M. Bruchac, "Lost and Found: NAGPRA, Scattered Relics, and Restorative Methodologies," *Museum Anthropology* 33, no. 2 (2010): 137–56.

14. Oliver Milman, "Archaeologists Denounce Dakota Access Pipeline for Destroying Artifacts," *Guardian*, September 22, 2016

15. Turner and Andrushko, "Partnerships, Pitfalls, and Ethical Concerns in International Bioarchaeology."

16. Donna Yates, "Archaeology and Autonomies: The Legal Framework of Heritage Management in a New Bolivia," *International Journal of Cultural Property* 18, no. 3 (2011): 291–307.

17. Federal NAGPRA legislation deliberately obviates the question of private holdings, in order to avoid constitutional entanglements. The US case is not only a contrast to Peru but also to several other formerly colonial states, including New Zealand and South Africa, whose cultural historic preservation laws apply to state and private property. For a comparative analysis, see Ryan M. Seidemann, "Bones of Contention: A Comparative Examination of Law Governing Human Remains from Archaeological Contexts in Formerly Colonial Countries," *Louisiana Law Review* 64, no. 3 (2004), http://digitalcommons.law.lsu.edu/lalrev/vol64/iss3/7.

18. Frank Salomon, "'The Beautiful Grandparents': Andean Ancestor Shrines and Mortuary Ritual as Seen through Colonial Records," in *Tombs for the Living: Andean Mortuary Practices*, edited by Tom D. Dillehay (Washington, DC: Dumbarton Oaks, 1995), 336.

19. Thomas A. Abercrombie, *Pathways of Memory and Power: Ethnography and History among an Andean People* (Madison: University of Wisconsin Press, 1998), 117–18.

20. It should be stated explicitly that my research was not designed as an ethnographic inquiry into local beliefs and practices surrounding pre-Columbian gravesites. I do not assert that feelings of attachment to ancestral remains do not exist, simply that they were not expressed in arguments made to me regarding the removal of human remains from Yuraq Qaqa.

21. Autoridad Autónoma del Colca y Anexos—AUTOCOLCA, *Reporte de ingreso de visitantes al Colca*, http://www.colcaperu.gob.pe/2018/04/18/reporte-de-ingreso-de-visitantes-al-colca (accessed November 2, 2018). Tourists come from the urban centers of Peru, as well as Germany, France, Japan, and the United States, among other countries. The arrival of tourists numbering anywhere from the lone explorer to dozens of gringos outfitted with hydration packs was a frequent occurrence during our field season.

22. The story of Juanita and her discovery has been the subject of several documentaries and popular books. See, for example, Johan Reinhard, *The Ice Maiden: Inca Mummies, Mountain Gods, and Sacred Sites in the Andes* (Washington, DC: National Geographic Society, 2005).

23. For a recounting of these events, see Yuji Seki, "Participation of the Local Community in Archaeological Heritage Management in the North Highlands of Peru," in *Finding Solutions for Protecting and Sharing Archaeological Heritage Resources*, edited by

Anne P. Underhill and Lucy C. Salazar (New York: Springer Science+Business Media, 2015). Shortly after her discovery, Juanita traveled to the United States for specialized laboratory analysis and later, in 1999, went to Japan for a museum exhibition, "Juanita, the Beautiful Maiden in Grief." Juanita's travels and exhibition also sparked national debates about the commodification and exoticization of indigenous bodies.

24. APP América Noticias, "Momia 'Juanita' no regresaría al Colca: museo fue construido sobre zona intangible," http://www.americatv.com.pe/noticias/actualidad/momia-juanita-no-regresaria-al-colca-museo-fue-construido-sobre-zona-intangible-n125126 (accessed November 4, 2018).

25. See, for example, Anna S. Agbe-Davies, "Concepts of Community in the Pursuit of an Inclusive Archaeology," *International Journal of Heritage Studies* 16, no. 6 (2010): 373–89.

26. Juan, an expert artisan and embroiderer, was also more familiar than most with the field of anthropology, having been a subject of an ethnography on the culture, production, and meaning of local clothing. See Blenda Femenias, *Gender and the Boundaries of Dress in Contemporary Peru* (Austin: University of Texas Press, 2005).

27. At the conclusion of the field season, the governor accompanied the excavated archaeological materials to Arequipa to observe their transfer to the Ministry of Culture and receive a copy of the inventory.

28. *Rimanakuy* roughly translates as "to speak with one another."

29. The results of this line of inquiry are published in Matthew C. Velasco, "Ethnogenesis and Social Difference in the Andean Late Intermediate Period (AD 1100–1450): A Bioarchaeological Study of Cranial Modification in the Colca Valley, Peru." *Current Anthropology* 59, no. 1 (2018): 98–106.

30. Miraculously (or thanks to the forethought of ancient Collagua builders), the tombs of Yuraq Qaqa suffered no visible damage from the 2016 earthquake.

31. Whereas Article 6.1 of the *Ley General del Patrimonio Cultural de la Nación* ("General Law of Cultural Patrimony of the Nation") previously stipulated that immovable cultural patrimony is *only* to be administered by the state, a legislative decree in September 2015 removed the word "only" (*unicamente*) and added two paragraphs that sketched out, however vaguely, what form shared management could take. Granted, the decree pertains exclusively to archaeological sites (not "movable" collections), and cultural patrimony remains the property of the state even in the context of shared administration. Nonetheless, this move can be seen as part of a broader shift in the ethos and logistics of heritage management, with the state recognizing the practical limitations of heritage protection without local involvement. See Kevin L. Ricci Jara, "Crónica de un decreto no anunciado" (unpublished manuscript in possession of author).

CHAPTER 5

Forgotten Faces, Missing Bodies

Understanding "Techno-Invisible" Populations
and Political Violence in Peru

José Ragas

José Ragas investigates the emergence of the
global biometric system in postcolonial societies and the current implementa-
tion of ID cards as a mechanism designed to grant citizenship and curb the
legacy of gender, age, and racial discrimination imposed by similar technolo-
gies in the past. In his doctoral dissertation he examined the genealogy of
the identification system in postcolonial Peru, arguing that the implementa-
tion of certain techniques and devices (fingerprints, mug shots, and identity
cards) reinforced archaic social structures that enabled policy makers and
technocrats to extract resources from citizens via the imposition of individual
identities. His research also shows how citizens turned those technologies into
generators of social and political rights, empowering them and allowing them
to gain official recognition. In an era of heightened concern over state surveil-
lance, Ragas's work offers vital reminders of the human and social agendas
behind the invention of such technologies: to be counted, literally; to be found
among a nation of others and recognized as yourself.

After completing a position as a lecturer at Yale, Ragas took up a position
as professor at the Pontificia Universidad Católica de Chile, where he is pursu-
ing new work focused on the transnational circulation of biometrics and other
technologies of identification during the long Cold War and their dissemina-
tion in contexts of political violence and struggle for civil rights.

In mid-2015, an announcement that an international forensic team had reconstructed the "true" faces of two of the most popular Peruvian saints was welcomed by an enthusiastic group of believers and commentators alike.[1] The "new" appearances of both Santa Rosa de Lima and San Martín de Porras were received amid crowded religious ceremonies in Lima that coincided with the anniversaries of their deaths (August for Santa Rosa, November for San Martín de Porras). Before the binational team of Brazilian and Peruvian experts could generate a full tridimensional image of the faces through photogrammetry, they examined the skulls of both saints to obtain information about their physical features. Despite the technology's novelty and despite enthusiasm for the outcome, the digital reconstructions of both Peruvian saints did not significantly differ from other representations of the saints that had circulated for centuries. As one of the experts reluctantly acknowledged, San Martin de Porras's 3D reconstruction looked very similar to an anonymous old painting of the saint. Even the particular form of his jaw, which experts attributed to his continuous effort while chewing due to his lack of teeth, was present in the old portrait long before 3D reconstruction was imagined (Correo 2015). The prior of the Convent of Santo Domingo, where San Martin de Porras spent his life, did not hide his disappointment with the digital reconstruction: "It is not suggestive or artistic" (Correo 2015). But if these "new" faces did not change our knowledge of those characters, what triggered the enthusiasm?

The fervor to apply identification technology to specific figures of the past—as in the case of the reconstructed faces of both San Martín and Santa Rosa—may obscure the existence of a significant number of individuals whose faces and identities remain unknown to us. Just few months after the new faces of both saints were unveiled to the public, President Ollanta Humala signed the Ley de Búsqueda de Personas Desaparecidas on June 22, 2016, as part of an official initiative to coordinate efforts meant to "design, establish, execute, and supervise" the search of national citizens who disappeared during Peru's era of political violence (1980–2000). Since the 1980s, a multifarious group of human rights activists, forensic scientists, and relatives have struggled to recover the remains of their beloved ones killed by state forces and terrorist groups, identify their remains, bury them, and attempt to end their grieving that has lasted nearly three decades for some. These groups have conjured both traditional and innovative strategies and technologies (e.g., forensic science and DNA analysis) to match the remains, bones, and DNA of the victims with their families and assign them an identity. Although technology and forensic science has been crucial to restoring some of the victims' identities and bringing some comfort to relatives, the enormous challenge remains of attaining justice for them and the hundreds of bodies that are still buried in clandestine sites (Cardoza 2016).

Bringing Back Invisible Populations through ID Technology

This essay offers an exploratory alternative to study the contentious relationship between identification technology and "techno-invisible populations." By "techno-invisible population" I mean a heterogeneous group of people who, for different reasons, have been or continue to be undetected by national identification systems and the technologies deployed to apprehend their existence over the last two centuries. National governments invested significant resources in building infrastructure, training experts, and designing artifacts to confer individual identities to citizens by capturing their faces, personal information, and fingerprints and inserting that information in digital and written databases and identity documents. Governments have made advances in the design and implementation of this particular technology, as witnessed by police departments' efforts to create lists of suspects and more recent and ambitious projects like Aadhaar in India, where one billion citizens are expected to receive a unique identification number. Wendy Hunter and Robert Brill assert that in Latin America these efforts have allowed registration of children younger than five years old to expand from 82 percent to 91 percent between 2000 and 2012 (Hunter and Brill 2016, 206). If we look at other regions, we will encounter similar projects whose ultimate goal is to incorporate vulnerable populations into national records.

Peru is part of this global trend of civil registration, and in the last years it has positioned itself as a regional leader in biometric and identification technology. Anyone familiar with Peru's recent history will be surprised to observe the transformation of a country with alarming high rates of undocumented people to one that is fully capable of providing an identity document (Documento Nacional de Identidad) to every citizen. An ambitious campaign carried out in the last two decades by RENIEC (Registro Nacional de Identificación y Estado Civil), the official entity in charge of identification, covered the territory in the coastal area, the highlands, and the Amazon, granting personal documents and curbing the number of unregistered national citizens. In addition, RENIEC expanded the original scope of ID card holders to include children, as a way to protect them from kidnapping and human trafficking.

My aim here is not to downplay the impressive accomplishments achieved by RENIEC or any of its global counterparts in providing identity cards to national citizens worldwide. Over the last few years, and during fieldwork for my dissertation, I spoke with officers at RENIEC and found professionals committed to curbing the number of undocumented people. Although there is cause to celebrate that more national citizens (especially children, senior citizens, and women) are receiving material proof of their existence, this essay seeks to look beyond this optimism and insist that the presence of an undocumented population is a problem that is far from being extinguished. What I propose here is to focus on those individuals and groups who for different reasons lack a proper identity document, in order to highlight the fissures in the identification systems and possible ways to close them. While counterarguments insist the undocumented population represents a small fraction of the total number of citizens, I argue that their enduring presence is a powerful and disturbing reminder of how governments, technology, and society foster the reproduction and perpetuation of individuals without proper documents.

There are a constellation of reasons why individuals lack an identity card or are unregistered with the state, reasons we have just begun to understand. It is difficult to encompass all of these cases under a single category, thus I will use the term "techno-invisible populations" for didactic and pragmatic purposes. As I demonstrate in my research, some populations were systematically excluded from having personal documents since they did not fit in the restrictive model of citizenship envisioned by postcolonial policy makers in the Andes who deliberately excluded women, poor people, and indigenous peoples from obtaining a voting identity card (Ragas 2020). In addition, becoming invisible to the system does not necessarily occur in remote areas or in the historical past. For instance, in the 2010s in the United States, the Republican Party pushed for the strict enforcement of the voter ID laws that obliged US citizens to present a photo ID in order to register to vote. Hundreds or thousands of people could not provide such proof and were prevented from voting in the 2016 national election. Not surprisingly, the majority of those belonged to minority groups. Alongside these scenarios, we should also consider groups that have never been contacted or are considered floating urban groups, like homeless people. Wars and natural disasters have also produced a high number of refugees and immigrants whose status represents a limbo for the host countries and local authorities.

Studying the roots of populations that exist "outside" the system poses both logistical and methodological challenges to researchers. Given the exploratory nature of this paper, my principal aim here is to revisit the history of identification technology by focusing on those who were not exposed to a certain type of devices (identity cards) and infrastructure (national identification systems) and who were deliberately neglected by experts and policy makers. In order to do so, I will focus on the case of the Peruvian nationals who were labeled "disappeared" during the internal armed conflict that ravaged the country between 1980 and 1992, and the ensuing difficulties in restoring one's identity given the lack of official documents. I aim to highlight the various strategies developed by relatives, authorities, and activists to circumvent the lack of official records and assign an identity to the victims or to their remains. Government efforts to reopen cases against the perpetrators and carry out exhumations represent an important step toward correcting the inadequate attention that the state and society gave to the victims and their relatives. That those largely affected are from an indigenous background helps explain the neglect and the lukewarm reception of the media toward the cases, burial rituals, and even trials, as Isaias Rojas-Perez has noted in a recent book (2017a).

By the time Shining Path was pushed back to the jungle and the Tupac Amaru Revolutionary Movement (another terrorist group inspired by 1960s guerrillas) had been defeated after their leaders were imprisoned or killed, Peru was transitioning from an authoritarian civil regime under Alberto Fujimori (1990–2000) to democracy under a president elected by the Congress of Peru, Valentin Paniagua (2000–2001). In his short tenure, President Paniagua created the Truth and Reconciliation Commission (TRC) to investigate the causes of the political violence and obtain recommendations to prevent them from happening again. The final report presented by the TRC in August 2003 is one of the most important and disturbing documents in the history of the country. One of its most shocking revelations was the estimated number of victims: 69,280 citizens killed by terrorists or the military. A significant number of these casualties had a specific profile: they were indigenous, Quechua speakers, poor and illiterate, and resided in the region of Ayacucho. The number of disappeared according to the final report was 4,000, but this figure was contested in 2011 by the Central Register of Victims (CRV), which had been receiving testimonies and collecting evidence since the 1980s. For the CRV, the number of people disappeared was 8,661. Finally, the United Nations Working Group on Enforced or Involuntary Disappearances added another estimate: "between thirteen thousand and sixteen thousand" (Rojas-Perez 2017b).

Disappeared citizens constitute a haunting presence not only in Peru but also throughout Latin America. Traditionally associated with the brutal military regimes that emerged in the Southern Cone and persecuted political opponents in the 1970s and 1980s, cases like the Colombian victims of the attack to the Palace of Justice in 1985 and the forty-three students who vanished in Ayotzinapa, Mexico, in September 2014, suggest that disappearances are neither confined to the Cold War nor to the military or civilian nature of a political regime. The search for justice for the disappeared questions the governments' democratic credentials and puts pressure on their existing efforts to find the remains. The ways in which Latin Americans remember the disappeared forms part of their national identity, though this commitment and degree varies from country to country. Therefore, "Una historia necesaria" ("A Necessary Story"), a 2017 Chilean TV production based on testimonies from victims and relatives, was aired on the anniversary of Augusto Pinochet's coup and presented short stories of arrested Chileans whose bodies were never recovered. In Colombia, one victim of the failed assault on the Palace of Justice in 1985 who had been buried in a common grave was identified as Héctor Jaime Beltrán Fuentes. While I was writing this essay, Argentinians had mobilized consistently in both the public sphere and social media to demand the appearance of the activist Santiago Maldonado.

Documents and Political Violence:
A Personal Approach

For those of us who grew up in 1980s Peru amid hyperinflation and political violence, the tension between exposure and invisibility was part of our daily struggle. Our adult lives were made official by ID cards made of thin paperboard, fragile and easily damaged, and possession of these could determine our fate in a highly militarized and violent milieu. Military patrols combed the cities, halting men and women, young and old, asking for papers and discerning whether people looked like potential subversives. Sometimes a bribe could do more than a proper ID card to avoid detention. For those who lacked one or another, their destiny was jail or worse. Throughout the twelve years of political violence in the country, identity documents, personal papers, and identification practices became part of the war itself, and they constitute an overlooked aspect of how Peruvians navigated their escapes from both terrorist groups and the military by masking their own identities or making themselves visible by taking advantage of their social privileges.

In retrospect, it still strikes me how just a simple and ill-designed rectangular piece of cardstock could determine the fate of many of my fellow nationals for such a long time. Identity cards served as virtually the only material proof of a complicated relationship between individuals and the state, and, by extension, between civil existence and nonexistence. One of my personal rituals every time I visit my parents in Lima is to spend some time looking at the multiple personal ID cards I keep in a drawer in my former bedroom. ID cards and conference badges are mixed among photo carnets, debit cards, business cards, and even an expired passport with the Schengen visa stamped on it. It is not difficult to observe the material evolution of such artifacts. Light cardstock was replaced by laminated plastic, and simple typography gave way to complex fonts not as easy to forge. Perhaps because I don't fear documents anymore (or perhaps because I do, especially with the most recent developments and the return of the Far Right), I usually carry more than one in my wallet.

In essence, we are documented organisms. Documents have accompanied us for a very long time, and we cannot imagine our own lives without them, regardless of their size, shape, or implications. Documents serve to authenticate our changing identities as organisms who are constantly evolving. This is an illusion, of course, since no single kind of identification device has been failsafe. However, our own nature forces us to believe in such an illusion in order to organize civil society and avoid chaos. If modern societies have been built upon this assumption, it is then urgent not only to revisit the genealogy of such devices and institutions but also to rethink the ultimate consequences of such techno-social foundations and how it has affected people in different times and places.

Over the last years, my personal and professional efforts have been devoted to studying the lives of vulnerable populations through their identification practices and artifacts. As a historian of technology, my first impulse was to trace such populations through written and visual records and the artifacts these individuals and groups engaged with in order to provide a valid identification to other parties. Nonetheless, very rapidly I realized that the conventional frameworks used to reconstruct human-artifact interaction in the past were insufficient to capture the complexity of identification and social identities. My professional training had involved reverence for print sources and embracing archives as the quintessential place to find those figments of the past. When I began doing research for my dissertation in Peruvian archives and online repositories, I soon came to realize that personal documents themselves were rare. Was this because individuals kept them with themselves? Or because documents were not the primary way to identify populations in postcolonial Peru? To make things worse, the extraordinary expansion of identity cards after 2000 was an obstacle to understanding how Peruvians identified themselves in the past. In order to assess the intricate trajectory of identification in postcolonial Peru, I needed a new perspective and to learn new methodological frameworks and evidence.

The Mellon Seminar provided the space, skills, and resources to explore these new avenues while I worked on a book manuscript. My decision to pursue a postdoctoral fellowship in an area (science and technology studies) different from my doctoral education (history of Latin America) proved to be the right call. The interdisciplinary nature of science and technology studies and the solid reputation of the Department of Science and Technology Studies at Cornell were both a challenge and a motivation to keep pushing the once compartmentalized analysis of the history of identification. While I reinvented myself as an STS scholar, the Mellon Seminar was a place where I could complement my research by absorbing inquiries and preoccupations with friends from other disciplines. The weekly meetings were a stimulating space to bring and discuss our doubts and inquiries.

For what I envisioned as my book project to develop during the seminar, the challenge was threefold. Firstly, I had to approach biometrics and identification in an analog era prior to the arrival of fingerprints, mug shots, and modern identity cards. For some researchers, identification can be examined only from this perspective, which has led to focus on a single institution: the police. I decided not to take this approach and to go back at least half a century prior to the advent of such innovations. My point of departure was the Peruvian War of Independence, in order to study the transition from colonial practices inherited from the Spanish rule in the Andean region since the sixteenth century. As I demonstrated, there was a rich and vibrant set of practices and artifacts that were embraced and rejected by colonial subjects long before modern technology.

Secondly, by deliberately disrupting the temporal arc and not starting in the mid-nineteenth century I learned more about the role of technology. Biometrics and the adoption of sophisticated methods might have helped authorities to identify citizens, but in the end these brought negative consequences for the majority of the population, especially in a postcolonial setting. Identity cards became more professional, but they were used to watch fellow nationals and to reinforce colonial structures based on racial hierarchies. Until the 2000s, these papers were not available to everyone; they were limited mostly to male, urban, literate, and "white" citizens. Their selective use created an invisible barrier between the coastal areas and the highlands, depriving the right to vote to those of indigenous descent, a legacy that was barely curbed in the late 1970s, when a new identity document, designed for the illiterate population, was issued by the government.

The final challenge seems to be how to move beyond the nation-state framework. Fortunately, the interdisciplinary nature of the seminar made it easy to learn from the multiple areas studied by its participants by inserting the Peruvian case onto a global stage. There is a tendency among scholars to emphasize the "peculiarity" of our own cases or to introduce them as part of perennial "peripheries." I disagree with this approach. Yet there are some peculiarities in the Peruvian case, such as how humans and societies dealt with identities and recognition in cases of political violence many decades ago.

For most Peruvians throughout the twentieth century, our lives gravitated toward two specific documents: the Libreta Militar (or military card) and the Libreta Electoral (or national identity card). Obtaining the military card in the 1980s was a rite of passage. Once we approached our eighteenth birthday (the legal age of adulthood in Peru), we had to approach the local military headquarters. The procedure was humiliating, to say the least. We had to wait for long hours under the sun, and then we were mistreated by the occasional clerk. Despite our concern obtaining the Libreta Militar, this was a necessary evil in the process of becoming citizens and discouraging unnecessary attention from the army. The military nature of Peruvian citizenship—a distortion from the liberal idea of "armed citizenship" that emerged in the early years of the Republic—was present through the numerous raids led by local caudillos to increase the number of soldiers in the barracks. When military service became mandatory, the military card was used to separate those who has already passed through the barracks from those who could be arrested and dispatched to the barracks without any notice or justification. This somber exercise also reinforced the hierarchy of the officials and the armed forces over civil authorities and the government, especially in those areas where the state had been historically absent, such as certain parts of the highlands and the Amazon.

The Libreta Electoral, on the other hand, was the civil counterpart to the military card. It granted political rights to its bearer, like the right to vote in presidential and municipal elections. Yet, like the Libreta Militar, it embodied a long history of inequality and segregation. It was created in 1931 amid the "perfect storm" of the Great Depression, the collapse of the government, and the rise of populist parties in Peru. The political and economic crisis led to the reorganization of the electoral system, which proposed the Libreta Electoral as the cornerstone of such reform. The pressure for mass parties contributed to its vast dissemination on the eve of a presidential election in 1931. Over the next sixty-five years, until it was replaced by a new ID card, the Libreta Electoral reigned as the primary proof of identity among Peruvians. Nonetheless, many did not hold the card, thus remaining invisible to the government on the brink of the violence unleashed by the Shining Path and the military in 1980.

It is not surprising that I have vivid recollections of how I got my Libreta Militar but none at all of receiving my Libreta Electoral. Getting the latter was a simple matter that entailed going to an obscure governmental office when we turned eighteen. Our major concern pertaining to that document was to protect it from being ruined. Meanwhile, obtaining the Libreta Militar, was a traumatic and abusive experience that is impossible to forget. Fortunately, that process is now extinct.

The Disappeared of Peru

In May 1980, the Shining Path, one of a myriad of radical groups that emerged in the upheaval of the preceding decade, announced the beginning of armed struggle against the Peruvian state. For the next twelve years, the Shining Path orchestrated a vast number of attacks against civilians, political leaders, and military and police officers, dragging the entire country into a bloodbath until the capture of its leader, Abimael Guzmán, known as Comrade Gonzalo, in an upper-class neighborhood in the capital city. During the initial stage of the conflict, the state proved to be ineffective against the rise of the Shining Path. In the early 1980s, President Fernando Belaúnde Terry (1980–85) irresponsibly dismissed terrorists as a band of thieves (*abigeos*) before he realized this mistake and declared a state of emergency in the southern highlands, which led the military to replace the police and take control of large portions of territory, deepening the intensity of the conflict. The Shining Path, on the other hand, was committed to a total war in order to create a "new" society following the destruction of the existing institutions and the state. Inspired by Maoism, terrorists carried out their own version of a cultural revolution in the Andes, which ultimately led to their defeat, leaving behind a legacy of victims and desolation.

After the army took control of the operations against the Shining Path in the southern highlands in 1983, Ayacucho was suddenly populated by soldiers and officers dispatched to the region to contain the terrorist group. The army also set up detention and interrogation centers. Not surprisingly, the number of those disappeared and victims rose abruptly after this. Bodies began to appear with visible signs of torture. Relatives approached human rights organizations as well as the military headquarters asking for their sons, daughters, and parents. To avoid any tangible proof that could incriminate them, the military destroyed the bodies, incinerating them in crematories, like the one built inside Los Cabitos, an infamous army headquarters in Ayacucho. In other cases they heaped the bodies in the *botaderos* (dumps) that appeared in the region, waiting for vultures to make them unrecognizable or for them to decompose. When Shining Path perpetrated similar crimes, they exposed their victims so everybody could see the signs displayed over the inert bodies, signs accusing them of being military informers (Hatun Willakuy 2014, 268). For relatives, it became a painful routine to visit these places and try to recognize the faces or clothes of their loved ones among the disposed bodies.

When the recognition of human features was impossible owing to the state of the body, clothes were a decisive marker to use in identification (Torres 2017). The exhumations conducted in Los Cabitos led to the recovery of clothes and belongings from those who had been detained, tortured, and then executed in that army base. The investigation determined that President Alan Garcia's visit to Ayacucho in mid-1985 pushed military chiefs to incinerate approximately 500 bodies buried at the base. Experts determined that the remains found there belonged to 109 bodies, but only five have been fully identified so far. In order to contribute to their identification, clothes and other items were displayed in Lima in September 2014 (Fowks 2014). Fragments of shirts, jerseys, shoes, and underwear constituted the macabre collection of remains exhibited to relatives (Castro 2017). Along with clothing, other objects were retrieved from those clandestine sites, such as combs, coins, belts, and even a notebook. It is moving to note how ordinary objects ended up serving as ultimate identifiers of their owners when other methods were not available. For some families, these objects act as representations of missing kin and thus provide some comfort despite the troubling circumstances.

In a few cases, the only tangible proof of existence of the victims was a *foto carnet* (passport photo). These small *fotos carnet* were very popular in the country throughout the twentieth century. With the increasing availability of cameras and the demand for an affordable portrait, more people gained access to black-and-white passport photos. As a first step toward their dissemination, these photos moved beyond the confined spaces of police stations and photographic studios, with itinerant photographers key in their availability. Given the nomadic nature of these traveling photographers, tracing their biographies or professional activities is very difficult. Still, their presence has been noted in small towns in the highlands, where villagers lined up as they waited for their turn to be photographed, posing for the camera with a light blanket serving as an improvised background. We also find these photographers in urban areas, especially in public spaces, offering portraits to bystanders. These photos were cherished by their bearers, who often annotated the date and place where they were taken. Sometimes they were sent to loved ones in the letters that went back and forth between the capital city and hometowns. Ultimately someone kept these photographs, which formed part of their personal archives. It is likely that the subjects did not imagine when they commissioned these photos that their relatives would one day use them not only to remember them but also to help find and identify their remains.

The lack of a portrait or a photograph meant less exposure and visibility for the victim's relatives who sought justice. And the amount of time that had transpired between August 1985, when a group of sixty-seven peasants was massacred by a military patrol in the town of Accomarca, and the 2000s, when the investigation was reopened, contributed to the deterioration of the few existing images of the victims. The attack against this community was particularly brutal. Lieutenant Telmo Hurtado led the raid against the *comuneros*, taking them from their homes and locking them—including twenty children—in three cabins and then ordering his subordinates to burn the cabins and to kill any potential witnesses. The case was reopened in 2002, and by then the portraits of the victims were hard to distinguish. While their families fought to have the case reopened, the images of their beloved ones were rapidly vanishing. Furthermore, not all of the victims had photographs, and when they were readily available it was difficult to enlarge the size of the small *fotos carnet*. Hence the possession of a photograph took an unexpected additional value: not only to remember the victims but also to secure their relatives a privileged position in press conferences. As journalist Jonathan Castro (2017) contends, without these images, families' demands for justice were "less visibilized," and those without a photograph were moved to a back row in their interviews with reporters and the media.

The relatives of Benedicta Quispe Martínez were among those who had to cede their spot to those holding a photograph. The only visual testimony they had of Benedicta was a poor-quality image found in a local electoral record. The photograph barely shows a face and some facial features (see fig. 5.1). In 2016, Jesús Cossio, a Peruvian artist who had documented the years of political violence in two acclaimed graphic novels (*Rupay* and *Barbarie*), attended the public hearings and committed himself to assisting the relatives in restoring the faces of their loved ones killed in Accomarca. Cossio sketched portraits of the disappeared based on photos relatives provided. In other cases, where photographs were not available, he used photos of relatives to reconstruct certain physical features that described the victims. In the cases of individual children, Cossio sought inspiration in photographs portraying other children of Ayacucho. Working in tandem with relatives and their organizations was key to correcting the initial sketches. The final portraits were given to the families in February 2017 in a ceremony attended by the Ministry of Justice.

BENEDICTA QUISPE MARTÍNEZ

FIGURE 5.1 Benedicta Quispe Martínez by Jesús Cossio. Reproduced with permission of the artist.

Lacking material evidence of the victims, whether an identity card, a photograph, or any other visual reminder, along with the absence of the bodies, altered social cultural practices associated with mourning, grieving, and burial during and after the conflict. As noted, not being able to show a photo of a disappeared person could undermine the public exposure of a case and relatives' ability to gain justice. On a more personal level, not having a body to mourn and bury changed the dynamics of death rituals in the Peruvian southern highlands, a profoundly religious area. Heavy coffins once carried atop shoulders by four or more people from the church to the cemetery were replaced by the carrying of small and light boxes, like the one containing the remains of Mr. Feliciano Huamaní, killed by the Shining Path in 1984 and buried by his son Feliciano (Luna Amancio 2017; Llakiy Times 2017). When neither bodies nor even remains have been recovered, rituals, such as the changing of clothes and the subsequent funeral service, cannot be performed properly. Even worse, during the height of the violence, burials were banned by the authorities, hence families had to perform inadequate burials (*malos entierros*) that impeded families' ability to deal with the pain and haunted them for the ensuing years (Hatun Willakuy 2014, 268).

Epilogue

This chapter shows the social and cultural impact of disappeared populations in a post-conflict area like the southern highlands in Peru. As this case demonstrates, the relationship between technology and "invisible" populations is way more complex than the possession (or not) of an identity document. As I aimed to demonstrate here, the undocumented nature of an individual or a group should be a point of departure to investigate the genealogy of such exclusions and how the mechanisms that prevented them from obtaining proof of identity continue to operate and block them from achieving full rights and participation. The investigation of identification and invisible populations urges us to rethink the history of identification and reexamine the sources and methodologies we have been using. In doing so, we need to descend into the most obscure regions of the human past, to learn about the victims of political violence, genocide, and, most recently, terrorist attacks and figure out how we can contribute to the restoration of their histories and identities. Technology has proved to be a formidable tool in assigning identities to bodies exposed to such inhuman acts, and new methods and advances will certainly help identify other victims, posing new challenges for experts, scholars, and relatives, as Jay D. Aronson (2016) suggests in his book on Ground Zero and the victims of the 9/11 terrorist attacks. In other cases, where such episodes of mass death took place in areas with a high percentage of undocumented people, it is necessary to complement forensic science to explain why such persons lived outside the scope of the large systems of which they were a part. We must examine how those same systems continue to exclude or overlook groups, making them more vulnerable to violence and poverty in the near future.

Note

1. Many friends and colleagues contributed to this chapter. I want to thank Debra Castillo and Anna Sims Bartel for organizing the Mellon Diversity Seminar at Cornell and also thank the fantastic group of scholars who participated. Patricia Palma, Griselda Jarquin, and Valérie Robin Azevedo read an early version and gave excellent feedback. Jesús Cossio kindly shared his material and allowed me to reproduce one of his works.

Works Cited

Aronson, Jay D. 2016. *Who Owns the Dead? The Science and Politics of Death at Ground Zero.* Cambridge, MA: Harvard University Press.

Cardoza, Carmen Rosa. 2017. "¿A dónde van los desaparecidos?" *Ideele* 267, February, 2017. Accessed April 4, 2020. https://revistaideele.com/ideele/content/%C2%BFa-d%C3%B3nde-van-los-desaparecidos.

Castro, Jonathan. 2017. "Accomarca: Retratos contra el olvido." *Ojo Público*, August 20, 2017. Accessed April 4, 2020. https://memoria.ojo-publico.com/articulo/accomarca-retratos-contra-el-olvido.

Correo. 2015. "Mira el verdadero rostro de San Martin de Porres." *Correo*, November 4, 2015. Accessed April 4, 2020. https://diariocorreo.pe/peru/mira-el-verdadero-rostro-de-san-martin-de-porres-630264/.

Fowks, Jacqueline. 2014. "Una prenda de vestir como último vestigio para reconocer un cadáver." *El País*, September 21, 2014. Accessed April 4, 2020. https://elpais.com/internacional/2014/09/21/actualidad/1411259334_734843.html.

Hatun Willakuy. 2014. *Hatun Willakuy: Abbreviated Version of the Final Report of the Truth and Reconciliation Commission* (Lima: Transfer Commission of the Truth and Reconciliation Commission of Peru). Accessed April 4, 2020. http://ictj.org/sites/default/files/ICTJ_Book_Peru_CVR_2014.pdf.

Hunter, Wendy, and Robert Brill. 2016. "'Documents, Please': Advances in Social Protection and Birth Certification in the Developing World." *World Politics* 68, no. 2 (April): 191–228.

Llakiy Times. 2017. "Los ataúdes pequeños guardan dolores grandes" ("The Small Coffins Keep Great Sorrow"). *Llakiy Times* (October): 4–5. Accessed April 4, 2020. https://www.scribd.com/document/417930297/Llakiy-Times-un-periodico-contra-la-impunidad#from_embed.

Luna Amancio, Nelly. 2017. "Las prendas que relatan el horror." *Ojo Público* (August 20). Accessed April 4, 2020. https://memoria.ojo-publico.com/articulo/las-prendas-que-relatan-el-horror.

Ragas, José. 2020. "The Official Making of Undocumented Population: Peru, 1880s–1930s." In *State Formation in the Liberal Era: Capitalism and Claims of Citizenship in Mexico and Peru*, edited by Ben Fallaw and David Nugent, 107–125. Tucson: University of Arizona Press.

Rojas-Perez, Isaias. 2017a. *Mourning Remains: State Atrocity, Exhumations, and Governing the Disappeared in Peru's Postwar Andes*. Stanford: Stanford University Press, 2017.

Rojas-Perez, Isaias. 2017b. "Making a Home for the Disappeared." Stanford University Press Blog, August 3, 2017. Accessed April 4, 2020. https://stanfordpress.typepad.com/blog/2017/08/making-a-home-for-the-disappeared.html.

Torres, Fabiola. 2017. "El Armario Infinito de los Desaparecidos" ("The Endless Wardrobe of the Disappeared"). *Llakiy Times* (Lima) (October), 2. Accessed April 4, 2020. https://www.scribd.com/document/417930297/Llakiy-Times-un-periodico-contra-la-impunidad#from_embed.

CHAPTER 6

A Ride to New Futures with Rosa Parks

Producing Public Scholarship and Community Art

RICHÉ RICHARDSON

Riché Richardson was born and raised in Montgomery, Alabama, the birthplace of the civil rights movement. She was an active student leader, developing a community initiative as a teen for children at the city's Cleveland Avenue YMCA, reflecting her aim to "make a difference," a goal that to this day shapes her public outreach and public voice as a scholar in the humanities. She attended Spelman College and majored in English, minoring in philosophy and women's studies. She received her PhD at Duke University in American literature with a certificate in African and African American studies. She is a 2001 Ford Foundation Postdoctoral Fellow. She spent the first decade of her academic career in the University of California at UC Davis; she is currently an associate professor in the Africana Studies and Research Center at Cornell University and works primarily in the fields of African American literature, southern studies, cultural studies, and gender studies.

Her recent courses include bell hooks Books, The Oprah Book Club and African American Literature, Introduction to Africana Studies, Toni Morrison's Novels, Black Panther Party Autobiography: Writing the Activist Self, 1966–2016, The Willard Straight Takeover and the Legacy of Black Student Movement, and Beyoncé Nation. She has published essays in numerous journals and the book Black Masculinity and the U.S. South: From Uncle Tom to Gangsta *(2007). Since 2005, she has coedited the New Southern Studies book series at the University of Georgia Press, and began serving as its editor in 2018. She is also an artist whose mixed-media appliqué art quilts have been featured in several solo and group exhibitions and in the films* A Portrait of the Artist *(2008) and* The Skin Quilt Project *(2010). Her chapter here details intersections between three interests—her quilt art, her deep roots in Montgomery, and the living legacy of civil rights—stitching together a compelling image of one particular public humanist and artist.*

As a black woman teacher, researcher, and artist, I frequently grapple with how systematically blacks were abused in the system of antebellum slavery, including slavery's assault on the black maternal body. In dealing with what the human means to someone who works in an interdisciplinary department of Africana studies in the humanities in fields such as African American literature, gender studies, southern studies, and black feminism, I think and talk a lot about the long history of black dehumanization within the system of Western slavery. Africana studies, a field founded on an embrace of activism and community service and outreach, is an ideal site from which to cultivate projects linked to public and community engagement, especially as the latter have gained more emphasis in academic institutions. Concomitantly, I frequently discuss the long history of freedom struggles in the black liberation movement that have been developed to confront subjection within slavery and Jim Crow, along with the lingering manifestations of these systems that have persisted. Because I was born and raised in Montgomery, Alabama, the civil rights movement, including the activism of Rosa Parks, is an aspect of this long history of black liberation struggle that has most viscerally impacted my life and work.

In retrospect, I can say that Rosa Parks's legacy began to influence my life profoundly during my teen years. At ages sixteen and seventeen as student council vice president and then president at the historic St. Jude Educational Institute, I developed a leadership program at the Cleveland Avenue YMCA under the supervision of its director Robert James with the goal of making a difference in the community. For two years, I volunteered every Friday afternoon coordinating this program for children and preteens in the surrounding community, the same community in which Parks had once lived. It was in Montgomery that Parks refused to give up her seat when bus driver James Blake ordered her to do so on that fateful evening of December 1, 1955. My work with children in the vicinity reflected Parks's longstanding commitment to supporting them through work such as her leadership in Montgomery's NAACP Youth Council, where she had mentored girls such as Mary Frances Whitt, a friend and federated club sister of my mother, Joanne Richardson. Parks's early work with this group was extended in her continuing engagement with children in her writings and in her outreach to them through her work in the Rosa and Raymond Parks Institute for Self-Development in Detroit. At age seventeen, I won a first-place prize in a poetry contest in Montgomery for a dramatic poem that I wrote honoring Parks, "Together We Will Win."

At this point in my life, nearly thirty years later, and in the work I do as a professor at Cornell University and as an artist, I continue to find deep inspiration in the legacy of Rosa Parks. When my book *Black Masculinity and the U.S. South: From Uncle Tom to Gangsta* was published in 2007, Troy University's Rosa Parks Museum in Montgomery hosted a book-signing and public reception.[1] As an art quilter, my first two solo exhibitions of my mixed-media appliqué art quilts in 2008 and 2015 were also both held at the Rosa Parks Museum, curated when Georgette Norman was its director. In 2008 and as part of the community-based programming for the first show, talking in a workshop with fourth and fifth graders from E. D. Nixon Elementary, a school located a few blocks away from the Y, brought me full circle and back to the community in which I had volunteered during my teen years.

Georgette and I first met after I graduated from Spelman College in 1993, when we were assigned to the same unit as volunteers for a week at a Girl Scout day camp for economically disadvantaged girls, Camp Sunshine. At the time, she was serving as director of the Alabama African American Arts Alliance, which she had founded to help support and promote African American and African diasporic art in the state. This was in keeping with her outstanding leadership legacy of building arts institutions in Alabama to make a positive and transformative community impact. Such cultural contributions have situated her among the South's foremost black women institutional leaders and arts curators. Like the girls, I called her "Miss Georgette" back then, and she and I kept in touch after sharing such an inspiring week together mentoring the girls. I had made my first quilt as a senior at Spelman, and she encouraged me to exhibit my artwork at some point. Our dialogues mirrored Rosa Parks's continuing investments in youth and demonstrated the difference that sustained commitment to mentoring and volunteering in the community can make, including building mentoring relationships among black women and girls.

On my visits home from graduate school at Duke University, I would visit Georgette and attend arts salons and parties at her home, also located in Rosa Parks's former community near the Y where I had once volunteered. Actors from the Alabama Shakespeare Festival and musicians from the Montgomery City Orchestra could often be spotted in this intellectually dynamic and lively arts community. Over the years, during these evenings

I enjoyed activities from participating in African drumming to hearing a blues band, and I even shared my quilt work informally in this setting several times.

On January 31, 2013, the historian Jeanne Theoharis was invited to the museum to speak about her newly released political biography, *The Rebellious Life of Mrs. Rosa Parks*. The talk was organized and introduced by Georgette and aired on C-Span2 to launch Parks's centennial birthday celebration in Montgomery. On February 4, I was honored to serve as the invited speaker for Rosa Parks's gala hundredth birthday celebration at the museum, which was an opportunity to present an excerpt from my academic work on Parks. The program also included a letter from First Lady Michelle Obama read by Georgette, a poetry reading by National Book Award recipient Nikky Finney, and remarks by Montgomery's mayor Todd Strange and other city officials, along with administrators from Troy University.

At the centennial event, I was presented with a framed set of soon-to-be-released Rosa Parks commemorative postage stamps and invited to be a part of the stamp unveiling with Montgomery postmaster Donald Snipes and Georgette Norman, along with Rosa Parks's family members who had traveled from Atlanta (fig. 6.1). Georgette had developed a "100 Birthday Wishes" community project in Montgomery in which children shared their thoughts about their city, their country, and the world and suggestions for

FIGURE 6.1   Montgomery postmaster Donald Snipes, Riché Richardson, and Georgette Norman, from *Montgomery Advertiser*, February 5, 2013. Photograph by Mickey Welsh.

changes to make them better places. These were shared in the daily *Montgomery Advertiser*, and on the night of the celebration, printed on paper made by children in a mobile studio traveling throughout the region, the hundred wishes were presented to city officials. Others and I were given a framed "Wishes do come true" commemorative print on the handmade paper.

I took the stage again as I unveiled my art quilt honoring the heroine and donated it to the museum. All of my life's work came together that day, and it has been one of the happiest days of my life. I felt as if I had been born for that day and saw my life's purpose far more clearly, to the point that I am humbled enough to say that I enjoyed celebrating Rosa Parks's centennial birthday far more than I have ever enjoyed celebrating a birthday of my own. My Rosa Parks art quilt is now on display in the permanent collection at Troy's Rosa Parks Museum, part of an art montage that greets guests as they enter (see fig. 6.2).[2] With a three-dimensional appliqué portrait of her against fabric featuring images of globes, my art quilt frames Parks in relation to the long history of the black freedom struggle while simultaneously linking her to diverse global populations. As someone who was born, raised, and educated in Montgomery through high school but who primarily lives and works in Ithaca, New York, far from my hometown, I value everything that keeps my work as both a scholar and artist connected to the Montgomery community.

Rosa Parks's gala birthday gave me a sense of what can happen when academics, especially humanists, are given a public platform on which to share ideas. It underscored my work's potential to begin up dialogues between people positioned at opposite political poles and people who typically do not have opportunities to meet or talk. In 2013 and 2014, the centennial event program aired regularly on the regional cable television network, Capital City Connection, typically three times a day when on the programming schedule. In the program, I talked about my research project related to Parks's legacy, which allowed me to share the project with a large and diverse television audience in Alabama, which means a lot to me as a scholar who was born and raised in the state. This is just one of the ways in which my project demonstrates the relevance and value of humanist-oriented academic research in the public sphere and its potential to make an impact on communities.

From January 10 to March 27, 2015, an exhibition of sixty of my art quilts, *Portraits II: From Montgomery to Paris,* appeared at Troy's Rosa Parks Museum, dedicated to the memory of my grandparents, Joe Richardson and Emma Lou Jenkins Richardson. It was designed to help launch both the fiftieth anniversary of the Selma-to-Montgomery March and the sixtieth anniversary of the Montgomery Bus Boycott. Rosa Parks was the centerpiece of the series that I developed for the exhibition in tribute to the Montgomery Bus Boycott, which also featured pieces honoring Martin Luther King Jr. and E. D. Nixon. A public reception held on Dr. King's birthday, January 15, drew a large audience, and on that occasion I also released a print card picturing my King quilt. Daily busloads of schoolchildren and many others visited the exhibition, and it was featured in stories in the *Montgomery Advertiser* and on local television. On the eve of the fiftieth anniversary of the Selma-to-Montgomery March, the museum held a gala reception in the gallery featuring my quilt exhibition, and local leaders attended along with such national figures as House Minority Leader Nancy Pelosi, Martin Luther King III, Jesse Jackson, and Bernice King.

The signature style of portrait art quilting that I have developed draws on intricate design techniques and incorporates painting, mixed-media, and hand-stitching to produce detailed, three-dimensional quilts. My 2015 show featured several large installation-style "torso quilts." The centerpiece among them was a large triple-panel quilt installation in the debutante series, a work that features my grandparents on either side of my aunt Pamela at age sixteen during her cotillion in Montgomery in April 1976 at Garrett Coliseum. The installation incorporates digital media for spotlighting and soundtrack, and I drew on principles of geometry, engineering, and architecture in developing it. In my art, I aim to depict the beauty of the human spectrum, including the body, sometimes acknowledging the beauty and dignity of black life and family in the Jim Crow South. My family quilts recall May Day celebrations in Montgomery dating back to the 1960s, as well as Easter parades, school programs, and birthday celebrations. They re-create family debutante portraits from the 1970s to the 2000s. Altogether they capture a side of black life, particularly in the U.S. South, that is not frequently discussed.

My work as a scholar and visual artist helped me to make a strong public impact during these events at the Rosa Parks Museum, which is fitting considering that her legacy has been a subject of investigation for me as both a scholar and artist. While my academic work has begun to draw public and media interest on its own terms, I have found my artwork to be tremendously useful in expanding my opportunities for public and community engagement. I often find myself working in my art on questions similar to those I am researching. The work is for very different audiences, but I value both opportunities. Those who may never read my writing can nevertheless reflect on philosophical questions my exhibitions raise when they encounter my visual work and attend receptions in public gallery spaces. Art audiences are often more dynamic and energizing than scholarly audiences and help to expand my platforms for teaching. As an academic, I find that also being an artist expands my access to public and media platforms and allows me to participate more extensively in public and community art projects. While I typically develop my work as an academic and artist for different audiences, public spaces often bridge the work that I do in each by simultaneously drawing on my voices as a scholar and artist. My art also helps to broaden my understanding and practice of research, in the sense that I routinely do research in developing my art projects. My sometimes overlapping research trajectories as an artist and academic unsettle and challenge the separate spheres into which I am inclined to categorize my work.

Rosa Parks, in honor of whom Congress commissioned a monument for the National Statuary Hall that was unveiled in the US Capitol on February 27, 2013, has often been reduced to a myth of "quiet strength" and described as having remained seated on the bus that day because she was "tired." Invoking Parks's long days of work as a seamstress at the Montgomery Fair Department Store in downtown Montgomery and thus physical tiredness obscures reality. It was *mental* exhaustion that Rosa Parks herself described: "People always said that I didn't give up my seat because I was tired, but that isn't true. I was not tired physically, or no more tired than I usually was at the end of a working day. I was not old, although some people have an image of me as being old then. I was forty-two. No, the only tired I was, was tired of giving in."[3] In such instances, invoking the weariness of her body as a laborer supersedes the emphasis on her mind and fails to frame the story of Rosa Parks at a metaphysical level, which would complicate the narrative that so insistently reads the bus encounter through her physical human body and exhaustion of the flesh.

From another viewpoint, the bus driver's response to Parks that night came from a reading of her as inferior and subhuman because of her status as a black woman.[4] In my own research, I foreground critical epistemologies from black feminism to interpret such views and to analyze the impact of gender alongside race and sexuality in fashioning Parks's body on the bus that night. Furthermore, I consider Parks's recurrent iconic imaging as the "Mother of the Civil Rights Movement," emphasizing its rootedness too in politics of race, gender, and sexuality, underscoring ways in which the title unsettles conventional pathologies of the black maternal body such as the mammy figure (I mean this in the sense of not being as stereotypical and pathological as the mammy, as my forthcoming book elaborates), while foregrounding themes related to children and futurity. I examine this title's manifestations in her own writings and its mirroring in some of her representations in culture.[5] In the process, I have aimed for a more nuanced portrait of Parks as a human subject by focusing on her own words.

In this essay, in light of my training in fields such as literary and cultural studies, and building upon my work on Rosa Parks and her scripts as a national mother who has challenged conventional white-centered images of femininity, I discuss the Children's Wing added to the Rosa Parks Museum in Montgomery in 2006. Its dynamic and futuristic engagement with Parks's legacy was designed to facilitate public encounters with her legacy at the site of her 1955 arrest, the intersection of Montgomery and Lee Streets.[6] The installation invokes Parks as a mother, echoes major themes that inflect her writings related to freedom, and challenges children to help eliminate injustice and create a better world in the future. Its primary exhibit is a futuristic bus that simultaneously situates Parks's action on the bus in relation to a longer history and draws on themes related to future time and space, including a virtual tour given by a robotic bus driver. I link these motifs to Afro-futurism. This installation frames Parks's message as a universal one and is developed primarily to speak to youth growing up in the twenty-first century in a digital age.

Though this museum draws visitors from all over the world and busloads of schoolchildren, its powerful message is not as widely known by those who have not had the opportunity to visit it. It is also useful to analyze and write about in my research from a scholarly standpoint because much of its design innovation and ingenuity flies under the radar. Too often, the legacies of black women leaders have been marginalized and their voices silenced in civil rights narratives, in spite of their pivotal contributions to the movement. This institution related to Rosa Parks is worthy of far more critical reflection than it has received. Moreover, it is all the more important to reflect on because it is now juxtaposed with the new groundbreaking Legacy Museum and National Memorial for Peace and Justice, a project of Bryan Stevenson's Equal Justice Initiative, which is nearby and has promoted, in national media, critical reflection on histories of slavery, Jim Crow, and civil rights in Montgomery.

As I think more about my own art quilt featuring Rosa Parks that helps welcome audiences into the Rosa Parks Museum, I also realize the ways the quilt mirrors and echoes the Children's Museum's framing of her as a figure who transcends time and space and as a universal symbol of freedom. I am thankful that this institution is a space that, over the years, has provided public platforms for me to engage the community in Montgomery as both

FIGURE 6.2   "Rosa Parks, Whose 'No' in 1955 Launched the Montgomery Bus Boycott and Was Heard around the World" (Commemorating 100 years, 1913–2013), *Civil Rights Movement Series, Black History Series,* and *Alabama Women Series.* Art quilt by Riché Deianne Richardson, dedicated to Georgette Norman. Photograph by Mickey Welsh.

a scholar and artist. My analysis also provides a more direct critical dialogue on the museum, which illustrates the role that it has played in shaping my research in recent years. My conclusion of this essay acknowledges how Rosa Parks's legacy has continued to shape my commitments to public and community art. Some of the opportunities that I have had for community engagement have also helped me to appreciate the value of organic intellectual voices and perspectives that operate at the grassroots level, beyond the context of academia.

The Rosa Parks Children's Museum and the Cleveland Avenue Time Machine

As someone who has come to view the Rosa Parks Museum as a kind of artistic home, in the sense that it has helped me to build upon my early work in life related to Rosa Parks and to remain organically connect to the Montgomery community, I cherish this institution. It is one of the premier sites in the nation for teaching and learning about her legacy, along with the Rosa and Raymond Parks Institute for Self-Development that she established with her friend and eventual caretaker Elaine Steele. Already intellectually invested in studying Rosa Parks, I increasingly began to draw on critical frameworks at my disposal to think about the ingenuity in the museum's design and particularly about how the Children's Wing builds on the conventional mythology of Parks as Mother of the Civil Rights Movement. Furthermore, I recognized the levels on which the Children's Wing operates subversively by presenting a counter-narrative to conventional stereotypes of black mothering, extending the platform that she outlines in her books and carried out in her activism related to reaching out to children around the world.

The Children's Wing draws a national and global audience of thousands of tourists annually. Its popularity points to the extent to which Parks has been embraced by an intergenerational audience and to the timelessness of her message, including its themes related to freedom. They are themes that run counter to narratives in popular culture and hip-hop that reductively frame Parks in relation to the past or dismiss her altogether, such as those of the rap group OutKast and Cedric the Entertainer, but relate her legacy to the future. In this sense, the young audience that the Children's Wing primarily draws and its futuristic themes demonstrate the limits and misperceptions in such popular readings of Parks.

In 2000, Troy University's Rosa Parks Library and Museum in Montgomery emerged as the nation's second major institution in the United States designed to honor the life, work and legacy of Rosa Parks and the history of the Montgomery Bus Boycott.[7] Georgette Norman was hired as the museum's director, and it opened to the public on December 1, 2000, in a ceremony that featured Parks as the guest of honor. The landmark 55,000-square-foot building on the site of the former Empire Theater, where

Parks's famous arrest occurred, houses not only outstanding installations but also extensive databases on Rosa Parks, the Montgomery Bus Boycott, and civil rights movement legal cases.

The Cleveland Avenue Time Machine, built to resemble a bus, is the centerpiece of the museum's Children's Wing, which opened in 2006, a year after Parks's death. Georgette spearheaded this addition to the museum. In March 2009, it won a TEA Award for Outstanding Achievement in the category "Exhibition on a Limited Budget" (from what was once the Themed Entertainment Association) at the fourteenth annual Thea Awards ceremony held at the Disneyland Hotel in Anaheim, California. The installation was a collective design effort by Eisterhold Associates of Kansas City, Missouri, Jan Bochenek of Virginia, Ben Lawless of Maryland, Peter Vogt of Washington, DC, and Hadley Exhibits of New York, whose primary features include special lighting, a seven-projector video, audio, and fog. The large bus installation most viscerally climaxes the museum's emphasis on temporal themes. The bus is painted green, gold, and beige to resemble the one on which Parks was arrested in 1955. However, a number of features accord it a futuristic aura: the size (larger than the historic bus and larger than average seats), the wide center aisle, and the robot driver, "Mr. Rivets," poised over a dashboard resembling the instrument panels on space ships in science fiction films.

As a space, the bus evokes the past through its color scheme while conveying the future through its design and features. The bus is framed through its name (Cleveland Avenue Time Machine) and its appearance. The installation of the giant bus is a space designed to look larger than life from the perspective of a child and to provide an imaginative tour to engage the history of the Montgomery Bus Boycott. The bus is parked in a large, open warehouse-like display space, framed by black metal posts, connected to a host of wires and steam pumps that one might see in an industrial factory, and it must be boarded by walking down a long, L-shaped ramp lined with metal rails that lead up to its entrance. Once a passenger is seated, Mr. Rivets starts the engine, and the bus uses a host of special effects, such as vibrations, flashing lights, steam and sound to create the sensation of motion, features that engage the senses and create the illusion that the bus *is* a machine. An overhead video screen on the bus becomes the focal point as a video narrated by the actress Tonea Stewart emerges, a parallel to the feature that begins the tour in the main museum.[8] The main exhibition casts its tourists as pedestrians and ushers them on a walk that alludes to the day-to-day material conditions and practices that led to the Montgomery Bus Boycott, but the Children's Museum alternatively stages and simulates an imaginative ride through history.

Time travel in the sense popularized through science fiction is the central motif in the video as the tourist goes back in time not just to the 1950s and 1960s but 150 years, an imaginative journey into the past signaled by the physical vibrations of the bus. It is notable that the naming of this bus installation invokes the H. G. Wells novel *The Time Machine*, which popularized the concept of time travel and expanded the possibilities for imagining the phenomenon. The novel was published in 1895, a year before the Supreme Court's *Plessy v. Ferguson* decision sanctioned the "Separate but Equal" doctrine segregating public facilities, including forms of public transportation. The Cleveland Avenue Time Machine conserves the original bus coloration but otherwise fully reimagines and redesigns the No. 2857 GM on which Parks was arrested. But navigating a trip *forward* in time emerges as the main purpose of Mr. Rivets.

The robotic Mr. Rivets manifests qualities associated with a cyborg and anticipates a post-human subject, even as his status as a male bus driver ("Mr.") might seem to conserve the conventional logic of gender. He is also marked as post-racial through his seeming race neutrality but situated in a context that acknowledges racism, contrary to post-racialism's evasion of the social impact of racism. In effect, Mr. Rivets replaces 1955 bus driver James Blake in his role as the navigator for a diverse generation of passengers. He facilitates their encounter with the past as he sits poised to transport them to a world of new possibilities in the twenty-first century and beyond. The video that unfolds on screens positioned outside of the bus windows create the sense that one is surrounded by and traveling through history as Parks's story is narrated.

To show the origins of the term "Jim Crow" that eventually emerged as a euphemism for segregation, Mr. Rivets goes back in time 1828, to Cincinnati, where stage entertainer Thomas "Daddy" Rice donned the burnt cork mask of minstrelsy and did a song and dance routine called "Jump Jim Crow." Narrator Tonea Stewart explains that minstrelsy propagated an image of blacks as foolish. The video displays a host of caricatures of blackness that were circulated in U.S. material culture and that were linked to notions of black inferiority. The year 1857 is the next time period to which the bus travels. The video's most compelling feature at this juncture features local actors portraying the family of Dred Scott to facilitate discussion of his famous legal case. An enslaved black man, Dred Scott sued for his freedom, but the U.S. Supreme Court held in its 1857 *Dred Scott v. Sandford* decision that citizenship rights did not apply to blacks. Thus, the video shows discrimination against blacks in the North and "how Scott became the most famous black person in America" at that time.

The video's next phase of time travel stages an imaginary conversation between Harriet Tubman and Henry "Box" Brown. After she escaped slavery to freedom via the northbound Underground Railroad, Tubman made numerous trips to the South to free black slaves, and the video tells the story of how Brown famously arranged to have himself boxed and shipped to freedom. The year 1892, in New Orleans, emerges as another signal juncture on the journey that pinpoints an early challenge of Jim Crow on public transportation by covering the case of Homer Plessy, the Supreme Court case upholding segregation as "separate but equal." The time machine's next major stop occurs in 1955, when the narrator raises the question, "How much has changed?" and says, "Not enough, I'm afraid, by this time." At this point, actors dressed in period clothes evoke the Montgomery Bus Boycott and Parks's heroic choice to remain seated. Stewart, narrating, says, "Something happened that changed America on that bus that evening," registering Parks's indelible impact on the nation.[9]

Besides examining the past, the video in the Children's Wing bus also takes its young audience on an imaginative journey into the future and draws on images associated with the space age. The Rosa Parks Museum, by tacitly casting Parks as a symbolic mother, reinforced references to her as the "mother of the civil rights movement" that had been increasingly mainstreamed and embraced in this nation by the 1990s. However, the museum effectively recasts romanticized motherhood within civil rights history by associating it with notions of futurity as much as the past. The name "Children's Wing" is also significant for alluding to the famous Children's March in Birmingham, Alabama, that occurred in 1963.

The young audiences the museum addresses in this bus tour can be thought of as an extension of the youth mentored by Parks during her lifetime. In the video they watch, the forced migrations of modernity that were linked to slavery are eventually displaced by images of a world in which travel is entirely voluntary. More than that: all limitations on time and space are removed. The containment and marginalization of black subjects is completely ruptured. In this future all humans are free from mental and physical constraints and have the entire universe at their disposal, including access to alternative and inclusive historical narratives. In this space, the hope and potential looking toward the year 2055 are indispensable in complementing a look back to the historic events of 1955.

The dynamic Cleveland Avenue Time Machine challenges passé narratives of the civil rights era by making Rosa Parks not only an emblem of past struggles against segregation but also as a harbinger of African American futurity. The installation registers an axis of temporal nodes that dislodges Parks from romantic and nostalgic narratives. It frames her as a premier revolutionary and a woman who not only made a national impact on ending segregation but also whose significance is global and universal. While the slavers' ship has recurrently functioned as a symbol of slavery in the Western world, it is the bus that emerges in this installation as the primary symbol of both civil rights struggles and the journey to new horizons.[10]

The Cleveland Avenue Time Machine creates an interactive and inter-subjective engagement with the past using video and animated sound and light effects to simulate movement backward in time. Yet the main move-ment suggested is travel forward. Even the historic bus boycott is seen as part of a transcendent narrative that signals the future. It exceeds earthly dimensions and temporalities by drawing heavily on science fiction, a genre in which black and female subjects have remained largely invisible or mar-ginal, with the exception of works by writers such as Octavia Butler. More-over, the video's narrative emphasizes Rosa Parks along with a range of black female precursors, unsettling conventional male-focused chronicles of Afri-can American history. Here Parks is situated within a futuristic aesthetic and simultaneously synonymous with the past, present, and future.

The installation's chronological narrative of the civil rights struggles goes well beyond the 1950s and 1960s, spanning the antebellum era to the twenty-first century. This in effect dislodges civil rights history, including the Montgomery Bus Boycott, from the stasis to which it has been linked in the national imaginary. This approach is particularly significant when consid-ering the exhibition's diverse audience of children and adolescents. Today's youth don't know much about civil rights history and internalize the myth of its obsolescence, but the Time Machine's technology and multimedia can reach them and position them to share this history with future generations. The representations of Rosa Parks that have emerged in the new millennium, as in this exhibit, also profoundly resonate with Afrofuturism.

In historicizing and remembering the Montgomery Bus Boycott and mon-umentalizing Rosa Parks as a civil rights leader via video, while drawing on technology and features derived from science fiction, the Cleveland Avenue Time Machine poignantly actualizes a visual and aural aesthetic in keeping with Afrofuturism. A critical and cultural discourse in areas such as literature and art, Afrofuturism draws on fantasy, magical realism, and science fiction to engage the past and present in relation to the lives of minorities, includ-ing people of African descent, while decentering Western-centered frames of reference. Mark Dery, author of the seminal essay "Black to the Future," introduced the term itself in 1993.[11] It has been further advanced and developed critically by scholars such as Alondra Nelson, who founded an internet site called Afrofuturism in 1998.

Nelson acknowledges that the site emerged in part because dialogues about blacks and technology proved limiting in their vacillation between focus on the utopian fantasy of technology in eliminating race and emphasis on the rhetoric of a digital divide. As she argues, "The racialized digital divide narrative that circulates in the public sphere and the bodiless, color-blind mythotopias of cybertheory and commercial advertising have become the unacknowledged frames of reference for understanding race in the digital age. In these frameworks, the technologically enabled future is by its very nature unmoored from the past and from people of color."[12] Enlightenment philosophy, most notably the perspectives of G. W. F. Hegel, famously excluded Africans in the schema of world history and posited them as being out of time, a framing that denied their humanity, marked them as inferior, and helped to rationalize their enslavement and subjection. Afrofuturism, along with queer and gay and lesbian studies, has played a primary role in shaping discourses on temporality in African and African diasporic thought as it provides a counter-narrative to conventional narratives that have marginalized and excluded blacks.[13]

Birmingham, Alabama, musician Sun Ra, who migrated to Chicago and founded his "Arkestra" in the 1950s, stood at the forefront in developing an Afrofuturist discourse in music, synthesizing sound with images of Africa, space, and science fiction in costuming and other visual displays. While his groundbreaking innovations in jazz and experiences in cities such as Chicago, New York, and Philadelphia typically link his Afrofuturist musical production to urban contexts, they were shaped by his foundational musical training and performances in clubs in Birmingham during the bitter years of the Jim Crow era. Sun Ra and his Arkestra challenged stereotypes of the South as backward and trapped in time. Their performances and recordings organically link the origins of Afrofuturism to Alabama, worth thinking about in connection with the Cleveland Avenue Time Machine.

The installation frames Parks's choice to remain seated on the bus as the outgrowth of a longer history of movement for freedom that continues to unfold, a movement that her transcendent legacy continues to impact. At the same time, this framing challenges the conventional perception of her choice to remain seated as being simply an individual act of heroism. It emphasizes that the boycott that Parks's arrest catalyzed was a collective and interdependent community initiative. The installation also enacts and stages the messages running through Parks's books for young readers, affirming their potential to help catalyze change in the world, just as she did, framing them as the hope of the future.

A paean to Parks as a symbolic mother in the nation, the Rosa Parks Museum's Children's Wing was designed to help spread the message that mattered to her most, and the Afrofuturistic digital Time Machine emphasizes its timelessness and universality. Like her books, it addresses a young audience and challenges narratives of the civil rights movement by linking the past to the future. In the Cleveland Avenue Time Machine, a black woman—Parks—is unfettered and embodies the triumph of a national ideal: freedom and democracy. As I conclude, I want to describe two ways in which my own art related to Rosa Parks has been used at the local level to help bridge her legacy to newer grassroots movements.

From Black Lives and Black Community Art

As I have acknowledged, the rap group OutKast and the actor Cedric the Entertainer have both been famously dismissive of Rosa Parks's legacy. The high-profile controversies reflect other contestations of Rosa Parks's legacy that have emerged in African American popular culture in music and film. In 1999, OutKast, along with its production company LaFace Records, was sued by Rosa Parks for the song "Rosa Parks" included on the 1998 album *Aquemini*. Parks's attorney Gregory J. Reed argued that OutKast illegally appropriated her name for a song that included vulgar lyrics. Similarly, the 2002 comedy film *Barbershop*, directed by Tim Story, garnered controversy because of a heated debate that it stages about Parks between two of its characters, Calvin Palmer Jr. (Ice Cube) and Eddie (Cedric the Entertainer), with Eddie crudely asking, "Who the hell is Rosa Parks?" and asserting that "Rosa Parks ain't do nothing but sit her black ass down." Such representations belie the dynamism that connects Rosa Parks's message to younger generations in her own work. In the years since her death, the aforementioned museum installation and national tributes to her, including the statue in the US Capitol, have compellingly underscored the continuing impact of her legacy.

A tragedy involving hip-hop closer to home in Montgomery was a catalyst for linking Rosa Parks to antiviolence activism in the area. During the final days of December of 2013, the popular Montgomery rapper named Doe B (Glenn Thomas) and two other people lost their lives in a shooting at a local night club. The city had witnessed multiple homicides that year. Doe B., who wore an eye patch after a 2009 shooting, was known for both his talent and generosity in the community. In July 2014, Michelle Browder, a grassroots community artist and activist in Montgomery, took an image of my Rosa Parks art quilt and replaced its broken arrest number with the words "#No More: Stand Up Against Violence" as a call to end the city's violence perpetrated by black youth. She posted her redesigned image of my quilt on social media and challenged others in her circle to join her in taking a stand against violence, and her message then appeared on posters and other paraphernalia. Encouraged and supported by Georgette Norman, Browder has worked on numerous public art projects and initiatives related to civil rights history and is well known for her colorful paintings and murals and visionary designs using Converse sneakers as canvases.

Browder's statement affirmed the continuing significance of Parks's civil rights legacy in Montgomery and its relevance to grassroots community organizing efforts to promote peace. At the same time, some local artists and activists began to question and rethink the use of the phrase "Stop the Violence." Instead of invoking the word "violence" at all, they began to express a preference for the use of the phrase "Start the Peace" or "Keep the Peace." Browder, who established a youth nonprofit and her own tour business, was also one of the activists in Montgomery's Black Lives Matter movement who helped to lead demonstrations after the death of Gregory Gunn in February 2016 at the hands of a Montgomery police officer. A relative of Aurelia Browder, one of the plaintiffs in the 1956 legal case *Browder v. Gayle* challenging segregation of public buses in Montgomery, she has engaged in critical reflection on Parks in her art and does workshops at the museum. It is among the institutions Browder visits when leading her popular "I Am More Than" public tours of civil rights movement sites.[14]

In fall of 2016, I was invited to speak and exhibit my civil rights quilts at the annual Westheimer Peace Symposium at Wilmington College in Wilmington, Ohio. I was also invited to contribute a block to a community quilt that was made in tandem with this event to promote messages related to peace, which I rendered in my typical appliqué style. Michelle Browder's provocative retooling of my Rosa Parks quilt and use of it as part of her campaign to raise awareness of her antiviolence campaign helped inspire my quilt block design. In it I used an image recalling an earlier work depicting Parks (see fig. 6.2) but replaced the arrest number of the earlier work with the name "JOHN," to honor John Crawford, a young African American man killed by a police officer in a Walmart in Beavercreek, Ohio, in August 2014. I was honored to have my art quilts installed in the gallery room alongside Gail Cyan's powerful quilt featuring Crawford, which depicted his image in juxtaposition with Black Panther Party women giving the Black Power salute. I appreciated the dialogism that Browder established with me as an artist, and it has also inspired me to continue designing Rosa

Parks quilt blocks that foreground the first names of victims to help ensure that they will not be forgotten.

For me, this peace quilt, like Browder's art and my representation of Parks in relation to John Crawford, links the global freedom movement that Parks catalyzed and the earlier black liberation movement to newer political movements, from Black Lives Matter to #SayHerName, that critique and protest police violence. Like the installation in the Rosa Parks Museum Children's Wing, such work links Parks's legacy to the future as well as to the present. At the same time, the initiative out of which this gesture emerged in Montgomery underscores the importance of working to combat crime in black communities.

My great-aunt Johnnie Rebecca Carr was a longtime leader of the Montgomery Improvement Association and the best friend of Rosa Parks. However, that background has nothing to do with why I embrace the latter in my own work and art. My own dynamic and visceral encounters with the legacy of Rosa Parks, whom I never met in person, were the outgrowth of my work and investments as a community volunteer, which began during my teen years. My work on her is an intricate part of my identities as both a scholar and artist and has inflected some of my most visible and meaningful public work. I remain invested in learning from and researching her life's work focused on freedom, which is all the more urgent to study, reflect upon, and draw on in a political climate shadowed by so much division and unrest. The peace and freedom that Parks symbolized are indispensable for building a better future for this nation and the world, including all of its children, whom she embraced continually in her public work and who were ever dear to her heart.

Notes

1. Riché Richardson, *Black Masculinity and the U.S. South: From Uncle Tom to Gangsta* (Athens: University of Georgia Press, 2007).

2. On this occasion I also released an art print card featuring this quilt in Rosa Parks's honor.

3. Rosa Parks and James Haskins, *Rosa Parks: My Story* (New York: Penguin Books, 1992), 116.

4. Danielle L. McGuire, *At the Dark End of the Street: Black Women, Rape and Resistance: A New History of the Civil Rights Movement from Rosa Parks to the Rise of Black Power* (New York: Alfred A. Knopf, 2011); Jeanne Theoharis, *The Rebellious Life of Mrs. Rosa Parks* (Boston: Beacon Press, 2013).

5. See Rosa Parks with Gregory J. Reed, *Quiet Strength: The Faith, the Hope and the Heart of a Woman Who Changed a Nation* (Grand Rapids, MI: Zondervan Publishing House, 1994); and Rosa Parks with Gregory J. Reed, *Dear Mrs. Parks: A Dialogue with Today's Youth* (New York: Lee and Low Books, 1997).

6. See Riché Richardson, "Framing Rosa Parks in Reel Time," *Southern Quarterly* 4 (2013): 54–65. See also Riché Richardson, "Monumentalizing Mary McLeod Bethune and Rosa Parks in the Post-Civil Rights Era," *Phillis: The Journal for Research on African American Women* 2, no. 1 (2014): 23–30.

7. Cofounded in 1987 by Rosa Parks and her longtime assistant Elaine Steele to promote community initiatives among youth in the city and around the nation, the Rosa and Raymond Parks Institute in Detroit is the most longstanding U.S. institution designed primarily to honor the legacy of Rosa Parks. It builds upon her work to promote civil and human rights.

8. Stewart is best known for portraying the mother of the nine-year-old girl raped by two white men in the 1996 film *A Time to Kill*, which is set in Mississippi in the post–civil rights movement era. Stewart also portrayed Johnnie Carr in the 2002 film *The Rosa Parks Story*.

9. It is noteworthy that the Cleveland Avenue Time Machine in the Children's Wing is complemented by a physical time line stenciled on museum walls. This time line features figures associated with the Montgomery Bus Boycott beyond its major players such as Parks and Dr. King. Furthermore, an interactive computer extends the time line and shows, for example, the records of citizens arrested for their boycott activities.

10. The ship has been a long-standing metaphor associated with movement in the African American experience. For analysis, see Paul Gilroy, *The Black Atlantic: Modernity and Double-Consciousness* (Cambridge, MA: Harvard University Press, 1993).

11. See Mark Dery, "Black to the Future: Afro-Futurism 1.0," http://www.detritus.net/contact/rumori/200211/0319.html.

12. Alondra Nelson, "Introduction: Future Texts," *Social Text* 20, no. 2 (2002): 6.

13. See Georg Willem Freidrich Hegel, *Introduction to the Philosophy of History*, translated by Leo Rauch (Indianapolis: Hackett Publishing, 1988).

14. Meghan Drueding, "One Woman's Guide to Hidden Historical Gems in Montgomery, Alabama," *Preservation Magazine*, Summer 2018, https://savingplaces.org/stories/heritage-tours-visit-hidden-gems-of-african-american-history-in-montgomery-alabama#.XpCUstJKg2w; Stacy Long, "More Than Just a Tour Guide or Teacher, Michelle Browder Is a Montgomery Inspiration," *Montgomery Advertiser*, September 24, 2018; and Jada Yuan, "The 52 Places Traveler: In Montgomery, a City Embedded with Pain, Finding Progress," *New York Times*, February 27, 2018.

PART III

Considering Resistance

In early November, Caitlin Kane and Sara Warner organized a formal story circle for us, and we all felt it was an important breakthrough moment for our ongoing project. Coming after several weeks of passionate debate and discussion focused around readings of published material, suddenly the main material was intimate, personal—vastly enriching, though we knew we could not share the particulars outside the circle itself. In preparation, Sara and Caitlin posted the following on our website:

Consider some of the definitions of public scholarship as scholarship *about public issues, for public purposes, with public partners,* or *creating public goods.* . . .

Consider frameworks that suggest we can do academic work *about, for,* or *with* our partners (and that these might be developmentally staged or specific to our interests and gifts). . . .

Consider the inevitable public-ness of teaching students who are or become members of publics. . . .

In an effort to help us dig in a little more, please come ready with a brief story of a time you felt most clearly the public purpose / practice of your work.

We'll share those together and try to build some common understandings of what it means to enact the liberal arts in public.

(And yes, this is kind of Part I of the story circle practice, with an emphasis on deliberative dialogue).

Story circles (a formal methodology for community building most famously codified by Roadside Theater) are more about active listening than telling, in some ways the opposite of much of what we understand as traditional academic performances. Yet, of course, stories are our most fundamental way of sharing our humanness with others, and stories are what most powerfully draw us together as community. Stories, whether in the condensed forms of memes, or the longer forms of theatrical performance, have power.

Many of the members of our group have a background as artists or performers; in this section we highlight a few of the ways that activist-artist-scholars are helping us explore the idea of the public, both in production and in engagement with audiences. Christine Henseler, Ella Diaz, Caitlin Kane, and Sara Warner all look at intersections of popular culture and activism, how deeply felt and deeply personal commitments can be honed through academic and professional training, through active listening/observing. It is worth noting as well that in each of these cases, the academic/humanistic issues at the core of the context (using humanities to critique the systems at work on us; meme sharing and interpretation; youth theater production; political resistance using theatrical strategies) are classic academic fare. But used in the ways they are used by these colleagues, they come to life, enhancing then not only their public impact but also their scholarly significance.

CHAPTER 7

Finding Humanity

Social Change on Our Own Terms

Christine Henseler

Christine Henseler should have become a set designer. Her first twenty years were spent drawing, painting, and making. She won prizes for posters in high school; she painted theater sets, and even wrote a short play. And because engineering is in her blood, she spends her time building, from wooden decks to transdisciplinary programs. So why did she become a professor of Spanish literature? Because some messages rarely change: she was told you can't get a job in the arts. So she gained a degree in Spanish and journalism/advertising, and the rest is history. Or is it?

Life usually comes full circle. Christine now encourages students to study the arts and humanities; she expands young people's understanding of career choices through websites such as The Arts and Humanities in the Twenty-first Century Workplace and guidebooks such as Arts and Humanities: Don't Leave College without Them. *In the hopes of reaching a broader audience and slowly reshaping national conversations, Christine codirects a public advocacy initiative known as 4Humanities and contributes to the* Huffington Post *and* Inside Higher Ed. *Her long-term hopes and dreams? To give more underserved youth the opportunity to build a meaningful and successful career with the arts and humanities.*

Changing the Story

When tasked with compiling their personal stories into a book to be self-published on Amazon, the class I started to teach in the spring of 2018—Students

Call for Social Change—buzzed with excitement, one student so elated that she immediately texted her dad. The students couldn't believe it. They would become published authors! They would write about an issue that was near and dear to their hearts, a "story of change" meant to inspire their friends, their communities, the next wave of changemakers.

The goal of the course was as exciting as it was urgent. Prospects of a climate apocalypse, the unavailability of basic public goods like drinking water, let alone social security and health care, are some of the many reasons our young adults are taking to the streets. They were literally marching for their lives, as was the motto of the student-led demonstration after the Parkland, Florida, shooting on Valentine's Day, 2018 that left seventeen high school students dead.

Despite the power of such youth activism today, many young adults feel helpless, anxious, frustrated. They might march to the drum of these protests, but what can they really do in their everyday lives to affect social change?

That's what I asked my students that first day of class in April 2018. My goal was to enhance students' understanding of their place in this world and their agency to change their piece of the world. That is why the case studies we examined, the critical readings and film assignments, centered on young people making a difference in their everyday lives, in small ways, with persistence, belief, and compassion. Through books like Adam Braun's *The Promise of a Pencil: How an Ordinary Person Can Create Extraordinary Change* (2014), and films like Nicole Nenhman's *Revolutionary Optimists* (2013), Grant Baldwin's *The Clean Bin Project* (2010), and *Living on One Dollar* (2013), by Chris Temple, Zach Ingrasci, and Sean Leonard, student sentiment began to shift from helpless uncertainty and frustration to feeling an inkling of individual agency.

Through intensive and constant workshopping of ideas and writings, students began to feel that they had the power to affect change by telling their own personal story. But grappling with a unique and personal issue that had significantly impacted their lives was no easy matter. And being in a traditional classroom was certainly not conducive to developing a more student-centered environment or to calling me "Christine" instead of "Prof. Henseler." So every Wednesday, at 3:00 p.m., a Union College shuttle took us to an office building in downtown Schenectady called Urban Co-Works. It was a cool, industrial-looking space with walls made of glass. In this space I guided students through design-centered activities meant to expand their thinking about issues they felt were critical to their lives and to develop a public narrative that joined their "Story of Self" with their "Story of Us" and "Story of Now," an effective structure first developed by Marshall Ganz of Harvard University, then modified by Serena Zhang and Voop de Vulpillieres in their "Public Narrative Participant Guide."[1]

To further the publication of the book, I also asked students to select a team to write, edit, typeset, market, and design the manuscript, a task that was prone to frustration and difficult moments but representative of the title they chose for their introduction: "You Get Out What You Put In." And what they ultimately got out was a book they titled *Generation Now: Millennials Call for Social Change*. They chose a price of $9.50 and decided to donate all proceeds to COCOA House, a youth after-school program in Schenectady, NY.

After the publication of the book, I was exhausted and drained, but I also felt fulfilled and deeply moved. I had never felt so intensely connected to my students, so affected by the deeply impactful experiences already marking their young lives, from domestic partnership abuse to suicide, from escaping a Hasidic community or rebelling against a Pakistani education to working with disabled kids or suffering through high school with an invisible illness. Yes, contrary to popular belief, these young adults had a lot to say.

The eighteen students' fearless courage to speak about their most personal experiences led to strong emotions in the class, even tears. Their willingness to share personal stories through writing became a testament to their deep desire to be heard and to change their surroundings. It was an emotionally exhausting process for them—and for me. But in the end, this group convinced me that public storytelling could change the course of our lives and that the quote by James Baldwin at the top of my syllabus did indeed ring true: "You write in order to change the world, knowing perfectly well that you probably can't, but also knowing that literature is indispensable to the world. . . . The world changes according to the way people see it, and if you alter, even by a millimeter, the way . . . people look at reality, then you can change it" (quoted in Romano).

The course taught me a lesson that is universally applicable: to shift the way we function in this world, we must allow ourselves to be seen. Vulnerably seen. That's what the students did in this class. By extension, they changed how I think of my work as a teacher and scholar. When I became a "scholar as human," I learned about my own agency in the building of a more humanistic and holistic future. I also learned that we have much to gain from listening to and engaging the next generation of youth, because they confront the social crisis that underlines our nation by seeking more humanity. It's time we faculty, we in higher education, did the same.

So here goes. . .

I Wasn't Always a Professor

When I was twenty, I ran. I did not run from a country or from an unbearable political climate. I ran from a messy parental divorce, from an emotionally abusive stepfather, and from a self that had been demoralized, stripped of a voice and made to feel worthless. Drugs or depression would have been a natural next step, my spouse repeatedly tells me, but I had something that was far more addictive and redeeming: reading, learning, and drawing. So instead I overdosed on natural curiosity and creative drive.

I was seventeen when my mother and I fled back to Germany from Spain, on a bus, one late night in the dark. We were scared. We hid out in a tiny studio apartment. Although just one room, it seemed a hundred times larger than the "golden cage" (as my mom and I used to call it) of the villa in Spain—with swimming pool and tennis court—that had imprisoned us for five years. Cages come in all shapes and forms, and the memory of this metaphorical cage and the courage to find my voice led me to today, to teaching the Call for Social Change class and helping empower my students to raise their voices.

Contrary to popular belief, I am an immigrant. I'm a non-native speaker of English. I come from a wealthy country. A middle-income home. I could never compare my alien past to that of the Central and South Americans, Syrians, or Afghanistanis now seeking refuge. I am blond. Tall. Light-skinned. German. I am not likely to be stopped, arrested, deported. And I can't even imagine—as we all so vividly should—how it feels to be targeted, denounced, ripped from the wombs of those we love.

I am almost embarrassed to call myself an immigrant. My story seems trivial, elitist, even inappropriate in today's political climate, especially given my current professional position. But I wasn't always a professor. I didn't always make a good living. I, like so many contributors to this volume, started at the bottom and arrived here to write this essay for a reason. My reason is that my story of hope, my American Dream—although quickly turning into a nightmare for some in today's political climate—has significantly influenced how I look at the world and the meaning I seek through my work. My hope is to help young people today break out of their cages, whatever their shape or size.

They say that when one door closes another one opens, but what they don't tell you is that some doors need WD-40; they take a while to open and screech in the process. That's how I felt when I learned that the high school degree I received in Spain—the *bachillerato*—would not allow me to attend a university in Germany. And with no German *Abitur*, and no money to speak of, my choices were limited. I had wanted to pursue graphic design, but with no art portfolio my dreams of going to an art academy also went up in smoke. I had no choice but to enter a retail sales apprenticeship that I never wanted or enjoyed. I took painting and French classes at night to make up for my boredom. But I had no mentor. No idea how to change my life, no resources either. I felt much like so many kids do today: wanting more but not knowing how to get there.

However, when I went through the German apprenticeship for two years I learned everything from sales to accounting, from packaging to fabric manufacturing. I worked, and I went to school. And this experience defined how I see the role of education today here in the United States. You see, although I am a college professor today, I do not believe that college should be the only path to follow. Let's build diverse educational pathways to allow for diverse entries for individuals with diverse talents and interests. As in countries like Germany or Italy, solid apprenticeships, in any and all fields, afford respected professional opportunities in shoemaking, plumbing, carpentry, welding, or boat building. Now imagine an entire network of apprenticeships spanning the United States and providing our youth with respectful alternatives to technical schools or colleges. It's about building meaningful lives, not following prescribed paths. And it is for this reason that when I advocate for the arts and humanities, I do so not in exception to (or rejection of) other models and programs of learning but in addition and in partnership.

As a naive twenty-year-old in 1989, I arrived in the United States to start my own life, in my own image. I felt lost, lacking funds, linguistically challenged, insecure and voiceless, culturally in-between, and overall unknowing of the US educational system. I took classes in art and design, but, not knowing about potential careers, I earned double majors in journalism and Spanish, with a minor in art history. I worked as a freelance graphic designer and photographer. And when I was offered the opportunity to teach—I was a senior undergraduate—I was both terrified and energized. And I got hooked. Thanks to wonderful mentors who believed in me, TA-ships and fellowships, a free ride through graduate school determined my fate as a professor of Spanish language and literature, sealed with a doctorate from Cornell University and a friendship with Debbie Castillo. Which leads me here today. Who would have thought. . .

There are more details to share. But what is important to know is that, yes, the moments that marked my young life's path defined my life's purpose today: expanding young people's understanding of what they can do with degrees in the arts and humanities; mentoring and supporting those who are making their way through difficult personal circumstances; pushing on the edges of the boxes and structures that are inhibiting creativity and leaving nontraditional voices out; advocating for more diverse educational pathways, making space for playful and creative problem-solving, believing in holistic and realistic practices that combine happiness with utility and deep learning; building bridges between people and fields and disciplines on and off campus to further engagement; and providing platforms for our youth that allow them to give voice to their perspectives and their opinions. Most important, I believe in facilitating more human communication and compassion, a need that, as this volume pronounces, is becoming ever more urgent, for young and old alike.

Finding Happiness in Our Growing Social Crisis

Mine might be a story set in a different place and time, but the truth is that the basic needs of young people today are relatively unchanging. All seek happiness, health, meaning, purpose, stability, safety, success. Love. What has changed is that this generation is having to find their purpose in a nation that desperately needs to find its own.

Rarely do we faculty members (or do our students) allow ourselves the time to connect or to reflect in this fast-paced society. Even in our courses we move from one assignment to the next, piling on the work, expecting ever more of our students and ourselves. We spend our days returning e-mails, writing reports, working to meet the ever-increasing demands of our scholarly output and our pedagogical needs, not to speak of our many service and leadership responsibilities. What are we losing in this fast-paced society? When I served as director of faculty development I heard consistently about the need for more time, the need for more human communication and human contact. Yes, the need to slow down the clock.

Our need to slow down reminds me of the emergence of the Slow Movement and its guiding principle "to step back from economic markers . . . and to examine what our behavior tells us about the connection between our beliefs and our actions" (45).[2] According to professor Guttorm Floistad, we need to remind ourselves that despite today's sped-up rate of change "our basic needs never change," and they include the need to be seen and appreciated, to belong, to be cared for, and to be loved. And to meet these needs, "we have to recover slowness, reflection, and togetherness" (quoted in Riddle, 45). It seems obvious, doesn't it?

This notion of our unchanging basic human needs ought to be self-evident, but is not: we need reminding. In this capitalist consumer culture in which financial success is conducting plastic surgery on humanity, we, the citizens of this seemingly great country, are increasingly feeling anxious, frustrated, depressed, and angry. There is no time more ripe than today to remind ourselves of the powerful connection between macro-level politics and everyday well-being and happiness.

It is also no coincidence that the happiness factor in the United States has been steadily dropping, down to 19 among over 150 countries studied in the 2019 *World Happiness Report*. Researchers found that in the case of the United States, although its "income per capita has been increasing, several of the determinants of well-being have been in decline, as witnessed in the increased numbers of people suffering under depression, obesity, and opioid addiction" (Helliwell, Layard, and Sachs).

Study after study concludes that countries with the happiest citizens are not necessarily the richest nations. They are those "with a more balanced set of social and institutional supports for better lives" (Helliwell, Layard, and Sachs). But the United States, they found, suffers under weakening social support networks, the perceptions of corruption in government and business, and waning confidence in public institutions. Is it any wonder that, according to a study in 2017 conducted by the nonprofit Mental Health America (MHA), mental health in youth and adults is worsening, yet the United States suffers under a mental health workforce shortage?[3]

The United States does not lack the means to address this and other shortages, but this country continues to suffer under a political system that fails "to address and understand America's growing social crisis" (World Happiness). How ironic, and how out of touch, that our politicians still call this the greatest country in the world. Let's call this country what it is: a country in a deep social crisis.

The social crisis of the United States manifests itself in everyday life in ways that we all recognize. It seems that on a daily basis we shake our heads in disbelief or say: "you've got to be kidding me," not to speak of the very real emotions of frustration, anxiety, and anger that destabilize our well-being. The good news, if one can call it that, is that precisely because our political systems are failing us, our troubles are staring glaringly into our faces. It is like being confronted by our own poor health, a stark reminder that we have to change the way we eat and the way we live, and we need to tell each other how much we care. Yes, we can call getting in touch with our emotions "soft" (as we do of the humanities), but from my experience, this is the hardest work any of us can do. And the most valuable.

Millennials and the Rise of the Everyday Changemaker

Our young people are suffering. They are living through this social crisis at a time in their lives when they are just waking up to the world, a world whose horrors are exponentially broadcast on their social media channels every day. The twenties and thirties are when students are trying to grow into healthy adults who balance personal discovery and well-being with professional path-making and -breaking. So while "64% of Millennials say it's a priority for them to make the world a better place" (Asgar), they are doing so at a time when every aspect of this acute social crisis is affecting their lives. The stories are many. The truths are right at hand. And by extension, the feeling of confusion and helplessness is constant (with anxiety levels at an all-time high). My students said it best in the introduction to their book:

> Millennials: a generation that was born and raised in an era of information and global communications, where even the smallest injustice, in the smallest town, in the smallest country, triggers a call for respect. In our day, everything is relevant and everyone deserves attention. Everyone is expected to know everything. Anything is possible, ironically making new discoveries seem impossible. So how can we care about everything when we have an almost overwhelming amount of information at our fingertips? How can we make an impact in this world if every time we tackle one issue, another one seems to arise? (Union College Changemakers 1)

This overwhelming sense of helplessness that our young people, and all of us really, feel is making many reevaluate their priorities. Finding humanity through a more balanced lifestyle is of utmost importance to this generation willing to give up higher salaries or create alternative employment opportunities to either be their own bosses or work in a more collaborative, supportive environment with flexible schedules and the opportunity to achieve purposeful work-life integration. This is not the same as work-life balance, since it defines the healthy level of control Millennials wish to have over their lives through flexible hours, freedom to work in different spaces, outdoor time to chat with colleagues, and the opportunity to make decisions on all levels of the company (Robinson). And if you think their wishes are nice pipe dreams out of touch with reality, think again, because "86 million millennials will be in the workplace by 2020—representing a full 40% of the total working population" (Asgar). Change is forthcoming, like it or not.

In *Cause for Change: The Why and How of Nonprofit Millennial Engagement*, authors Kari Dunn Saratovsky and Derrick Feldman underscore the need for our organizations to adapt to the more human-centric interests of the Millennials. What drives Millennials, they explain, "even more than technology and social media are the personal relationships and human connections they forge along the way" (14). Attention to social causes, volunteering, and "making the world a better place" are driving motivators of this highly diverse and global generation interested in collaborating and, most importantly, building their "own system, on their own terms" and enthusiastically bringing along others who share the same vision (xv–xvi).

Individual agency to affect concrete change "on their own terms," is an attractive proposition in this political climate, which is the reason why the "everyday changemaker" concept has become such a driving force. The overarching idea has been most notably expressed by former president Barack Obama when he said: "I am asking you to believe. Not in my ability to bring about change—but in yours."[4] It has also been popularized by social entrepreneur and founder of Ashoka, Bill Drayton—"Everyone a Changemaker"—to point to the agency of all, but especially our young people, to build a more civic-minded and caring world. As *New York Times* columnist David Brooks highlights in a conversation with Drayton in February of 2018, "Social transformation flows from personal transformation. You change the world when you hold up a new and more attractive way to live. And Drayton wants to make universal a quality many people don't even see: agency."

But claiming our own agency does not come easy to any of us, young or old. It's a messy process that demands that we connect what we feel inside with our place in the world. As Doris Sommer in her fascinating book *The Work of Art in the World* thoughtfully expresses: "The appropriate question about agency is not if we exercise it, but how intentionally we do so, to what end, and what effect" (4). She believes agency to be "a modest but relentless call to creative action, one small step at a time," living somewhere "between frustrated fantasies and paralyzing despair" (4). Her words readily speak to the experience of my students, who admitted that, "this book did not come together flawlessly. We faced obstacles, large and small, every day. It was those obstacles that helped us learn, and without which we would have produced a very different book. Combining 18 brains is easier said than done. It was inevitable that when communicating our different ideas, we were bound to bump heads, but it was those bumps that shaped the book and made it that much more authentic" (Union College Changemakers 3).

Agency demands the inclusion of more humanity, and humanity comes with uncertainty, failure, frustration, and often organically emerging discoveries and, yes, the unknown. That's why it is high time that we as scholars, and the organizations and associations that support our work, embrace our humanity and make space for the personal and the organic in our conversations, in our projects, and in our grant applications. With trust. Because when we can include play, laughter, creativity, compassion, authenticity, and honesty into our scholarship, our engagements can gain in personal and communal agency. It's what Drayton conveys as the holding up of a new and more attractive way to live. Is it all rosy? Definitely not. But who ever said that becoming human was easy?

Making It Personal

That's where we faculty members come in. Although not exclusively, those of us working in or at the intersection of the arts and humanities have influential roles to play at this moment in history. We are well-versed in the critical art of analytical self-reflection, the art of expression across all mediums, ethical and logical thinking, and the building of cognitive empathy, which is "the ability to perceive how people are feeling in evolving circumstances" (Brooks). We don't need to stretch the imagination to connect the qualities of our disciplines in the arts and humanities with the "evolving circumstances" of the next generation, namely with meaningful everyday change that is born from a critical understanding of changing social structures and narratives, reshaped into their own image, on their own terms, in their own languages.

But who are the Millennials in "their own image"? One telling identity marker is that "to a degree not seen in any previous generation, Millennials see themselves in the shoes of others who don't look like them, speak the same language, have the same education or come from the same background, perhaps because of their high level of diversity" (Case Foundation). Therefore, when the personal stories of my students began to emerge through genuine engagements with each other's topics, from education to immigration and the environment, that's when this seemingly homogenous student body began to expose their deep-seated and diverse life circumstances. Students came from black, brown, and white upper-, middle- and lower-class backgrounds. The group included Japanese, Tibetan, Haitian, and Pakistani Americans, first-generation immigrants and students living between two countries, gay and lesbian students, individuals affected by sexual abuse and long-term health afflictions and disease, liberals and conservatives, and even a royal—yes, we had a real live prince among us (and I dare you to read the book and figure out who it is).

In essence, as scientist Brené Brown expressed in her TED talk "On the Power of Vulnerability," when we let ourselves "be seen, deeply seen, vulnerably seen," that's when we can recognize our human potential in each other and ourselves. Here's how my students described their travails:

> Throughout this journey, each one of us Millennial changemakers went through our own process. We quickly realized the gargantuan task we were taking on. It would not be easy and we each grappled with this challenge in our own way. For some, choosing which movement they were passionate about seemed impossible. For others, it was coping with trauma or hardship and having the courage to share that story. We were reminded that our voices matter and that our generation has the capacity to ignite that change that we all desperately wish to see (Union College Changemakers, 3).

The students that got the most out of my class spent hours finding the changemaker within themselves: "We researched issues that mattered to us, and we wrote a story of change about the communities we so care about. It was when we stumbled upon obstacles in the creation of our social change narration, that we were reminded: our voices matter. Our generation has the capacity to ignite that change that we all desperately wish to see. And we knew that if we didn't throw ourselves into this opportunity for our voices to be heard, nobody else would" (Osterholz and Paneth, et al.)

"Nobody else would." That's a powerful assertion. Much like the ways in which our young are reacting to the social crisis of this nation, seeking happiness and well-being in more integrative work-life environments and reshaping the future in their own image, so can those of us faculty and administrators working in higher education. We must look beyond the structures that are no longer serving the good of our youth, or of us. We built them. We can change them. We can expand them. We can reshape them.

We must continue to ask ourselves: Which voices do our current structures and conversations favor? Which individuals are falling through the cracks? What ideas are stuck in the middle, with nowhere to go? In what ways are we limiting ourselves to traditional ways of thinking and doing that are out of line with today's needs? Where is the place for creativity, humanity, and happiness in all that we do? What is our purpose?

I do not consider these questions, this call to action, a rosy, theoretical exercise. Doris Sommer reminds us that, "It won't do to indulge in romantic dreams about art remaking the world. Nor does it make sense to stop dreaming altogether and stay stuck in cynicism" (4). It's time we claim our own agency in the remaking of the social good that the arts and humanities can promote as they interact with and in the world. And it's time we work *with* the next generations to affect everyday social change. As articulated by

Saratovsky and Feldman, involving Millennials, who comprise most young professionals in all fields and disciplines, is key to several aspects needed for the health and well-being of our shared arts and humanities. Their involvement will:

- connect our scholarly and civic engagement work in the arts and humanities from perspectives and through linguistic and visual registers and platforms that are not only our own.
- change top-down advocacy and educational approaches for more participatory and peer-to-peer engagements.
- engage more diverse voices and visions in new and surprising or unusual spaces.
- support the professional development of our next generation of artists and humanists and, by extension, build new leadership into our organizations.
- develop applied or solution-based environments that speak to the interests and passions of the next generation.
- make it personal by taking more organic and playful approaches that allow for individual vulnerability and connection-building.

If we want to find humanity in this growing social crisis, then we also need to do our part; we need to show the way, with the next generation by our side. Yes, we need to "make it personal"—because what we claim to be a crisis of the arts and humanities is only a crisis insofar as it reflects the larger malaise affecting our nation. As such, we must not only point to the obvious, the present connection between the arts and humanities to sustain and maintain our common good, but we must also question our own role in the building of a healthy future, for ourselves, for our kids, for this nation.

Being a "scholar as human," then, is a necessity. It is time we rebuild our "own system, on [our] own terms" and enthusiastically bring along others who share the same vision. If we don't, who will?

Epilogue

It was the middle of June 2018, when the Call for Social Change class had already ended. I was finalizing the book manuscript. I was editing and typesetting when I noticed a section I didn't recognize. It was titled "For Christine." Where did that come from? I started reading. My eyes welled up with tears. The students had written notes of thanks, expressing how much the course had meant to them. They felt transformed. They had learned to see themselves as agents of change. To see each other, authentically. To connect to each other on a human level, in ways they had never done before. I read on and on, and I began to sob. I sobbed so deeply, for so long. I knew right then that this was the kind of work I wanted to pursue from now on. I became viscerally aware of the transformative power of working with purpose. And I vowed to keep the tears flowing. Because we all need to dig a little deeper to find and share a bit more of our humanity.

Notes

1. Public Narrative Participant Guide, https://www.ndi.org/sites/default/files/Public%20Narrative%20Participant%20Guide.pdf.

2. World Institute of Slowness, http://www.theworldinstituteofslowness.com/.

3. MHA's "2017 State of Mental Health and America" reports that one in five adults has a mental health condition ("that's over 40 million Americans; more than the populations of New York and Florida combined), that youth mental health is worsening ("rates of youth with severe depression increased from 5.9% in 2012 to 8.2% in 2015" and "even with severe depression, 63% of youth are left with no or insufficient treatment"), and that here is "a serious mental health workforce shortage." Mental Health America, http://www.mentalhealthamerica.net/issues/2017-state-mental-health-america-report-overview-historical-data#Key.

4. Wayne Lee, "President Obama: 'Change Happens When Ordinary People Get Involved,'" Voice of America, January 10, 2017, https://www.voanews.com/.

Works Cited

Asgar, Rob. "What Millennials Want in the Workplace (And Why You Should Start Giving It to Them)." *Forbes*, January 13, 2014. https://www.forbes.com/.

Brooks, David. "Everyone a Changemaker." *New York Times*. February 8, 2018.

Case Foundation. "Millennial Engagement." https://casefoundation.org/program/millennial-engagement/.

Helliwell, John F., Richard Layard, and Jeffrey D. Sachs. *World Happiness Report 2018*. http://worldhappiness.report/ed/2018/.

"Millennials Seek Social Change in Their Everyday Lives, Study Finds." *Philanthropy News Digest*, March 16, 2017. https://philanthropynewsdigest.org/.

Osterholz, Kate, Hayden Paneth, Kathleen Sinatra, and Christine Henseler. *4Humanities* Feb. 17, 2020. https://4humanities.org/2020/02/social-change-through-storytelling/

Riddle, Dorothy. *Principles of Abundance for the Cosmic Citizen: Enough for Us All*, vol. 1. Authorhouse, 2010.

Robinson, Ryan. "Millennials, Control Your Own Work-life Integration." *ZenDesk Relate*. https://relate.zendesk.com/articles/millennial-work-life-integration.

Romano, John. "James Baldwin Writing and Talking." *New York Times*, September 29, 1979.

Saratovsky, Kari Dunn, and Derrick Feldman. *Cause for Change: The Why and How of Nonprofit Millennial Engagement*. New York: Wiley Jossey-Bass, 2013.

Sommer, Doris. *The Work of Art in the World*. Durham: Duke University Press, 2014.

Union College Changemakers. *Generation Now: Millennials and Social Change*. Independent Publisher, 2018.

CHAPTER 8

Performing Democracy

Bad and Nasty Patriot Acts

SARA WARNER

Sara Warner studies the art of activism. This means that she looks at the ways political actors use performance in programs for social justice and the ways stage actors use the theater as a laboratory for reimagining notions of community, citizenship, power, and responsibility. Sara is deeply committed to the co-creation of knowledge; as she says, she wants to "find ways to work with people to not tell people's stories for them but to create platforms where people can tell their own story, in their own words, what it means to them." Sara's award-winning book Acts of Gaiety: LGBT Performance and the Politics of Pleasure *examines the role of humor and play in experiments to create a more perfect union. She also publishes cultural criticism in a variety of news outlets, including* Time, HowlRound, *and* Huffington Post, *where she has her own column. In 2016, Sara was named a Stephen H. Weiss Junior Fellow, Cornell's highest teaching honor for a recently tenured faculty member.*

As an associate professor in the Department of Performing and Media Arts, Sara conducts research that takes many forms, from collaborating with incarcerated women to researching suffragist pageants. She coproduces a series of "patriot acts," political performances on national holidays, with the Bad (Hombres) and Nasty (Women) collective—the topic of her contribution to this book. Sara continues her multifarious pedagogical-research-performance-activist work in her current project, a collaboration with climate scientists to dramatize the human impact of global warming in the Finger Lakes. This project has led to Climates of Change *and* The Next Storm, *plays collaboratively created with Ithaca's community-based Civic Ensemble. These activities, with their collective genesis and performance, constitute one kind of political resistance through engaged scholarship, which is a relevant model for our times regardless of party or ideological affiliation.*

As scholar and a human, I spend a lot of time thinking about and producing political theater. I am interested in the ways social actors use performance in experiments for social justice (from the spectacular pageantry of suffragist demonstrations to the ritualized rage of AIDS die-ins) and the ways stage actors use the theater as a laboratory for creating new worlds. I attended my first protest march in college, wrote a dissertation on prison theater, and recently co-taught a course in which students collaborated with a Cornell climate engineer on community-based plays about the human impact of global warming on our local community. I am drawn to the theater as a mechanism for social change because it dramatizes human relations and in so doing invites us into civic conversations about who we are—as individuals, a people, a nation, and global citizens. Through the magic of performance, people can rehearse solutions to problems big and small. The theater is a space of make believe—an intentional pretending that something fictive is true—but it can also be a place of "make belief"—a liminal realm in which we can make and remake reality, creating the universe as we would like it to be, in a full-scale model![1] And, if we can dream it and build it, then—perhaps—we can live it, inhabiting this alternative reality outside of the theater. This world-making capacity is performance's utopian potential.[2]

For the past several years, I have been involved with a collective that on national holidays stages what I call "patriot acts," political theater designed to catalyze public debate and promote the active participation of citizens in the democratic process. This collective—a loose- knit coalition of artists, academics, media makers, web geeks, and left-of-center progressives— emerged as a response to the 2016 election, in which Hillary Clinton lost the US presidential election to Donald Trump, despite winning the popular vote by almost three million ballots. Because a participatory democracy thrives when everyone in society has an equal vote and an equal voice, we called our group Bad and Nasty as a way to counteract the phobic slurs Trump used to denigrate and disenfranchise Mexicans ("bad hombres"), females ("nasty women"), and other minority groups during the campaign.[3]

We held our first patriot acts on February 20, 2017, under the heading Not My Presidents' Day.[4] What began as a small group of friends—Holly Hughes, Lois Weaver, Mary Jo Watts, and me—using social media to plot political cabarets in our hometowns soon swelled to more than nineteen hundred participants who staged upwards of sixty protest events across the country and

FIGURE 8.1 Bad and Nasty logo, designed by Michael Quanci.

around the globe. In performances of democracy that reverberated with the Women's Marches, airport protests against the Muslim travel ban, spirited town halls on the Affordable Care Act, and rallies to denounce immigration raids, members of the Bad and Nasty collective staged ingeniously inventive patriot acts to oppose the discriminatory policies of the Trump administration and to dramatize their visions of a more perfect union.

The variety of patriot acts on Not My Presidents' Day astonished us almost as much as the diversity of locations. The most animated responses didn't come from what we think of as political epicenters of the country or cultural meccas, such as Washington DC or Chicago. They came from Republican outposts in historically red states: South Carolina, Oklahoma, Virginia, and Texas. While many Bad and Nasty cells staged protest marches and demonstrations, several organizers opted for more affirmative, family-centered forms of gatherings. Iowans created a community picnic capped by a conversation between Trump and Abraham Lincoln, represented by balloon puppets, on the steps of the Iowa State Capitol in Des Moines. Organizers in Baltimore also staged activities for adults and children during the day, followed by a political cabaret for mature audiences at night. Columbus, Georgia, held a candlelight vigil for our endangered Constitution, complete with an outdoor reading of the document in a public square.

There was a great deal of discussion among these cells about whether the name Bad and Nasty was too radical for red state constituents (meanwhile denizens in blue states feared it was too tame). Many of our coordinators (we call them Head Groovies) in the South and Midwest felt the moniker was too brazen and risked alienating the very audiences they hoped to attract. One self-described nonconfrontational artist in the Heartland decided that she did not have the luxury of being dignified and polite. The times demanded that she (and we) be angry and loud, Bad and Nasty. Other coordinators—those drawn to fierce, campy, in-your-face enactments—not only embraced the appellation, they also pushed the envelope. Take, for example, revelers in the Lone Star State, whose patriot act was titled "Pussyhood Is Powerful," an evening of lesbian and feminist punk music with Girls in the Nose, Les Nez, MyDolls, and Kegels for Hegel.

New Yorkers had their pick of seven different patriot acts on Not My Presidents' Day, most of them political cabarets. In the East Village, a historically bohemian section of the city, there were two different events on the same street, one at the WOW Café, the artistic home of Bad and Nasty cofounders Lois Weaver and Holly Hughes, and one a stone's throw away at La MaMa Experimental Theatre Club. Headlining the latter was Karen Finley, one of the famed NEA Four who—alongside Hughes—fought artistic censorship all the way to the Supreme Court in the 1990s.[5] A train ride away in BedStuy, one of the city's oldest and largest African diasporic neighborhoods, there was a benefit performance for Amnesty International, *Anna Asli Suriyah (I Come from Syria)*, by Sarah Badiyah Sakaan.

Farther afield, bad hombre Brian Herrera hosted a salon and pop-up art exhibit in Princeton, New Jersey, to debut his "Dichos" ("Sayings"), inspiring aphorisms rendered in a stylized form that he calls AcaDoodle (academic doodle). Herrera had doodled one "Dicho" every day since the election for

FIGURE 8.2   Performance artist Karen Finley at LaMama in Manhattan. Photo courtesy of Carolina Restrepo Loaiza.

a series titled "#ImWithUs—the 1st 100 Days." Bad and Nasty cells in Vermont, Bernie Sanders's home state, produced two events. Marlboro College presented *Two Spirit Resistance* featuring Kuna and Rappahannock Nations performer Muriel Miguel, artistic director of Spiderwoman Theater, the longest-running Indigenous theater company in the United States, on a bill with visual artist Kent Monkman and Canadian dramatist Waawaate Fobister.[6] Meanwhile Flynnspace in Burlington mounted *Trumpuboo Rex (King Turd Revisited)*, an adaptation of Alfred Jarry's dystopian political allegory *Ubu Roi (King Ubu)*.

The indefatigable Lois Weaver did double duty in Los Angeles, a live performance with her Split Britches collaborator, the "menopausal gentleman" Peggy Shaw, in a cabaret at the Lyric Hyperion, and a virtual performance on Facebook live as her avatar Tammy WhyNot, a country and western singer turned lesbian performance artist who longs to be an internet sensation. For her event in Ann Arbor, Hughes opted for a "not my circus" theme. Flying their freak flag of resistance high were some of the hottest talent in the Midwest, including Erin Markey, Lisa Biggs, and Lola Von Miramar (the drag persona of Lawrence La Fountain-Stokes).

Our Bad and Nasty website includes a detailed archive of patriot acts staged on Not My Presidents' Day.[7] In Ithaca, New York, I produced a standing-room-only event with my friend Ross Haarstad, founder and artistic director of Theatre Incognita. In the spirit of community collaboration, we teamed up with a number of local theaters and artistic troupes, including the performing arts departments of both Ithaca College and Cornell University. The Kitchen Theater, which donated their space, was booked on February 20, so we held our cabaret on the eve of Not My Presidents' Day. Tickets were free, as was a buffet reception after the show (thanks to a grant secured by my colleague and collaborator Debra Castillo, coeditor of this volume), and guests were encouraged to donate to Planned Parenthood of the Finger Lakes and Ithaca Welcomes Refugees. (We raised over $2,000 that night.)

When Ithacans entered the Kitchen, they were greeted by a drag queen and king (Haarstad and Ned Asta) singing show tunes played by a local musician on a baby grand piano. This pre-show entertainment stalled guests while I assembled the performers, who had not rehearsed together, for a quick run-through. Our master of ceremonies, Honey Crawford, was a Prince impersonator who electrified the crowd with a riotous opening number, a lip sync rendition of "Pussy Control." I took us back to the women's liberation movement with a staged reading of *SCUM Manifesto* by Valerie Solanas, one of history's nastiest women, which I performed with Jayme Kilburn and Mary Jo Watts (Bad and Nasty's social media coordinator and my partner of more than twenty years). Saviana Stanescu, an award-winning Romanian-American dramatist, delivered a monologue about her play *Aliens with Extraordinary Skills*, which has been produced to critical acclaim all over the world.

FIGURE 8.3 Ithaca master of ceremonies Honey Crawford, as Prince. © Thomas Hoebbel Photography.

FIGURE 8.4 Ithaca Bad and Nasty coproducers Sara Warner and Ross Haarstad. © Thomas Hoebbel Photography.

Ithaca's cabaret featured more than thirty patriot actors who riffed on a panoply of topics, from rape and backroom abortions to anti-Semitism and the Arab Spring. An undergraduate trio brought the audience to its feet with "Pantsuit Nation," a song in homage to Hillary Clinton, but the act that stole the show was a nine-year-old first-time performer who strode on stage in a leather jacket and baby Doc Martins and served up an original spoken word poem titled "Donald Trump Is Not Voldemort." To close out our cabaret, Chrystyna Dail led the audience in a sing-along of "Freedom Road," a 1944 antifascist race record with lyrics by Harlem Renaissance poet and dramatist Langston Hughes and music by Josh White. This song, which White intended as rousing plea for democracy, provided a pitch-perfect conclusion to Ithaca's Not My Presidents' Day.

Not My Presidents' Day was Ithaca's way of enacting, if only fleetingly, our hamlet's vision of a more perfect union. Admittedly, our inaugural event was staged by liberals for liberals. This kind of preaching to the converted (that political theater so often does) is of vital importance for creating and maintaining community.[8] As a form of "creative survival," political theater revitalizes activist energies and strengthens social bonds, which in turn provide the necessary conditions for people to collectively imagine political alternatives.[9] The proliferation of patriot acts across the country and around the globe on Not My Presidents' Day provided a necessary counterweight to the media circus Trump created during the presidential campaign and to his nefarious use of theater for totalitarian ends. "Performance," Richard Schechner reminds us, "is as useful to tyrants as to those who practice guerrilla theater."[10] We have only to study American history to know this to be true. Theatricality has played an important role in our democratic experiment since the country's founding, from revolutionaries costumed as Native Americans at the Boston Tea Party to gruesome spectacles of lynching in the Jim Crow South. An understanding of both the progressive and regressive aspects of performance, of who it includes and excludes, is necessary in order to use theater critically in a participatory democracy.

The Greeks, who invented both theater and democracy, used performance to educate audiences through complex dramas that served as privileged sites for reasoned debates about ethics, norms, and laws. Tragic competitions, held in conjunction with annual civic festivals, were rooted in the notion that the struggle to make sense of the world is a duty, a collective obligation that people must undertake together, in full view of one's compatriots. Greek drama teaches us that democracy requires the active participation of an enlightened and engaged citizenry. Conflict and contestation are not only inevitable parts of the political process, they are also essential to it. Fifth-century Athens was not unlike the contemporary United States insofar as it was hardly a utopian experiment in equality and freedom for all. The civilization that gave birth to the West's earliest democratic experiment also celebrated art (e.g., *The Trojan Women*) that justified the oppression and subordination of foreigners, women, and slaves, all of whom were denied citizenship and a formal role in the political structure of the polis. Most Greek tragedies (and more than a few comedies) are concerned with justice; some even stage the revolt of subaltern subjects against tyranny (e.g., *Antigone*). These dramas have for centuries served as models of patriotic dissent for bad hombres and nasty women everywhere.

An Appetite for Justice: Baking America Great Again

Based on the success of Not My President's Day and the increasingly complicated drama unfolding in the White House, many members of Bad and Nasty wanted to continue organizing, staging additional patriot acts on national holidays. The Ithaca cell did not want to produce another cabaret, which has a limited, self-selected audience and does not foster dialogue across the political aisle. After asking ourselves what kinds of patriot acts would play well in rural America, engaging in earnest those with different political views without sacrificing the radical, campy spirit of Bad and Nasty, we came up with the idea for a campaign called "Bake America Great Again"

(BAGA), a play on Trump's campaign slogan: "Make America Great Again." What follows is an analysis of our community bake sales as a model of "hospitable" political theater, one that provides food for thought, nourishes the social imagination, and provides sustenance for the body politic.[11]

Ithaca Bad and Nasty held its first BAGA patriot act on Flag Day 2017, June 14, which just so happened to be Trump's birthday, a perfect confluence of events. Flag Day is a working holiday, which meant we would have a captive audience on our public commons during the lunch hour. Most people who work in Ithaca do not live in the city (Cornell is the largest employer in the county), in part because they cannot afford the inflated rents typical of a college town. The poverty rate (20.1 percent) in our district is considerably higher than the national average (14 percent).[12] Many of the rural communities surrounding Ithaca are news deserts and lack high-speed internet. Trump carried Tompkins County, as he did many districts dominated by white, working-class constituents, by double digits. (Ithaca was the only blue spot in an electoral sea of red on the upstate New York map.) Ergo, many people who work in Ithaca voted Republican in 2016. We hoped a bake sale would provide a delicious opportunity to attract and talk with Trump supporters.

To whet people's appetites, we pitched a canopy decorated with stars and stripes and hung a huge sign proclaiming "Bake America Great Again." Musicians Andrés Pérez Hernández and Mijail Martínez played guitar and sang, and I donned a spangled top hat to entice passersby. As people approached the tent, they saw rows of delicious treats, which upon closer inspection were politically themed pastries. We had im-peach-mint pies, covfefe cake, (un)ethical wafers, "fudge the truth" brownies, "he's bananas" muffins, let them eat Ivanka-cakes, Kellyanne Conway nut clusters, Sean Spicer cookies, "may his term be short(bread)," and other cleverly titled delicacies. A handful of people turned away in anger or disgust when they realized this was no ordinary bake sale. Some folks complained about the sneaky tactics of the liberal elite but bought treats anyway (just as some of them held their noses after Trump's racist and sexist remarks, voting for the tycoon and reality TV star who promised to "drain the swamp" in Washington). Most people, however, laughed at our jokes, purchased a snack, and indulged us in a conversation about politics. A few liberals admitted they were initially reluctant to approach our tent because they thought we were hosting some kind of Republican fund-raiser. We successfully courted confusion on both sides of the political divide, and our first BAGA raised $600 (in four hours) for the Foodbank of the Southern Tier.

Bake sales provide a unique way to gauge the gut reactions of citizens. They also present a casual way to initiate conversations about the relationship of food to politics, and to immigration in particular. Without being too heavy-handed, we tried to talk with people about the underbelly of upstate New York's agricultural industry, which relies heavily on immigrant workers, and about the way food production is related to the reproduction of racial, social, and economic inequalities.[13] We asked our neighbors if they knew who served them their coffee at the Starbucks across the street, who farmed the milk for their latte, whether the beans they used were imported, and, if so, were they fair trade. A bake sale created the perfect foil for talking about earlier waves of immigration and trade, including the history of chocolate and sugar, which are deeply imbricated with the history of slavery and colonialism, which is to say with the history of democracy. In turn, we listened to people tell us why they voted for Trump and why we should try to stomach his policies.

We staged another Bake America Great Again event on Labor Day 2017, at Tompkins County's Worker Community Picnic. For this patriot act we chose a carnival theme, complete with a barker (my father), food stations, and midway games. We had a "Pin the Tiny Hands on the President" booth, a "Can This Administration" ball toss, an impossible "Hole in One" mini golf set-up, a "Shut Your Corn Hole" bean bag throw, and a GOP Game of Thrones contest (where people tried to pitch a roll of toilet paper through a gold-painted toilet seat). We raised over $500 for survivors of Hurricane Maria with this BAGA—at a community picnic that provides free food and drink to the entire county. Given the theme of this event—a celebration of labor—we talked with people about the various kinds of work they do to sustain themselves, their families, and their politics. In talking about labor with our neighbors, we found that we talked a great deal about hands.

The hands that bake and buy desserts and the hands that play a game of mini golf and sign presidential proclamations denying immigrant visas have a history, and they are shaped by history. Hands make history flesh, notes cultural theorist Sara Ahmed in her book *Living a Feminist Life*.[14] The hand that bakes a cake can make a fist, a fist that can be raised in protest for oneself and for others whose hands can't be raised because they are undocumented, digging themselves out of a national disaster, or restrained in handcuffs. Our Bad and Nasty bake sales represent one way of making connections between hands and histories.

Trump's first eighteen months in office offered progressives a taste of the bitter banquet the nation would be forced to consume, but few among us were prepared for the family detention crisis at the border that erupted in the summer of 2018. In response to this national tragedy, Ithaca's Bad and Nasty staged a patriot act in collaboration with the Immigrant Rights Coalition of

Tompkins County and the Cornell Farm Worker Program at our community Fourth of July fireworks celebration. We called this event an ICE Scream Social, and it featured a snow cone fund-raiser alongside a number of performance art installations. We erected a cage furnished with space blankets (a mirror of the structures erected by the government in makeshift tent cities along the border). Inside stood cardboard figures with cut-out faces. The cage sat near a cardboard wall on which people could write messages to the families at the border and to ICE agents. Forming a perimeter around the art installation were dozens of black umbrellas, representing our mourning and rage at the way our fellow humans were being treated. The umbrellas were stenciled with various verbs: "Resist," "Vote," "Impeach." Periodically a group of people would pick up the umbrellas and proceed around the park in an improvised routine inspired by choreographer Pina Bausch's 1982 public performance "Nelken Line." This procession was coordinated by multimedia artist Leeny Sack, a member of the internationally renowned avant-garde collective The Performance Group, in collaboration with Sierra Carrere, an Ithaca native and a devotee of anticapitalist political theater troupe the Church of Stop Shopping, led by Reverend Billy (the artistic avatar of Billy Talen). Community members were invited to take part in the procession, to come together under the same umbrella, share a snow cone, and talk about immigration, asylum, and family detentions.

We did not create these bake sales from scratch. Our BAGA events are based on recipes we have inherited from different movements for social justice, from the Black Panther Party's free lunch program to lesbian separatist potlucks. Food-based activism has a long history in this country because America is the great melting pot, though it has fed and nourished certain bodies at the expense of others. Patriotism, like the ICE Scream cones we served on the Fourth of July, comes in many flavors: chocolate, vanilla, dulce de leche, and rainbow swirl. If our policies are not intersectional, if they are racist and xenophobic, they can leave a very bad taste in one's mouth. Second-wave feminist adage "the personal is political" reminds us that staging bake sales can be a form of political labor.[15] Like the struggle for social justice, baking is a job that never ends; it must be practiced daily to ensure our survival.

Political work includes domestic and reproductive labor, both the labor of reproducing life and the labor of reproducing the conditions that make life possible. Being freed from the labor of feeding ourselves (including the kinds of back-breaking agricultural labor that many migrants perform) should not be confused with freedom, as this simply means that someone else is providing this labor for us. An "other" pays the price of our liberty. To engage in collective activism is to acknowledge our complicity in a system that feeds some citizens well while starving others—and the hungry often find themselves fighting with their neighbors for scraps, too busy with basic survival to combat effectively the ones with their bellies bloated from consuming more than their fair share. Baking, like all forms of political labor, is messy work; it is dirty work. It can also bring us tremendous joy and pleasure, feeding our bodies and our souls.

One of the greatest joys is breaking bread together. Our Bake America Great Again campaign strives to create spaces that are hospitable and open (though not devoid of conflict), where people can share both the work of political organizing and the fruits of our labor. I have milked this alimentary metaphor long enough, but I hope my wordplay is instructive in thinking about the kind of change progressive activists hunger for. In our bake sales, we strive to make a place for everyone at the table while at the same time serving up a biting critique of discrimination and oppression. Our decidedly domestic patriot acts promote collectivism and caring in a moment epitomized by narcissistic individualism, offering rich alternatives for a common good.

Notes

1. Richard Schechner, *Performance Studies: An Introduction* (New York: Routledge, 2013), 42.

2. Jill Dolan, "Performance, Utopia, and the 'Utopian Performative,'" *Theatre Journal* 53, no. 3 (2001): 455–79.

3. Participatory democracy is the concept guiding many of the political movements of the 1960s and is articulated most cogently in "The Port Huron Statement" by the Students for a Democratic Society. See Tom Hayden, *The Port Huron Statement: The Vision Call of the 1960s Revolution* (New York: Thunder's Mouth Press, 2005).

4. Sara Warner, "Calling All Bad Hombres and Nasty Women for a Nationwide Day of Performance Protest," *HowlRound*, January 20, 2017, http://howlround.com/. See also Sara Warner, "Transforming Anger into Art: Bad and Nasty Collective's Not My President's Day," *HuffPost*, February 17, 2017, http://huffpost.com/.

5. Anthony Haden-Guest, "How Karen Finley Turned Trump and Hillary into Brilliant Performance Art," *Daily Beast*, August 21, 2016, http://thedailybeast.com/.

6. Lois Weaver was a founding member of Spiderwoman Theater.

7. Bad and Nasty, http://badandnasty.com/. You can also find us on Facebook, Twitter, YouTube, and other social media platforms.

8. Tim Miller and David Román, "Preaching to the Converted," in *The Queerest Art: Essays on Lesbian and Gay Theater*, ed. Alisa Solomon and Framji Minwalla (New York: New York University Press, 2002), 220–51.

9. "Creative survival" is Rhodessa Jones's term for the motivational force behind community-based theater. See Sara Warner, "Restorytive Justice," in *Razor Wire Women*, ed. Ashley Lucas and Jodie Lawston (New York: SUNY Press, 2011), 229–45.

10. Richard Schechner, *The Future of Ritual* (New York: Routledge, 1993), 1.

11. Bad and Nasty cofounder Lois Weaver has developed a number of performance strategies for creating "hospitable" conversations about controversial topics. Her models (e.g., the Long Table and Porch Sitting) and her Public Service Announcement (PSA) project have greatly influenced our conception and staging of the BAGA campaign. See Lois Weaver and Jen Harvie, *The Only Way Home Is through the Show: Performance Work of Lois Weaver* (London: Intellect Live, 2016).

12. "Tompkins County, NY." Data USA, 2014. http://datausa.io/.

13. A recent two-volume special issue of the journal *GLQ: A Journal of Lesbian and Gay Studies* explores the processes by which food, flesh, and the alimentary tract are integrally related to the production and reproduction of systemic inequality. See Sharon P. Holland, Marcia Ochoa, and Kyla Wazana Tompkins, eds., "On the Visceral: Race, Sex and Other Gut Feelings," *GLQ* 20, nos. 4–5 (Fall 2014).

14. Sara Ahmed, *Living a Feminist Life* (Durham: Duke University Press, 2017).

15. Carol Hanisch, "The Personal Is Political," 1969, http://carolhanisch.org/.

CHAPTER 9

Making Law

GERALD TORRES

> I asked him how he came to be a painter. He said,
> "I liked the smell of paint."
>
> —Annie Dillard, *The Writing Life*

> Law reflects but in no sense determines the moral
> worth of a society. The values of a reasonably just
> society will reflect themselves in a reasonably just
> law. The better the society, the less law there will be.
> In heaven there will be no law, and the lion shall lie
> down with the lamb. The values of an unjust society
> will reflect themselves in an unjust law. The worse the
> society, the more law there will be. In hell there will
> be nothing but law, and due process will be meticu-
> lously observed.
>
> —Grant Gilmore, *The Ages of American Law*

Gerald Torres is Professor of Environmental Justice at the Yale School of the Environment and the Yale Law School. He was previously the Jane M. G. Foster Professor of Law at Cornell. He is a leading figure in critical race theory, environmental law, and federal Indian law. He previously served as the Bryant Smith Chair at the University of Texas School of Law and taught at the University of Minnesota Law School, where he served as associate dean. He is also a former president of the Association of American Law Schools. Torres has served as deputy assistant attorney general for the Environment and Natural Resources Division of the U.S. Department of Justice in Washington DC and as counsel to US attorney general Janet Reno. His book The Miner's Canary: Enlisting Race, Resisting Power, Transforming Democracy *(Harvard University Press, 2002) with Harvard law professor Lani Guinier was described by* Publishers Weekly *as "one of the most provocative and challenging books on race produced in years." He is also a poet, musician, and a seriously committed Mexican chef, with a standout recipe for mole. Torres says: "I love law, and I love humanities, because of the doorway through language that you have to pass to reach the imagination of others." His chapter in this book looks at this synthesis of how law and humanities together are practices that have a deep connection to shared beliefs, to what we care about, what we know, what we take to be meaningful about the community, and what we hope the future will produce.*

Because I am a lawyer, there can be little doubt that the lens through which I view most things is distorted by that training. Training in law requires (like most disciplines, I suspect) the capacity to hold multiple mutually exclusive ideas in your head at the same time. For example, every law student knows that a house can be legally haunted despite the nonexistence of ghosts.[1] Similarly, every first-year student learns to plead in the alternative: (1) I do not have a dog; (2) he did not bite you; (3) you kicked him first. The famous legal scholar and lawyer Thurman Arnold once paraphrased Thomas Reed Powell saying something to the effect of this: to think that you can think of something that is inextricably connected to something else without thinking about the thing to which it is connected, *that* is called thinking like a lawyer.[2] We must commonly do that, and initially it produces a kind of psychological unease, but, and perhaps this is worse, the dissipation of that unease passes almost unnoticed.

As the training takes hold, a strange thing happens. You forget what you know, and you start to believe that imagined things are real and that things are the way they are because they *had* to be that way. Instead of recognizing the inherent contingency of life and of the institutions that structure social life, that contingency is boiled away even as this abstract mind-set permits the expression of new forms of creativity that are prized.[3] The comedy of regulating lived life based on the make believe is lost on most people but perhaps especially on people who give their lives over to legal training.

The deleterious effect of this process of abstraction is that the social and historical contingency that makes change possible remains hidden behind a screen of false necessity. Of course, most people believe that the world is as it is because it could be no other way (or, for the religious, that it is the expression of some unknowable grand plan). Yet the belief in the necessity of certain social states of being is especially debilitating for the idea of democratic agency that lies at the core of the legitimacy of the modern democratic state.[4]

One of the problems for democratic society is that if institutions are abstracted from the people who created and run them, responsibility for the consequences of institutional action seems to exist nowhere. It is as if the institutions operated according to the laws of nature, like gravity, rather than according to human social convention or rules. Of course, constitutional institutions are the substrate on which all other institutions of governance rest. The meaning of constitutional powers and limitations (I will discuss those more later) is where the most serious political contestation occurs. Social contestation, what my colleague Sid Tarrow calls *contentious politics*, is where we make and remake our social life and write or rewrite our political commitments. This process affects all our social and political institutions, including courts and other formal venues for lawmaking. One consequence of recognizing this is that it requires legal theory to accommodate legal change that is made outside of the formal mechanisms that typically govern legal changes. There is great resistance to this idea, because there is no generally agreed upon moment when it can be said with assurance that this or that activity outside of the formal processes has made law. Retrospect can provide the evidence and the guidance but not the predictability.

Among legal scholars and those who attend to the ways in which legal institutions channel the popular understanding of the relationship between law and politics, the idea that "the people" can produce real legal changes outside of the normal institutional pathways is often considered deeply troubling. One of the problems, of course, is that for many commentators "the people" works well as metaphor but not as description. "The people" as an empirical reality are difficult to categorize. Their passions are messy, their ideological commitments are fractious, and their respect for authority is often both too strong and too weak. One need only look at the current debates over populism to see that. Yet "the people" cannot just be metaphor in a political system predicated on consent. The solution to this problem has always been to rely on elites to channel the passions of the mob through the structures of institutionalized decision-making in order to make their desires politically intelligible. Structurally, this is the constitutional method for domesticating politics, for keeping the distinction between law and politics clear.

When conversations begin over the relationship between law and politics there is always the tacit understanding that there is "law," and then there is "politics." No one really believes that there is a hermetic seal separating one discourse from the other, only that law should not *just* be politics. Of course, discourse is not just a way of talking. A discourse is the whole ensemble of activities that constitutes a subject and which derives its power by what it can exclude. Thus, the rhetorical move to logically separate law from politics serves a specific end. The domain of law can be insulated from politics understood as partisan claims as well as the rhetorical moves associated with ordinary politics. Within this discourse, law is the precipitate of politics, and the conventional story is that only those passions that survive the formal institutional gauntlet to enactment are worthy of being called law. That story, as everyone knows, is radically incomplete. Yet it continues to exert power in the realm of ordinary law and in the realm of constitutional law. After all, the constitution is not only the operating system through which we constitute ourselves as a people, it is also the backstop that prevents popular passions of the majority from running roughshod over the minority.

Constitutional democracy as we have understood it is premised in this context on a liberal constitution and a liberal democracy. The thin version of that idea is that both the constitution and the democracy that it constitutes grant priority to the right over the good as well as recognizing the formal equality of all members of the polity. Democracy is supposed to protect the plurality of the good, and politics is the forum where that struggle over the good is supposed to take place. Surely the role of mobilization and engagement through contentious politics cannot merely be to tee things up for the formal actors. Instead, correctly understood, contentious politics are a means through which the actions of the formal players are constrained. To this extent, the discourse constructed through the process of social movements creates the conditions within which laws are made. In addition, to the extent that they reframe the justifications for formal action, social movements can themselves create law. I recognize that is a complex and contestable claim, but, without wanting to rehearse the varieties of ways that law can be made, it seems indisputable that if social movements limit or expand the range of acceptable interpretations available to formal legal actors they have, in fact, made law. It may not have the crisp edges of a rule, but that is not a dispositive inquiry.

Nonetheless, the possibility of the people making law unmediated by democratic institutions is terrifying to democratic theorists, even if popular sovereignty is the bedrock of legitimacy. It is the constitution that modulates this possibility and quiets the fear. Whether it should is one of the questions that popular social movements ask. If the people themselves can make ordinary law, can they make constitutional law as well? The framers of the constitution purposely made it hard to amend. Nevertheless, as Bruce Ackerman has demonstrated, the people themselves can amend the constitution in ways other than the formal processes contained in the operating system. Yet this seemingly untethered power revives that fear. The constitutional scholar Reva Siegel puts that concern this way:

> There is reticence to analyze these pathways of responsiveness as providing goods we expect formal constitutional lawmaking to provide, because we see no ground to distinguish licit from illicit forms of constitutional change, in the absence of any procedure or metric for measuring democratic will. Without such criteria, it is easier to conceive of such pressures as threats to the Constitution's democratic legitimacy than as sources of it. Thus, even as Americans regularly mobilize to shape the ways that officials enforce the Constitution's commitments, Americans are deeply ambivalent about acknowledging the influence of movements on constitutional meaning.[5]

The contradictions in that characterization are troubling, because it is precisely constitutional meaning that is at stake in the most important moments of social contestation. We are always constituting and reconstituting ourselves as a people. American history in particular, but perhaps most of modern world history too, is replete with popular efforts to shape a nation's constitutional commitments. We are in one of those moments now. It is a particularly fraught moment because it arises when questions of nationhood have supplanted questions of the state and its role. It is an old story, usually told at ceremonial gatherings, that the United States arose from a commitment to capacious liberal ideas of political community rather than being an expression of a particular ethnic idea. Perhaps that is why "Song of Myself" may come closest to an America epic poem. We have no *Iliad*, *Aeneid*, *Beowulf*, *Gilgamesh* or *Song of Roland*.

> Stop this day and night with me and you shall possess the origin of all poems,
> You shall possess the good of the earth and sun, (there are millions of suns left,)
> You shall no longer take things at second or third hand, nor look through the eyes of the dead, nor feed on the spectres in books,
> You shall not look through my eyes either, nor take things from me,
> You shall listen to all sides and filter them from your self.

We know what Whitman means when he says; "For every atom belonging to me as good belongs to you. . . . I am large, I contain multitudes." He is speaking the voice of Americans, as he understood it. It a capacious vision, muscular and spiritual at once. First published just before the war that would rend the country, it was already looking toward the essence of our reconstitution, which would not be found in some preexisting ethno-nationalist identity but in an amalgam of selves that would confirm the motto *e pluribus unum* and be reconstituted in Lincoln's Gettysburg Address.

These moments and sentiments lead us to consider what binds us together. The law provides a way to lace together the partial visions, a way that limits us all. Constitutional law, however, is not the only law that matters. The people can change the law at all levels, and, as I will argue, it is though the contentious politics of social movements that this lawmaking occurs. My argument will proceed in the following way. First, I will propose a version of what professors Reva Siegel and Robert Post call *constitutional culture*. Constitutional culture has a thick version, a thin version, and perhaps a liberal version and an illiberal version. We have seen one expression of a thin version of the illiberal concept in the attempted implementation of an immigrant ban and perhaps a thick liberal version in the judicial repudiation of that ban. More importantly, we have seen a thick illiberal version in the administration's construction of the idea of a unitary executive with extensive plenary power and a liberal version of constitutional culture in resistance to that idea by ascribing constitutional meaning to presidential speech.

Second, I will describe what I mean by law. My version is in opposition to many of the brute positivist ideas of law and takes seriously the notion that law is the expression of bounded social consensus that is both fixed and fluid. Thus, contingency of social institutions as well as the felt fixity of institutional systems make law both real and indeterminate. It is a version of law that does not need a sovereign, and thus, despite the coercive power of existing institutions, we should not mistake their power for legitimacy. Nonetheless, as Professor Renato Rosaldo once said to me in conversation, the fact that witches do not exist is meaningless to the witch who is being burned at the stake.

Third, I want to describe social movements and suggest the ways in which such movements create law. Social movement theory is vast and conflicting. While I base my accounts on the literature, I also base them on experience with movements and my experience as an activist. Out of this experience, my frequent coauthor Lani Guinier and I have developed the concept of demosprudence, which we define as the study of lawmaking by the people. This kind of lawmaking entails both formal and informal methods reflecting the various interpretive methodologies that govern our legal system and that account for the fundamental indeterminacy that is at the heart of law.

Bruce Ackerman has written a magisterial account of constitutional amendment by concerted social movement activism validated through statute and elections. As we wrote of Ackerman's *We the People*:

> Our essay largely agrees with this aspect of Professor Ackerman's book: it is the people in combination with the legal elite who change the fundamental normative understandings of our Constitution. We argue that social movements are critical not only to the changes Professor Ackerman chronicles, but also to the cultural shifts that make durable legal change possible. We believe that the role played by social movement activism is as much a source of law as are statutes and judicial decisions. Our goal, therefore, is to create analytic space to enable a greater understanding of lawmaking as the work of mobilized citizens in conjunction with, not separate from, legal professionals.[6]

If this account of lawmaking is accurate, we are in an especially critical time. Resistance is thus not just opposition but also certification of an existing constitutional understanding that is under assault. Resistance is also the repudiation of an ethno-nationalist construction of the state and its various illiberal tendencies.

Constitutional Culture

According to Professor Siegel, "Constitutional culture mediates the relation of law and politics."[7] The nature of the mediation is crucial. In a recent lecture, Professor Siegel proposed two different visions of constitutional culture. The first views law as a mere reflection of the norms of the polity. The second entails a view of the law that reflects an understanding that is shared by professionals as well as nonprofessionals. In many ways, a historic dispute over the meaning of *Brown v. Board of Education* illustrated this distinction. One of the leading constitutional lawyers of the time declared the decision lawless. Yet the response of another, in my view one of the most profound constitutional scholars, reflects the second view of constitutional culture. In defending the decision in *Brown* against the charge of lawlessness, Professor Charles Black said simply: "If the cases outlawing segregation were wrongly decided, then they ought to be overruled. One can go further: if dominant professional opinion ever forms and settles on the belief that they were wrongly decided, then they will be overruled, slowly or all at once, openly or silently. The insignificant error, however palpable, can stand, because the convenience of settlement outweighs the discomfort of error. But the hugely consequential error cannot stand and does not stand."[8]

It is in the confluence of a popular view of the meaning of the Constitution (popular, though highly contentious) and the dominant professional view that social dispute is capable of being integrated into the meaning of the Constitution. We see this phenomenon happening right now. It has refined, vulgar, violent, and peaceful elements.

Of course, the anti-immigrant, anti-birthright citizenship movement is not new. The original Constitution engrafted that nativist tradition onto its structure even if it largely avoided direct statement. That is what gives it the weight of historical and professional pedigree. Yet it has been the minority professional opinion even as it has garnered wide popular support at least since the end of the Second World War and certainly by the middle of the Great Society. The crucial question of constitutional culture in this moment is which view of constitutional culture will prevail. The decisions enjoining enforcement of the immigrant bans promulgated through executive order have channeled the nativist anti-immigrant bias of the current administration through a broader understanding of acceptable constitutional argument. That is why the president's speech (through tweets and otherwise) are held to have a legal rather than merely a political dimension. It is not just that words matter but also that those specific kinds of words matter in particular ways. Just as *Brown v. Board of Education* was not about "freedom of association," the ban on immigrants from specific countries is not about "keeping America safe." It implicates norms of religious liberty that nativists themselves are constrained to recognize or to mount a campaign against. We are seeing elements of both activities in the rhetoric surrounding the effort to exclude a subset of immigrants and refugees. The rhetoric of fear is the cauldron used to dissolve the idea that the state must be neutral when it comes to religious belief.

The campaign against Mexicans has a different constitutional valence. That campaign uses tropes marked by naked nativist and white supremacist rhetoric but also uses the language of trade, crime, family values, and economic nationalism. The constitutionality of this ideological stew really does implicate notions of constitutional culture. Which arguments have valid legal and not just political weight? Which political arguments are most likely to be convertible to legal arguments? The arguments over the plenary authority of the president loom large because the Constitution is mute and because the exercise of what has come to be recognized as constitutional presidential power is at stake. Remember, in passing NAFTA the Congress gave away its trade regulatory powers granted to it in Article I of the Constitution. Yet, in a similar but exactly reverse move in 1871, the Congress prohibited the president from exercising one of his express constitutional powers. Both of those changes now are part of what we understand the Constitution to permit. Considered professional and lay opinion agree. What are the terms of engagement that will show one side or the other in the immigration struggle to be speaking through the Constitution rather than against it? How will the people instruct the formal political actors what they may do rather than what they can do? As Professor Siegel puts it: "Constitutional culture preserves and perpetually destabilizes the distinction between politics and law by providing citizens and officials the resources to question and to defend the legitimacy of government, institutions of civil society, and the Constitution itself. Constitutional culture both licenses and limits change."[9]

It is within these conflicting versions of constitutional culture that social antagonists engage. It is an old field of battle, but it is consistently fresh. If not, then the statues honoring the Confederate dead that line the capitol grounds in Texas would not carry the legend they bear: "Erected in honor of those brave soldiers who gave their lives in defense of the Constitution."

What Is Law?

Among legal professionals, the most common idea of law in circulation is one now largely discredited, although it has such staying power that it is often trotted out to deny the legitimacy of international law even by those who should know better. The idea is that law is a command of the sovereign backed by a sanction. The sovereign is the one whose will must be followed. The sovereign is the lawgiver. Of course, not all laws are commands, and it is often unclear from where a law emerged. E. P. Thompson dedicates an entire book to detailing the ways in which the law (understood as a formal rule) emerged from customs and practices of communities such that any effort to command a different result would precipitate revolt or some other crisis of legitimacy.[10]

A better understanding of law is to see it as "a construction of social rules, which are themselves constructed from practice."[11] From this angle, law is a congeries of social rules that are sorted out by practice and by the interactions of formal institutional actors (judges, legislators, administrative agencies, court clerks, etc.) and the people. Of course, the hazard, as discussed in the consideration of constitutional culture, is that there need to be some criteria of validity to claim that this or that rule is a law.

Law is the collection of rules that derived from practice. However, they are special kinds of rules. They are the rules that create obligations rather than merely oblige conformity. If someone has a right, then someone else necessarily has a duty, for example. Social practice creates this network of claims. There is an additional requirement to satisfy the criteria of valid-ity: there must be a rule that says, in effect, that these other rules are law. Nevertheless, of course, that rule itself is a function of practice. Take, for example, the idea that prior decided cases (even in the case of statutory or constitutional construction) govern present cases. This is a practice that has become a rule of decision and is thus one marker of validity, and every first-year law student learns that you never know what a case means until a sub-sequent court uses it to decide a case. (The decisions always have meaning for the litigants, but that is a function of the rule that created jurisdiction and finality.) Importantly, it is precisely this process that permits meaning to change over time. The fluidity of meaning rather than any static meaning is what gives law its legitimacy. Thus the idiocy of so-called originalism or vulgar textualism. The better way to understand those interpretive gambits is to see them as methods for keeping the people out of the way of "experts" in the process of saying what the law is.

Social Movements and Making Law

Social movements are engaged in saying "what the law is." Social move-ments are different from interest groups because, whereas interest groups work within established institutional structures, social movements challenge those structures. As Sid Tarrow teaches us, the centrality of "contentious politics" practiced by actors whose "core 'indigenous population' . . . tends to be 'the nonpowerful, the nonwealthy and the nonfamous'" is what char-acterizes social movements. Social movements are also typically animated by a moral vision of a better society and frequently reflect that vision in their own practices. There is no inherent ideological valence to social movements. They can be, to use the conventional typology, movements of the Right or the Left.

When social movements challenge the existing set of social practices and the rules that those practices reflect, they are, almost by definition, engaged in a form of lawmaking. They urge a normative vision that claims its legiti-macy by reference to the actions of its members whose advocacy establishes a normative guide to conduct. Through their resistance, these social actors are always in conversation with elites. The mobilization of popular resis-tance requires the elites to justify the rules they are applying. Viewed from the perspective of judges, what effective social movement advocacy does is make certain interpretations of existing law either more or less persuasive. One way to test this hypothesis is to see how the meaning of the legal canon has changed over time in response to social movement activism.

To take a recent example, Black Lives Matter and Say Her Name have put the conduct of police in the spotlight, such that what would have passed muster for a "reasonable" stop or "reasonable force" are now fit subjects of political debate. By generating a reaction to the idea that black lives and, perhaps more importantly, black deaths at the hands of officials or quasi-officials matter, the Black Lives Matter movement has made the devaluing of black lives visible. Black Lives Matter and Say Her name insist on membership in the community of mutual respect and are reminders that race and gender are too often markers of the reverse. This movement arose from the bottom. Its initial advocates were the "nonpowerful, the nonwealthy and the nonfamous," but the challenge became a source of power to reimagine how the state interacts with the powerless and to call out as illegitimate what passed for business as usual. Black Lives Matter, like the civil rights movement before it, stands for the proposition that if rights matter, then they have to matter for all. Less than that is mere authoritarianism, not the legitimate exercise of state power. Black Lives Matter is also a part of the environmental justice movement, and it gives us, with Occupy, a way to understand the criminal environmental debacle in Flint, Michigan.

Occupy, which most people like to write off as a failure, in fact put the issue of economic inequality on the national agenda. Without the call of the 99 percent, would even the timid efforts at financial reform have been possible? Would the distributional impact of trade deals be subject to scrutiny? Without the questions Occupy put on the table it is likely that the role of the state in curbing private power would not even be seen as legitimate. The wholesale rush to embrace neoliberalism was stopped not by those who discuss the theoretical foundations of global integration but by those who experienced its material expression in their daily lives.

Standing Rock has not only revealed law enforcement as a source of lawlessness but has also given environmental justice a profound and historical rhetorical footing. The morality of nonviolence in the face of state-backed private violence triggered veterans to stand by their pledge to defend the Constitution against enemies foreign and domestic. By standing shoulder to shoulder with the tribes who were trying to protect the health and religious integrity of their land, those veterans reaffirmed basic normative commitments that define us as a people. It was a constitutional moment in the most profound sense.

The resistance on behalf of the undocumented is as much about the power to include as it is about the power to exclude. Resistance to the executive order banning immigration from certain countries has raised the issue of religious liberty in a way that reveals the racialist and nativist content of previous iterations of the claims, and it exposes the gravity of this particular time in our constitutional history. Nativism and racialism are recurring themes in our national history. The recent events that have exposed the ugly side of our history also give, in resistance, the chance to redeem the brighter promises that the meaning of America contains. Law and lawmaking are about the creation of meaning. They are not limited to the experts, but they are a crucial part. The humanities permit us to understand what we see in the streets, and law is part of that too. Law and the practices that instantiate it are contained in the stories we tell about others and ourselves. It is the power of those stories that animates resistance. We should listen well to all of them. We should reject those that paint us smaller than we are. As Lisa Guenther and Abigail Levin put it when analyzing the white nationalist march in Charlottesville:

> Today's white nationalists seem less interested in the nation-state than in the nation as against the state (or at least, against "government"). If we understand a nation as an ethno-cultural concept defined by a sense of shared identity, history and ancestry, and the state as a political concept defined by a set of institutions, documents and structures, then it's pretty clear that most white nationalists want precisely that: a white nation (although Cantwell and others want an "ethno-state"). But the fact that white men already occupy most positions of power in the United States is tangential to their primary interest in the nation. Trump seems to share this affection for America the Nation, and accordingly finds America the State's institutions irrelevant and bothersome.[12]

This is why the origin stories about our shared national life matter. This is why coming to terms with the rejection first of slavery but then of any ethno-state definition of who we are matters.

Whether social movement resistance can transform social practices sufficiently to create real and durable legal change is an open question. What is not open to question is that even when resistance feels futile, it is not. The riddle of constitutional change is capable of being solved by the people themselves, and the validating rule is found in the collection of formal decisions, large and small, that ratify the vision of resistance even as the formal institutions seek to domesticate social movements. Resisting domestication is what real democracy is about.

Notes

1. See, for example, *Stambovsky v. Ackley*, 169 A.D.2d 254 (N.Y. App. Div. 1991).

2. Thurman Wesley Arnold, *The Symbols of the Government* (New Haven: Yale University Press, 1935).

3. See, for example, the invention of credit-default swaps or the various financing devices used to promote the internal slave trade as documented in Edward Baptist, *The Half That Has Never Been Told* (New York: Basic Books, 2016).

4. "The effective practice of the programmatic imagination requires us to retain the idea of structural change while affirming the basic contingency of institutional histories, the divisibility and part-by-part replaceability of institutional systems, and the legal indeterminacy—the multiple possible forms—of abstract institutional conceptions like the market economy and representative democracy. . . . These enabling ideas come under the heading *false necessity*." Roberto Mangabeira Unger, *Democracy Realized: The Progressive Alternative* (New York: Verso, 1998), 23–24.

5. Reva Siegel, "Constitutional Culture, Social Movement Conflict and Constitutional Change: The Case of the de facto ERA," *California Law Review* 94, no. 5 (2006): 1323, 1326.

6. Lani Guinier and Gerald Torres, "Changing the Wind: Toward a Demosprudence of Law and Social Movements," *Yale Law Journal* 123, no. 8 (2014): 2740, 2743.

7. Siegel, "Constitutional Culture, Social Movement Conflict and Constitutional Change," 1323, 1327.

8. Charles L. Black, "The Lawfulness of the Segregation Decisions," *Yale Law Journal* 69 (1960): 421.

9. Siegel, "Constitutional Culture, Social Movement Conflict and Constitutional Change," 1323, 1327.

10. See, for example, E. P. Thompson, *Customs in Common: Studies in Traditional Popular Culture* (New York: New Press, 1993). See also Douglas Hay et al., *Albion's Fatal Tree: Crime and Society in Eighteenth Century England* (New York: Pantheon Books, 1976).

11. H. L. A. Hart, *The Concept of Law*, 3rd ed. (Oxford: Oxford University Press, 2012), xxvii.

12. Abigail Levin and Lisa Guenther, "White 'Power' and the Fear of Replacement," *New York Times*, August 28, 2017.

CHAPTER 10

What's It All Meme?

ELLA DIAZ

Ella Diaz is from Northern California and is now living in Ithaca, New York, working as an associate professor of English and Latina/o Studies at Cornell University. As a child, Ella had a passion for reading, writing, and making art, particularly line drawing that matured into mixed-media collages of ink and watercolor on paper. While she studied American literature as an undergraduate student at the University of California at Santa Cruz and pursued an M.A. and PhD in American studies (literature, art, and history) at the College of William and Mary in Virginia, Ella continued to create visual art. Working on community projects and art exhibitions deeply impacted the trajectory of Ella's scholarly work as she completed her dissertation on the Royal Chicano Air Force (RCAF), a historical Chicano/a art collective that emerged during the 1960s and 1970s. Based in Sacramento, California, the RCAF implemented numerous community-based programs that fostered a rich and vibrant art and cultural scene in California's capital city. In many ways, Ella was not only studying and theorizing the RCAF but also practicing and experiencing the tools of consciousness-raising that the RCAF and other vanguard artists of color of the era espoused as they reenvisioned themselves and their communities.

Her chapter here is playful in tone but looks seriously at what so many people disregard as a doodad of twenty-first-century digital technology and mainstream culture: the meme, which is typically a recognizable image from a popular film, TV show, or cartoon, with brief text written on it. Every other *year, Ella teaches a course on US Latinx popular culture, exploring both the current and historical representations of people of color in US mainstream culture. This chapter, then, participates in cultural studies as a Western field of knowledge but extends traditions of Chicano/a art that refuse mainstream representations of people of color perpetuated by the culture industry. Teaching students how to see themselves and one another, and creating civic spaces in which representation is more real and more human, Ella's chapter offers a hopeful and generous kind of scholarship and one necessary if we are to retain a sense of our own humanity in the digital age. Recognition of one another's basic humanity is the foundation for any kind of civic thriving. Ella invites readers to think about both the visual representations that they encounter in their everyday lives and the historical layers of meaning in our evolving mainstream culture of imagery that we often encounter as meaningless or without consequence. Both perspectives are critical to how we think of ourselves and other people as human beings.*

On the first day of my Latinx popular culture class, I ask my new students to sit quietly and look at a PowerPoint slide of images that I project onto a screen. The images are memes that I have cut and pasted from social media websites. While standalone photographs and advertisements have the potential to convey multiple messages to viewers about race, class, gender, and sexuality, I focus on memes. These are images that anyone with a smartphone or a laptop and Wi-Fi connection can make by manipulating and captioning film stills, celebrity selfies, or news photos and then sharing them on social media. A meme can become more recognizable than the actual event, public figure, or issue on which it comments or pokes fun at when other social media users repost it and it *trends*. A phenomenon of popular culture in the digital age of social media, a *trending meme* is understood by the majority of its viewers, whether or not they agree with its intended meaning.[1]

Each year I update my slide of memes without any concern that I will run out of material. As an American studies scholar, I know that not much has changed in the representation of nonwhite peoples in mainstream US culture since the conquest and colonization of Indigenous and African peoples in the fifteenth and sixteenth centuries.[2] 2016 proved to be an abundant year for memes on racial representation. I copied and pasted one that was tweeted by talk show host Ellen DeGeneres in which she appears to be riding on the back of Olympic champion sprinter Usain Bolt. I also included one of Harambe, the gorilla who was shot to death at the Cincinnati Zoo in May 2016, after a Black child fell into his habitat and the primate grabbed him (see fig. 2). The Harambe meme was captioned by the line, "If I throw my baby on stage at a concert will they shoot Kanye?"

On the first day of class in the fall of 2016, I welcomed my students to Latinx popular culture with these memes and caused them much discomfort. I have learned that Millennial and, now, Generation Z students are unaccustomed to viewing racist images together in a "public" setting, like a classroom. Typically memes are made when one is alone, and they are reposted alone. Memes are indirect, passive, and considered authorless, and interactions with people regarding memes take place on social media. Unlike a tweet, which is a statement written in less than 280 characters, a meme uses an image and a few words to inject silly, ironic, political, and sometimes racist and sexist commentary into a seemingly public sphere. Often, memes stand in for coded statements and judgements about race, class, gender, and/ or sexuality, and their implicit meanings circulate through their reposting by other social media users.[3]

For my purposes, the memes of Ellen DeGeneres and Usain Bolt and that of Harambe framed the first reading assignment from Stuart Hall's *Representation: Cultural Representations and Signifying Practices* (1997). Hall's textbook is concerned with teaching people how to think about mainstream visual culture—which is a dominant one and a dominating force in our society, despite the cultural nuances we may read onto what we see in an image, given our different racial, gendered, and classed perspectives (Hall, 25). A mainstream culture as a shared visual culture is a space in which we encounter or access the same images, catchphrases, hashtags, and their combinations on various screens that we engage with or pass by throughout the day. Nowadays, the virtual world deeply influences how and what we perceive as the physical one, where we may or may not interact with people we assume are different from us.

Where do assumptions of our differences come from? My use of the pronouns "we" and "our" here is intentional, focusing our attention on the viewership that a meme assumes—which is a dominant cultural one, both a perspective and a gaze, or way of looking at and understanding a picture with words. But "we" and "our" are problematic because many of us may not feel the same about what a meme represents or part of the audience for which a meme is intended. Beyond their use in unpacking theoretical frameworks and teaching cultural analysis as a critical-thinking skill, memes are a useful strategy for community-building in the digital age. They can be mulled over in a classroom or discussed around a kitchen or conference table. In other words, *we* can go against the dominant cultural norm of posting memes alone on social media and, instead, come together to talk about how we are represented versus how we see ourselves and how we see and represent other people.

Ellen DeGeneres ✔
@TheEllenShow

This is how I'm running errands from now on. #Rio2016

♡ 99.8K 2:47 PM - Aug 15, 2016   ⓘ

💬 42.5K people are talking about this   >

FIGURE 10.1 A tweet posted by Ellen DeGeneres following Jamaican sprinter Usain Bolt's 2016 Olympic victories.

A Teachable Meme

I acknowledge different levels of access to technology across the United States, but I am also comfortable stating that all Americans are aware of, if not literate in, mainstream culture and a system of representation that conveys dominant messages. While all Americans may be aware of the main message of a cultural representation, they may not be aware of the impact the message has on different viewers. Conflict arises when a group of viewers objects to the intended meaning of an image, picture, comment, text, caption, et cetera. Often the public debate that ensues is one of intention versus impact. In May 2018, for example, celebrity comedian Roseanne Barr tweeted, "muslim brotherhood & planet of the apes had a baby=vj," referring to Valerie Jarrett, a former top aide to President Barack Obama. The vast majority of Twitter users read Barr's tweet as a comparison of Jarrett, a Black woman, to an ape. Barr, however, claimed she did not intend her tweet in this way and also that she was abusing Ambien when she typed and posted it. Public opinion disagreed, and the court of social media decided that what Barr intended did not negate the impact of her tweet.

Similarly, a year after the cultural phenomenon of the #MeToo movement, a photograph trended of pop singer Ariana Grande and pastor Charles H. Ellis, who officiated the public memorial of Aretha Franklin.[4] In the photograph, Ellis's arm drapes around Grande and his hand grabs the side of her breast. Grande appears uncomfortable. Social media users reposted the photograph, adding commentary on "toxic masculinity," patriarchy, and incessant sexual assaults against women. Pastor Ellis released a statement shortly after the photograph went viral: "It would never be my intention to touch any woman's breast. . . . Maybe I crossed the border, maybe I was too friendly or familiar, but again, I apologize" (Wootson 2018). Pastor Ellis's apology was seemingly accepted since discussion of the photograph on social media largely fell silent.

Barr's tweet and the photo of Ellis and Grande reveal that we see and read things differently when they are presented in a mainstream visual culture to which all of us have access as well as a vested stake. The intention and impact of a picture, statement, or text, however, are typically framed in mainstream culture by reductive binaries of right and wrong, guilty and innocent, or good and evil. Any opportunity to think beyond the surface of political correctness is lost, and systems of power remain in place as structural problems such as racism and sexism are attributed to individual people. For example, Roseanne Barr is seen as a racist (which she may very well be, but what about the fact that we all knew the anthropomorphic reference to *Planet of the Apes*?). Meanwhile, Pastor Ellis is probably not a sexual predator, but why did so many people, especially women, see the photograph as indicative of sexual harassment or patriarchal abuse of power? One wonders how we can build or engage community in our classrooms, workplaces, neighborhoods, and other hubs of societal interaction if we do not first start unpacking the meaning of what we all see in our shared visual culture and the assumptions we bring to the table about each other.

Stuart Hall is particularly helpful in understanding the process of meaning making in a shared visual culture for Western societies. He asks, how do we represent difference through the human being, and how is humanity represented over time?[5] In picturing the Black male athlete, as with the Usain Bolt meme, Hall considers advertisements and photos of Black male runners in the 1980s and compares them to Black men in the Western Hemisphere in the colonial era and after slavery ended in the United States in 1865. He then tracks the representation of Black people in early twentieth-century vaudeville performances, 1970s blaxploitation films, and the representational ruptures made by Black artists and activists in the 1960s and 1970s US civil rights movement. Introducing the term *regime of representation*, Hall asks, "How do you 'read' the picture—what is it saying? In Barthes' terms, what is its 'myth'—its underlying message?" (Hall, 226). For my students, many of whom were new to cultural studies, I explained the complex rumination of Roland Barthes on the myth of objects by reframing Hall's question. I asked them to look at the meme of Ellen DeGeneres riding on Usain Bolt's back as I read aloud the tweet that captions it: "This is how I am running my errands from now on #Rio2016." I next asked the students, "But isn't this how Black men have *always* run errands?" Positioning Bolt as "the speaker" or the subject of the picture unsettles its intended meaning.[6] The meme's caption connotes that Ellen speaks directly to the viewer, but I asked the students, "What if the caption is Usain Bolt speaking to you, the viewer?" Redirecting the meme's caption destabilizes the dominant cultural assumption of what is wrong (or racist) with the picture. Millennial and Generation Z college students are adept at calling out racism in mainstream culture, but they may not fully understand what is racist about a given representation— where it comes from, how it happened, and why it persists.

One of the reasons this meme is racist derives from the fact that the subject (who is human) and the object (who is not) rarely ever changes in the regime of representation in US mainstream culture. The racial problem with the meme was obvious to my students: Usain Bolt is objectified because he serves as a means of transportation for Ellen Degeneres, a white woman.[7]

Regardless of the particularities of my students' perspectives based on their racial, ethnic, class, and gendered identities, they agreed that the meme was racist—of course, to differing degrees; but they could not explain how it came to be so.

To move the students closer to understanding the origins of the meme's racism, I proposed that another message about racial difference is transmitted through the meme and is connected to a repetition of images like it. "If the meme is racist," I wondered aloud, "whose problem is it?" At first glance, the problem of racism in the meme is Bolt's problem. "But what if Ellen is the problem?" I asked, adding that Degeneres is recognizable as a human being in the picture not only because she is famous but also because of the contrast that Bolt's objectification provides her. This is the meme's myth—that whiteness *has always been* human. My questions were unsettling for the students because they raised the idea that the definition—the truth—of being human is a construction and that it is largely produced through representational difference.

In order to continue unraveling the idea that the human being is not natural or biological but constructed, and largely through representational difference, I next asked questions that led to concepts such as "visual indices" and "image banks," which each of us possess and that we reference as we look at visual culture across our lifetimes: "Have you seen this image before? Does the meme remind you of anything from history or assumptions of who works and who is at leisure?" I had the students turn to a page on which Hall presents a drawing of a "creole lady" in the West Indies, riding a horse as a Black male slave runs next to her with an open parasol. The students were now confused over the intention and impact of the meme after confronting an illustration that they immediately perceived as racist. Surely Ellen did not intend the meme in this way—"as a visual echo of slavery," one insightful student remarked, adding that, after the television host was publicly criticized on social media for the meme, she tweeted, "I am highly aware of the racism that exists in our country. It is the furthest thing from who I am" (Lockett 2016).[8] Perhaps racism is the furthest thing from who Ellen is, but it is the nearest thing to our mainstream culture's regime of representation that gleans what is funny from a spectrum of dehumanization, established in colonial structures of power that degraded Black and Brown human beings for the economic prosperity of white people. Ellen didn't mean it. *But the meme still means.*[9]

This exercise of thinking critically about the meme of Ellen DeGeneres and Usain Bolt was simultaneously compelling and depressing for my students on the first day of class. I imagine it is the same for anyone now reading my long-winded analysis of digital doodles as abridgements of complex cultural histories produced through processes of empire, colonialism, and economic expansion. We watch and click, after all, to escape and zone out—not to think. But this raises another important point: outside of a college class on cultural and visual analysis, how often are the representations on the myriad screens we encounter thought about in this way—examined, pondered, and discussed for the sake of making and understanding meaning that matters more than we are willing to admit?

The Family Feud Is Not a Game

Certainly memes can be funny without being racist or sexist, and the point of thinking critically about them is not to moralize or judge the decency of a joke. Meaning floats, Hall argues, and it is the floating that distresses people—the lack of a definitive conclusion, a right or wrong answer, a black and white issue. In our distress, we should ask ourselves what the impulse is, or the need for meaning to arrive at an outcome or an exact point. But, if points are needed, then one of the points that memes make (their function) is the fleeting role they play as cultural barometers, bringing together current events and cultural references typically to make a joke. Another point of memes, albeit unintentional, is that they expose the continuum of dehumanization on which human difference continues to be represented. Memes can also be a point of departure for friends, families, colleagues, and coworkers, leading to breakups and disruptions in kinship networks.[10]

In February 2016, celebrity rapper Kanye West made several statements on social media in which he ranted about Grammy winners and announced the release of a new album. Kanye became the center of social media debates over whether he was right about the racism of mainstream award shows or whether his antics were a publicity stunt. In May 2016, social media turned attention to the shooting death of Harambe, a gorilla at the Cincinnati Zoo, after a three-year-old Black child climbed into the gorilla's habitat and Harambe grabbed him. Zoo officials and several primatologists stated that the staff had no choice but to shoot the gorilla because a human child was in danger. Nevertheless, public outcry over Harambe's death escalated to condemnations of the child's parents over their poor parenting skills.

In early June, I opened my Facebook page to see a meme posted by one of my cousins. It was a picture of a gorilla captioned with a quip about shooting Kanye (fig. 10.2). I glanced at the meme and immediately reacted, commenting on my cousin's post that the meme was "flat out RACIST." I also mentioned our shared experience of racial-ethnic representations in mainstream

FIGURE 10.2 A meme that circulated during the summer of 2016 on social media following the shooting of Harambe, a gorilla at the Cincinnati Zoo.

culture as Mexican Americans. Amid the escalating "illegal immigration debate" in the presidential election campaign and the ongoing police killings of Black people (Alton Sterling and Philando Castile would be killed by police later in the summer of 2016), I told my cousin to be more thoughtful about her online posts. "But that's not how I see it," she wrote back, adding, "It reminds me of when my mother calls me a 'gorilla mom.'" She concealed the humor she experienced through the Harambe meme, which is a joke predicated on the shooting of a Black man (Kanye West), within a personalized version of its meaning and, thus, one that I could not access. This is a common strategy for negating the effects of dehumanizing digital doodads like memes: to disassociate one's intention from the impact a meme makes when posted in the virtual public sphere. "But that's not what I meant" is the refrain of the twenty-first century. As if systemic oppression and structural power is on a first come, first served, individual basis.

My solution to our disagreement was to "unfriend" my cousin on Facebook. The consequences of such virtual choices in the real world are the subject of another essay, but I continued to press the issue with a different family member who asked why I was so mad about the Harambe meme; after all, it was *just* Facebook. I replied that comparing the shooting of a gorilla to the shooting of Kanye West is racist and participates in a regime of representation of Black people figured as monkeys and gorillas. My family member responded, "No, that's not what it means." I elaborated my case, citing eugenics, a popular pseudoscience in the late nineteenth century and prominent in the popular culture of early twentieth-century vaudeville, as well as the backdrop of Nazi Germany's visual campaign to dehumanize and then exterminate Jewish people in support of their racist and economic agenda.

My family member's response to the historical contexts for the racism of the Harambe meme was that it was privileged knowledge—"ivy tower stuff." Let us pause for a moment and think about this response. The notion that the "coon caricature" of nineteenth-century American advertisements and twentieth-century cartoons, the "mammy" stereotype of early American film (and the symbol of a famous pancake mix and syrup brand), the radio-turned-television show *Amos 'n' Andy* that was popular for over forty years, and anthropomorphic representations of Jews as rats, are the exclusive domain of the ivy tower—that privileged space for conversations in difficult language.[11] How has it come to pass that the most lowbrow and mass-produced popular culture has somehow been reconceived as the domain of the intellectual elite? I continue to hold my position, however, that what my family members found funny about the Harambe meme hinges on a disavowal of the regime of representation in which "the black" was first constructed to dehumanize and then rationalize chattel slavery.[12] Despite their lack of awareness of the visual echoes of slavery in the Harambe meme, the lesson my family members taught me is twofold. First, there is a difference between ignorance and willful ignorance, and, second, they both produce the same outcome: a defense of dehumanization as only or merely a device of humor. Perhaps I should lighten up.

Visual Shorthand: Memes Are Tropes

"The black" is an archetype of US mainstream culture: a visual, literary, and aural trope. By this I refer to figures of speech, sounds, and images that signal an all-too-familiar idea of Blackness that frightens viewers as it entertains them. "Tropes are not abstract, nor neutral," writes Vorris L. Nunley (2013). Rather, they serve aesthetic ends, driving the content and form of a given "image, entity, symbol, speech act, or gesture." There are other tropes that function like "the black" in twenty-first-century mainstream culture in the United States that reflect de facto and de jure definitions of who is human. The "undocumented," the "illegal," and the "transgendered" are euphemisms for *the other*, each coded with implicit meanings that differentiate human beings from what is defined as human, which is also a construct but in mainstream culture is defined by what it is not. While tropes are culturally understood, and used in television, film, art, and other visual mediums, they are also legislated. The United States has a history of laws for determining categories of humanity—witness the "three-fifths" rule for Africans and African Americans in the eighteenth century that determined the fraction of their political representation, the nineteenth-century Chinese Exclusion Act that made kinship ties impossible for many Chinese Americans to maintain throughout their immigration journeys, and the ninety-year period of Jim Crow laws across the US South, under which all public space was racially segregated.[13] In 2018, the United States separated children from parents after they crossed the US-Mexican border, and the headlines and pundits referred to these people not as "refugees" or "asylum seekers," but as "illegal aliens" and "criminals." Tropes, as figures of speech, can articulate, perform, and visualize such categories, dehumanizing people through interrelated modes of representation. Memes are twenty-first-century tropes.

Being seen as a trope when you are a human being has grave consequences, one of which was made powerfully clear in the 2012 shooting death of Trayvon Martin and the 2013 trial of George Zimmerman. Upon hearing the jury's "not guilty" verdict for second-degree murder and acquittal of the lesser charge of manslaughter, Trayvon's mother, Sybrina Fulton commented, "They didn't *see* Trayvon as their son [or] Trayvon as a teenager. They didn't *see* Trayvon as just a human being" (interview with Tracy Martin and Sybrina Fulton, my emphasis). Seen as a trope of Black masculinity in the moment of his death and at the trial of his killer, Martin's murder was the consequence of his "misbehaving Black body (that is, any Black body challenging White notions of proper Black civility and decorum in fact or in fearful projection)" (Nunley 2013).[14] The consequence of the Black male trope is the destruction of a human being, and ironically it is also the very "kind of Blackness Whites are often attracted to in movies (re: *Training Day*), music (Hip-hop), sports and news programming (take your pick)" (Nunley 2013). The paradox of a viewing audience that demands to be entertained by a threatening trope of Black masculinity while simultaneously demanding its destruction in real time and space reveals a desire for contingent categories of humanness and the differentials they produce.[15] In the year following Trayvon's death, a meme circulated in which young people, mostly white, performed his deceased body, discernable through the hoodie Trayvon wore and the Skittles and Arizona Iced Tea he carried with him. Captioned "Trayvoning," the meme transformed a human being into a verb. Outraged by the meme, many social media users condemned it, but to do so *they reposted it.*

"Trayvoning" happens on a visual field of dehumanization, where cultural representation mixes with de facto and de jure definitions of who is and who is not a human being. The political status quo, colonial histories of slavery, and US mainstream culture are entangled in this meme. It is only funny if it is not a human being depicted but a trope—a stereotype of the Black male that viewers, mostly white (but really all of us who look at it first through the dominant gaze of mainstream culture) see and are then outraged, disgusted, or not affected at all. Over the last thirty years, the role of the injured, deceased, and disassembled body has evolved in American dramatizations of death—from making television shows appear grittier and more realistic (*Law and Order*), to becoming the central driving force of their

FIGURE 10.3 One of many "Trayvoning" memes that appeared on social media following the death of Trayvon Martin in 2012.

dramatic plots (*Bones*, *NCIS*, *CSI*, and *Criminal Minds*.) American audiences are familiar with incessant images of death, both as mise-en-scène (background) and as central plot lines.

Certainly, in documentary films on the US-Mexico border, the US prison system, the horrors of modern wars, and now the global refugee crisis, dead bodies, pieces of bodies, and skeletal remains are used to strike viewers' visual field with the visceral impact of social injustice. But one wonders if the footage works in the way it is intended or if it is part of a visual spectrum of dehumanization that hinges on the conditioned sensory experiences of watching such violence. Is there a difference between witnessing crimes against humanity and watching it as entertainment? Do we access or experience such imagery differently than we do when watching the dead bodies of prime time? Again, I do not seek a moral outcome. Rather, I argue that memes like "Trayvoning" participate in what Alicia Schmidt Camacho calls the "discourse of the cadaver"—cultural production ranging from mainstream representations to fine art and scholarly analyses of human beings that ultimately figures people as objects for the sake of conveying an intellectual point or eliciting a reaction from an audience.

Proposing the "discourse of the cadaver" as a critical lens for evaluating representations of femicide in Ciudad Juárez, Mexico, which is the consequence of an exploitive labor system following the implementation of NAFTA in 1994, Schmidt Camacho directs our attention to the names and titles of artworks, exhibitions, songs, and various publications, by artists and scholars, that anticipate a category of dead women. "'Las muertas de Juárez/The dead women of Juárez,' 'The City of Dead Women,' [or] 'Para las muertas'" (Schmidt Camacho, 36) are each titles that "coincide in their depictions of the victims as the inevitable causalities of globalization, effectively dead prior to their killing" (32). These catchy titles presume the "disposability" of brown women by literally creating a space for the passive acceptance of human beings that Lisa Lowe says are "exploited and then thrown away." Lowe calls this "necrospace," a "dehumanized social space . . . of complex and pervasively gendered violence."[16] Adding to Lowe's notion of necrospace and how one would move within it, Michel de Certeau contemplates "walking as a space of enunciation" and the grammars of speech used in movements through urban spaces that are performed and identify a city dweller (Certeau, 98). I wonder what it means when one makes a verbal shortcut and refers to an art show about femicide in Mexico with the title "For the dead women." I wonder what the verbal shortcut means when one makes a "Trayvoning" meme with a few clicks and posts it, intending it to be funny, or reposts it in outrage, ironically to counter its existence.

The Better to See You With: Eyes, Not Screens

So, *what does it all meme*? How do we reclaim our eyes from the screens that bombard us with dominant and dominating images that *de-mean* our humanity? How do we relearn how to *see* and not just *glance*? In writing about contemporary art (and not the mainstream stuff I have been ranting about), Nicolas Bourriaud characterizes the art world's turn in the late twentieth

FIGURE 10.4 "I Am Trayvon Martin," poster by Jesus Barraza, Melanie Cervantes, and Maztl (Dignidad Rebelde 2013).

century to "relational aesthetics," which is a fancy way of describing the realm of human relations and their potential, as artists disengage from their individual desires to create singular works of art, and instead choose to foster community by building relationships with people by making art together. Bourriaud further argues that "relational aesthetics" is both symptomatic and transcendent of our age of the screen: from online banking and shopping to social media sites, the flow of capital happens visually as we privately touch screens with fingertips, making and doing nothing, really, except transacting (Bourriaud, 14, 66). Screens are communication spaces bound up in market economies that drive our desires, but ultimately they decide what we want because they control the options and thus the outcomes.[17] Relational aesthetics, then, is an opportunity to produce something beyond individual and transactional desires through artful social engagement.

Bourriaud perhaps doesn't have Facebook, Instagram, and other social media sites in mind with "relational aesthetics," but it resonates. We are definitely in the age of the screen, yet there are screens that still require participation in the physical world, both with our hands and our voices as we talk to each other about our ideas (what we see) and create different representations of ourselves. There is the silkscreen poster, for example, and, its digital counterpart, the downloadable poster, which is something like a meme in the sense that it is a picture with words and accessible online. Beyond that, however, the downloadable poster diverges from the meme, disrupting the spectrum of dehumanization in popular culture by representing moral values that *rebel* against the status quo through *dignified* images of people. Dignidad Rebelde (Rebel Dignity) is a graphic arts collaboration between artists Jesus Barraza and Melanie Cervantes, based in Oakland, and they believe that "art can be an empowering reflection of community struggles, dreams and visions." Alongside their silkscreen posters and fine art, Barraza and Cervantes produce downloadable posters that "amplify people's stories," they assert, putting representations of Black, Brown, and marginalized peoples "back into the hands of the communities who inspire it" (Dignidad Rebelde).

Dignidad Rebelde continues a tradition of protest art that emerged during the 1960s and 1970s civil rights movements in the United States, in which artists such as Rupert Garcia, Yolanda López, and Emory Douglas disrupted the mainstream regime of representation of people of color. These artists were inspired by the posters of Cuban artists (such as Félix Beltrán) emerging out of the Cuban Revolution, alongside the Third World liberation movements and the Taller de Gráfica Popular founded in Mexico after the tumultuous years of the Mexican Revolution. In each of these historical moments, artists built new relationships between words and images, reconfiguring state-issued propaganda, mass media advertisements, and work by pop artists in the mid- to late twentieth century as powerful tools of intervention on mainstream culture. A few weeks after sharing the meme of Ellen Degeneres and Usain Bolt and that of Harambe with students in my Latinx popular culture class, I countered them with posters from the 1960s and 1970s civil rights era in the United States, especially portraits of revolutionary leaders, journalists, political prisoners, and community activists, all of which are joined with textual abbreviations of larger political points of view that upend the domi- nant gaze of the mainstream culture industry. Writing about Rupert Garcia, for example, a vanguard Chicano artist of the 1960s and 1970s, art historian Lucy Lippard calls his posters "ideological portraits," and the description fits all artists of the twentieth century who created "images intended to bring justice and radical change to life, to bring the faces of history's Third World protagonists up on the screen of the dominant culture" (Lippard, 28).

Dignidad Rebelde's downloadable poster series began during the barrage of police killings of young Black and Brown people that came to national attention following the death of Oscar Grant in 2009, the young Black man shot to death by a Bay Area Rapid Transit (BART) officer at the Fruitvale Sta- tion in Oakland. "To commemorate Oscar's life, Melanie designed a poster on the one-year anniversary of his death," Jesus Barraza writes, adding that it had the following text: "I Am Oscar Grant and My Life Matters." This poster and others were shared via Facebook and Dignidad Rebelde's website, creating an "online deployment" of their ideological portraits with abridged declarations of human rights (Barraza and Cervantes, 216).

And then there was Trayvon, whose death at the hands of a self-appointed neighborhood watchman was followed by another murder—the assassina- tion of his character in mainstream media. Circulating images of Martin that he had posted of himself on social media, with gold fronts or flipping off the camera, the news media largely framed Martin as a delinquent teenager, a "black male thug." The succession of murdered Black people over the next decade followed suit, as each human being was represented through a reduc- tive binary of good and evil, right and wrong, and ultimately, as a *black and white* issue. These visual binaries were augmented by statements from the officers or vigilantes that they felt threatened when the "suspects" did not obey their commands. Meanwhile, body cameras and eyewitness cell phone footage continue to reveal otherwise, as in the May 2017 killing of Jordan Edwards and the March 2018 killing of Stephon Clark. To make sense of the senseless killings and maintain the political status quo rooted in colo- nial definitions of who is and who is not a human being, mainstream media depict Black victims of state violence and its paramilitary forces as either being noncompliant "thugs" (Michael Brown, Eric Garner, Sandra Bland,

and Alex Nieto), or as exceptional students and athletes (Jordan Davis and Jordan Edwards). They are never simply human beings who, ultimately, were killed wrongfully and partly due to a regime of racial representation beyond their control.[18]

In collaboration with artist Mazatl, Dignidad Rebelde created a downloadable poster of Trayvon in which we see a vivid Black teenager staring directly at us with a kind smile that suggests he sees us too. Through a color-saturated background and a closely cropped portrait, the artists present Trayvon in the midst of life and not in death, and the caption tells us in clear, simple language that *his life matters.* Dignidad Rebelde is committed to remembering people in life. They want to honor and raise awareness of the injustices and the killings that are happening but do not want to further exploit people in death or do more harm to those that have been harmed so deeply. As simple as a meme in its design, content, and accessibility, the downloadable poster redirects the relationship between text and image, the viewer and the viewed, and the act of looking and glancing. Reconfiguring the representational and the tools of the digital age, the posters of Dignidad Rebelde and their collaborators insert a momentary pause into the visual status quo and mainstream media machine that pushes us further away from a shared sense of our humanity.

Notes

1. Limor Shifman defines memes as "groups of digital items that (a) share common characteristics of content, form, and/or stance; (b) are created with an awareness of each other and (c) are circulated, imitated, and transformed via the internet by multiple uses." He also notes that the word "meme" dates to "Richard Dawkins in 1976 to describe small units of cultural transformation that are analogous to genes." Limor Shifman, "The Cultural Logic of Photo-Based Meme Genres," *Journal of Visual Culture.* 13, no. 3 (2014): 341.

2. I introduced students to Saarjite Baartman, for example, an indigenous South African woman also known as the Hottentot Venus and who was on display for European audiences in the nineteenth century. I reference other indigenous bodies on display, like that of Ishi, a Yahi man who lived in the Museum of Anthropology located on what is now the site of University of California, San Francisco. Covering Guillermo Gómez-Peña and Coco Fusco's performance *Couple in a Cage* (ca. 1989–1990), I turn to music videos by Nikki Minaj, Jennifer Lopez, and other pop stars. For more, see Magdalena Barrera, "Hottentot 2000: Jennifer López and Her Butt," in *Sexualities in History: A Reader*, ed. Kimberley Phillips and Barry Reay, 406–17 (Routledge, 2002).

3. Walter Benjamin also makes this point in his 1936 piece "Art in the Age of Mechanical Reproduction," *Illuminations*, ed. Hannah Arendt, 217–20 (London: Cape, 1970), concerning the lack of an aura in mass-produced art that simulates an original or are copies of single works of art. Jean Baudrillard furthers this idea with

the simulacrum or copies of things that have no origin or original and thus are bound up in our desires for the real, a desire driven by capitalist consumption.

4. A hashtag on social media that went viral in 2017, #MeToo focused national and then international attention on the sexual assault and harassment of women in the workplace.

5. Hall actually asks, "How do we represent people and places which are significantly different from us? Why is 'difference' so compelling a theme, so contested an area of representation? What is the secret fascination of 'otherness', and why is popular representation so frequently drawn to it? What are the typical forms and representational practices which are used to represent 'difference' in popular culture today, and where did these popular figures and stereotypes come from?" Stuart Hall, "The Spectacle of the Other," in *Representation: Cultural Representation and Signifying Practices*, 225–90 (London: SAGE Publications, 1997).

6. Although too elaborate for this essay, Barthes's framework of the "stadium" and the "punctum" of a photograph in *Camera Lucida* is important here and in the analysis of all memes.

7. Limor Shifman provides types of memes, defining "stock character memes" as "the overt construction of stereotypes" through the association of a "certain (negative) feature with a specific social category." While the Ellen DeGeneres meme is more reflective of the category he calls "reaction Photoshops," Shifman fails to acknowledge that all memes trade in stereotypes of who is and is not a human being, since stock character memes like "Sheltering Suburban Mom" are predominantly white women. Unlike his examination of the "successful Black Man" meme where race is both central and the center of the text, Shifman does not address how white signifies or is marked in the stereotype of who is a suburban mother. Shifman, "Cultural Logic of Photo-Based Meme Genres," 348.

8. I will add that the students also discussed the improbability that Ellen DeGeneres actually made the meme or even tweeted her response to the backlash online, but the ambiguity of its authorship only furthers the point that memes only exist when they are reproduced.

9. The contemporary context of the 2016 Olympic Games in Brazil and the meme in which Degeneres rides on Bolt's back included the political protests of poor Brazilians and student uprisings against the country's subsidization of infrastructural projects created solely for sport. The construction of athletic venues and transportation to these venues occurred amid dilapidated neighborhoods called favelas, underfunded schools, and inadequate public hospitals, all of which heightened the absurdity of DeGeneres's meme in a national context. From afternoon talk shows to the nightly news and morning programs, the "spirit" of the Olympic Games was celebrated as the errands of industry and economic progress were run the same old way. Marie Auxiliadora, a Brazilian resident of the Mandela favela, summed up the reality in Rio de Janeiro succinctly: "The rich play, and we die" (Michael Powell, "Officials Spent Big on Olympics, but Rio Natives Are Paying the Price," *New York Times*, August 14, 2016). The televised pictures of Brazil transmitted a national vision mixed up in the colonial logic of sixteenth-century empire. Proclaimed as a promise of more jobs and shared economic prosperity through the tourism that the buildings and transit systems would bring, the reality of the Olympic Games was the continued economic exploitation of resources and dehumanization of Black

and Brown peoples—or who runs the race for the patriotic pride of the nation, and whose home is destroyed to make way for the venue in which the race is run. The meme of DeGeneres riding on Bolt's back is only funny if the past and present are forgotten simultaneously.

10. While a personal rift with my family does not demonstrate a larger cultural impact of a meme, individual outcomes provoked by memes are evidenced in popular culture. See note 11 which references public servants who posted and commented on social media regarding First Lady Michelle Obama.

11. During my fall 2016 Latinx Popular Culture class, the mainstream media picked up a story about a teacher's aide in Georgia calling Michelle Obama a gorilla in a Facebook comment that she posted with a picture of the First Lady. Around the same time, a West Virginia mayor commented that her day was made better by another public administrator who referred to Michelle Obama as an "ape in heels" on Facebook. Rachel Paul Abrahamson, "Teacher's Aide Fired after Calling Michelle Obama a 'Gorilla' in Racist Facebook Rant, *Us Weekly*, October 4, 2016; Nick Allen, "West Virginia Official Who Called Michelle Obama an "Ape in Heels' Fired Following Outcry," *Telegraph* (UK), November 15, 2016.

12. Judith Butler, in *Undoing Gender* (New York: Routledge, 2004), examines state failure to recognize transgender people as human and references Frantz Fanon's claim that "the black is not a man" and his "critique of humanism that showed that the human in its contemporary articulation is so fully racialized that no black man could qualify as human" (13).

13. The three-fifths compromise, decided at the Philadelphia Constitutional Convention in 1787, counted an enslaved African or African American as three-fifths of a free person in determining representation in the United States House of Representatives. The Chinese Exclusion Act (1882) undermined the human rights of Chinese immigrants and people of Chinese descent by requiring people who were "nonlaborers" to obtain certification from the Chinese government that they were qualified to immigrate; it also made it impossible for many families to be together in the United States, breaking down the construct of heterosexual kinship along racial lines. I don't intend this to be an exhaustive list of historical rulings and US policies concerning who is enfranchised and has the legal right to be here; rather, I seek to briefly expose how race, ethnicity, and gender as categories of the state can get in the way of one's humanity, causing an unlivable life for many.

14. Overwhelmed by the image of a singular Black male walking through a residential zone—an environment that connotes kinship ties and communal belonging, Zimmerman didn't see "an average teenager that was minding his own business, that wasn't committing any crime, that was coming home from the store," as Sybrina Fulton describes her son's movements on the evening of his death. "Interview with Tracy Martin and Sybrina Fulton," *Anderson Cooper 360 Degrees*, July 18, 2013, http://transcripts.cnn.com/TRANSCRIPTS/1307/18/acd.01.html. Likewise, Zimmerman's jury didn't see Trayvon as a human being but only judged his reaction to the presumption of his criminality—or the trope of the Black male that Trayvon Martin was most certainly aware of—or why he stayed on the phone with his friend, walked fast, and ultimately confronted his stalker.

15. The simultaneous desire *for* and destruction *of* the Black male trope coincides with tropes of "[t]ransgendered and transsexual people [who] are subjected

to pathologization and violence," Judith Butler writes, pointing to the "continuum of the gender violence that took the lives of Brandon Teena, Mathew Shephard, and Gwen Araujo" (Butler, *Undoing Gender*, 6). Along this continuum of gender violence, black, trans, and migrant people are pathologized and harmed. While there are distinctions between categories of race (the black), gender (the transgender), and citizenship (the undocumented), they are all based on de facto and de jure categories of difference.

16. The examples of the discourse of the cadaver and its intersection with Lisa Lowe's necrospace are endless. But one event that brings together both frames is the 2010 collaboration between MAC Makeup and designer brand Rodarte, which scheduled the release of a makeup line with colors and names "inspired" by the border towns of Mexico, from "Juarez," a pale pink nail polish, to "Factory," a pale green polish. MAC faced public outcry over the profiteering on the labor exploitation of young, female factory workers and the ongoing and unsolved murders of young women in Ciudad Juárez. For more, see *Of Faces and Fingers*, July 18, 2010, http://musicalhouses.blogspot.com/2010/07/mac-rodarte-collection-how-to-give-your.html.

17. The artists that Bourriaud writes about, then, disrupt this exchange by re-centering human interaction and engagement: they prepare food in a staff break-room in a museum and invite patrons to eat; they stage happenings in galleries that disrupt customary use of the space, et cetera.

18. I am not suggesting that the killing of Black youth and other people of color is not due to the individual racism of the persons who killed them. Rather, I am arguing that the regime of representation in US mainstream culture reifies and perpetuates the dehumanization of Black people and other human beings deemed "other."

Works Cited

Barraza, Jesus, and Melanie Cervantes. 2016. "Empujando Tinta: The Work and Politics of Dignidad Rebelde." *Aztlán: A Journal of Chicano Studies* 41, no. 2: 209–20.

Bourriaud, Nicolas. *Relational Aesthetics*. Trans. by Simon Pleasance & Fronza Woods. Dijon, FR: Les presses du réel, 2002.

Certeau, Michel de. 1984. "Walking in the City." In *The Practice of Everyday Life*, 91–110. Berkeley: University of California Press.

Dignidad Rebelde. "About Us." http://dignidadrebelde.com/.

Hall, Stuart. 1997. "The Spectacle of the Other." In *Representation: Cultural Representation and Signifying Practices*, 225–90. London: SAGE Publications.

"Interview with Tracy Martin and Sybrina Fulton." 2013. *Anderson Cooper 360 Degrees*, July 18, 2013. http://transcripts.cnn.com/TRANSCRIPTS/1307/18/acd.01.html.

Lippard, Lucy. 1990. "Rupert García: Face to Face." In *Rupert García: Prints and Posters, 1969–1990*, 13–42. The Fine Arts Museum of San Francisco and Northeastern University Press, Boston.

Lockett, Dee. 2016. "Ellen DeGeneres Responds to Accusations of Racism over Usain Bolt Meme." *Vulture.com*, August 16, http://www.vulture.com/.

Lowe, Lisa. 2008. "The Gender of Sovereignty." *Borders on Belonging: Gender and Immigration. S&F Online*. 6:3 1–7. http://sfonline.barnard.edu/immigration/index.htm

Nunley, Vorris L. 2013. "Cicero's Tongue: 'Hey! It's Me, Trayvon!'" *Los Angeles Review of Books*, July 19, 2103. http://lareviewofbooks.org/essay/ciceros-tongue-hey-its-me-trayvon.

Schmidt-Camacho, Alicia. 2004. "Body Counts on the Mexico-U.S. Border: Feminicidio, Reification, and the Theft of Mexicana Subjectivity." *Chicana/Latina Studies* 4, no. 1: 22–55.

Wootson, Cleve R., Jr. 2018. "Pastor Apologizes to Ariana Grande for Squeezing Her Breast at Aretha Franklin's Funeral." *Washington Post*, September 1, 2018.

Part IV

Using Humanity/ies

In our very first meeting, as we sat around a big table with our sandwiches, we asked ourselves what we wanted to achieve during that year and how we wanted to interrupt and reframe the familiar academic conversations around the humanities, around the role of scholars and scholarship, and around our socialization process and pedagogical practices. How do we have a more human humanities? How do we expose and celebrate the messiness of the human? What is the change we want to see, and how do we contribute to that?

We agreed that while our dialogues were institutionally framed (we were up on the hill, after all, sitting in what was formerly the house of Cornell's cofounder and first president), we all felt strongly that it was important for us to get off campus—with our website, with this book, and with public events that truly welcomed the wider community. Yet . . .

While all of us were "community-minded," to use Ella Diaz's term, and are committed to "humanities in action" (Christine Henseler), not everyone was directly involved in concrete collaborations with off-campus community members, and some of us found it challenging to imagine spaces of true collaboration. For those of us who were involved in such collaborations, in the midst of the rich exchanges that were the highlight of our Wednesdays there was a slightly melancholic note. The very structures that made these conversations possible also prevented us from including our community partners in these dialogues except indirectly. (For example: the funding that brought us together was limited to Cornell faculty and graduate students, and our community leaders couldn't get off work to come to campus for regular midday meetings.)

This section explores three different ways that some of us who are deeply invested in community collaboration have thought about the interdisciplinary intersections and challenges of our work, how what we bring from our academic background is enriched by what we learn from our partners, and how we try to understand the formal structures, constraints, and opportunities. Above all, we want to convey the joy of humanities work, the love for the things we make and the things we do.

CHAPTER 11

Performing the Past, Rehearsing the Future

*Transformative Encounters with American
Theater Company's Youth Ensemble*

CAITLIN KANE

> If there was a time I'd go back to in my life, I'd go
> back to day one of doing *Greensboro: A Requiem*—a
> stormy day in June, meeting up at Next Door Café
> and reading the whole script in the noisy café where
> we could hardly hear one another. I didn't know what
> I was getting into. It felt like another play with high
> schoolers in it. Looking back at it now, the process
> had a huge impact on my life and shaped my thinking
> about one of the most important social problems we
> face in America today.
>
> —Michael Sandoval

*Caitlin Kane is a PhD candidate in Cornell's
Department of Performing and Media Arts, where her research interests include
the politics and ethics of documentary theater, queer and feminist performance, and theater historiography. Caitlin was a New York Public Humanities
fellow in 2017–18 and a Fulbright Fellow in 2011–12 (Bulgaria). Alongside
her scholarly interests, Caitlin is a freelance director, dramaturg, and teaching
artist based in Chicago. Recent projects at Cornell include cowriting and associate directing* The Loneliness Project, *a new documentary about intergenerational loneliness in LGBTQIA+ populations, with Kelli Simpkins and directing
Leigh Fondakowski's documentary play,* Spill, *about the 2010 explosion on the
Deepwater Horizon offshore oil drilling rig. She is currently collaborating with
Fondakowski on her newest play* Casa Cushman, *about the nineteenth-century
lesbian actress Charlotte Cushman.*

*This chapter was written in memory of PJ Paparelli, Cesar Cauce, Dr. Michael
Nathan, William Sampson, Dr. James Waller, and all the men, women and children who have lost their lives to state-sanctioned violence. Caitlin would like to
express her deepest gratitude to the members of American Theater Company's
Youth Ensemble and members of the Beloved Community Center who made the*

production of Greensboro: A Requiem *discussed here possible. She would not be the scholar or artist that she is today without their ongoing support and inspiration.*

In this chapter, Caitlin examines the ways in which an intergenerational collaboration between Chicago public high school students and a collective of seasoned civil rights activists allowed for a cross-temporal retelling of the 1979 Greensboro Massacre. The essay argues that the members of the ensemble and their counterparts at the Beloved Community Center in Greensboro exemplify the potentialities of the public humanities outside of academia. Both groups used the documentary process to reexamine Greensboro's often forgotten history and its implications at a time when Black Lives Matter was rapidly gaining national recognition. These collectives dreamed into being visions of what a more equitable and just world might look like and then worked to embody those visions in the microcosm of their communities. "Performing the Past, Rehearsing the Future" considers what these processes of envisioning and embodying alternative futures through theater and activism might tell us about the potentialities of the public humanities within and beyond academia.

On the evening of June 17, 2015, a young white man entered Emanuel African Methodist Episcopal Church in Charleston, South Carolina, and took part in almost an hour of Bible study before pulling out a handgun and firing at members of the congregation. He killed nine people, including the pastor.[1] Halfway across the country, I was seated at a crowded table with two teaching artists and eleven Chicago public high school students, discussing the distinctions between the civil rights movement and Black Lives Matter. The news of the shooting would not hit social media until later that night, but when we returned the next day for another evening of research and table work, the tenor of our conversation turned quickly from unbridled enthusiasm about the project at hand to righteous anger about the state of our nation.

The eleven students crowded around that café table were members of American Theater Company's Youth Ensemble, a two-year tuition-free college preparatory program that combined professional acting training with individualized college planning. Underlying these professional aims, the program served primarily as a space for young artists and activists to explore and deepen their commitment to working toward social change. In pursuit of these intersecting goals, the program culminated each year in a production of a documentary play that engaged the ensemble in both a professional production process and the study of a social issue that concerned them.[2] This intensive process, which was the highlight of the ensemble's year, involved a multi-day research trip, six weeks of rehearsal, and two weeks of performance. On that rainy night in June, we had just begun to prepare for the ensemble's production of Emily Mann's *Greensboro: A Requiem*, a documentary play that examines the miscarriage of justice following the 1979 murder of five young activists by members of the Ku Klux Klan. The ensemble, our artistic director (the late PJ Paparelli), and I (then the director of the program) decided to produce *Greensboro* because the play allowed us to examine the history of racial and economic oppression in the United States from the perspective of the massacre's survivors, most of whom were members of a multiracial, antiracist collective that, in many ways, resembled the ensemble itself.

Our focus on racial and economic justice that summer was not happenstance. The 2014–15 school year had already been a year of too much loss, too many deaths, and too little action on the part of those in power. That fall, the Black Lives Matter movement gained national recognition when Darnell Moore and Patrisse Cullors organized a "freedom ride" to Ferguson, Missouri. There they joined local activists in protests against the murder of a

FIGURE 11.1   Members of the American Theater Company's Youth Ensemble, graduation 2015.

young, unarmed black man named Michael Brown Jr. by a white police officer (Garza). Two months later, Laquan McDonald, a seventeen-year-old high
school student, was shot sixteen times by a Chicago police officer on the
southwest side of the city, effectively bringing the fight for black lives home
for many members of our ensemble and staff. For much of that academic
year, similar stories of black men, women, and children being killed by police
inundated the national news, while gun violence in Chicago seemed to soar,
impacting far too many friends and loved ones.[3] This state-sanctioned violence repeatedly found its way into the discussions at our biweekly workshops, and the consistency and urgency of those conversations led to our
unanimous decision to produce *Greensboro: A Requiem* that year.

We had spent much of the spring semester anxiously preparing for the
production when, that May, less than a month before rehearsals began, PJ
Paparelli, our artistic director, mentor, and friend, died in a car accident. The
news left the ensemble, members of our staff, and much of the Chicago theater community reeling, and for a moment the future of the theater company
seemed to be in peril. On June 17, we had just begun to regain our footing,
when the news of the Charleston shooting broke. For the second time in
as many months, the play's director, Kelly O'Sullivan, and I met to discuss
whether we should move forward with the production. The shooting had
inspired vigils and protests across the country, but in many southern states,
including North Carolina, there were threats of white supremacist counter-
protests. We were scheduled to leave for our research trip to Greensboro four
days later, and parents who had already been worried about their children's
emotional well-being were now concerned about their physical safety.[4] Taking
those concerns seriously, we consulted with other members of the theater's
staff, our contacts in Greensboro, and the ensemble members themselves
before finally deciding to continue with the trip and production as planned.

In that moment, our collective sense of purpose was threatened by an overwhelming sense of anger and despair. The Charleston shooter's ties to white
supremacist organizations and stated desire to prompt a "race war" tied the
omnipresence of racially motivated violence in 2015 directly to the Greensboro Massacre in 1979 and, in so doing, left many of us feeling that the racial
and economic injustices that had inspired our production were insurmountable (Block). Documentary theater felt like a woefully inadequate mode of
response to the rampant racism surrounding us, and we were all—staff and
ensemble members alike—suddenly and profoundly uncertain of whether
we had the capacity to contribute to social change in any meaningful way. In
light of these uncertainties, our decision to produce *Greensboro: A Requiem*,

rather than another documentary play with similar themes, proved to be fortuitous. Our study of Emily Mann's process and the play's impact on her public partners restored our faith in documentary theater's capacity to serve as a form of corrective historiography. At the same time, our interactions with members of Greensboro's Beloved Community Center—the collective of seasoned civil rights activists whose story the play tells—placed that year's events into perspective and challenged us to reconsider the aims and practices of our activism. Ultimately, our engagement with the documentary process established an environment in which we, as students and professionals, could recognize ourselves as engaged citizens who had the skills necessary to contribute to an informed and empathetic public.

Engaged Artistry: Making Sense of Insurmountable Problems through Documentary Plays

Emily Mann has never shied away from difficult subject matter. As a playwright, she is primarily known for her works of "theater of testimony," which use direct quotations from archival documents, public records, and interview transcripts as the primary source of their language. In order to craft each of these works, Mann spent years conducting research and interviews, transcribing those materials, and then sculpting that content into dramatic form. Through this methodology, she crafted a series of plays that confront challenging and often controversial subjects, including the Jewish Holocaust, the Vietnam War, and various acts of hate-based violence. *Greensboro: A Requiem*, which premiered in 1996, was the last play that Mann created using this methodology, and it is one of her most dramaturgically and narratively complex works. In it she uses the remembrances of dozens of individuals to address the miscarriage of justice that occurred in the trials following the Greensboro massacre when appeals to emotion—particularly race-based and anticommunist fear—overrode readily available factual evidence. Mann uses theater as a form of critical historiography that works to simultaneously restore faith in objective facts while also addressing the ideological forces that so often distort the ways historical events are remembered. Her plays also serve as powerful reminders of the ways documentary theater can help make sense of seemingly insurmountable sociopolitical issues and highly contested narratives.

On the morning of November 3, 1979, members of the Communist Workers' Party—a diverse collective of young activists committed to racial and economic justice—gathered at the Morningside Homes public housing

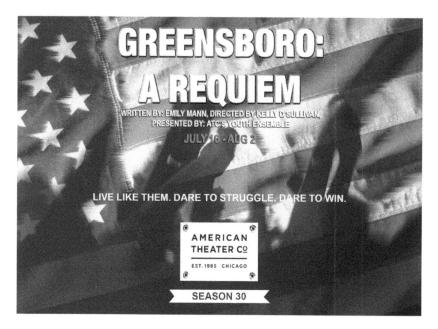

GREENSBORO:
A REQUIEM
WRITTEN BY: EMILY MANN, DIRECTED BY KELLY O'SULLIVAN,
PRESENTED BY: ATC'S YOUTH ENSEMBLE
JULY 16 - AUG 2

LIVE LIKE THEM. DARE TO STRUGGLE. DARE TO WIN.

AMERICAN
THEATER CO

EST. 1985 CHICAGO

SEASON 30

FIGURE 11.2   Poster for American Theater Company production of *Greensboro: A Requiem*.

complex in Greensboro to protest the resurgence of the Ku Klux Klan and its violent intimidation techniques, which they believed were thwarting their efforts to organize unions in local textile mills (Dawson, 37). The spirited but peaceful rally quickly became violent when members of the KKK and American Nazi Party drove through the neighborhood and shot into the crowd, killing five people and injuring nine others in only eighty-eight seconds. The Communist Workers' Party had acquired the necessary permits for the rally and had, therefore, been guaranteed police protection, but when the shooting began there were no police officers on-site (Mann, 279). It would later become clear that members of the Greensboro Police Department and the federal Bureau of Alcohol, Tobacco, and Firearms had prior knowledge of the threat but did nothing to prevent the violence (Jovanovic, 6). In its immediate aftermath, the massacre garnered widespread media attention on both local and national levels. The narrative of the day's events, however, quickly became distorted as the Communist Workers' Party's radical, leftist views became equated with the violent white supremacist ideologies of the groups that attacked them. Early reports rightly described the November 3 attack as an ambush, but by the end of the first day of reporting, members of the media had begun to label the event as a "shootout" (Institute for Southern Studies, 14). When the Iran hostage crisis began the following day, national media shifted their attention away from Greensboro, leaving many of those reports uncorrected. On a local level, misrepresentations of that day's events worsened as Greensboro city officials worked to minimize negative media coverage, which they worried would tarnish Greensboro's reputation. In their attempts to distance themselves from the violence, the city claimed that Greensboro was "the innocent victim caught in the middle of extremist groups' ideological warfare" (Jovanovic, 7). They went on to argue that outside actors were to blame for the violence and called into question the racial motivations of the confrontation. Within a week of the massacre, local Greensboro papers had begun to place the blame for the violence on members of the Communist Workers' Party by suggesting that the protestors use of "Death to the Klan" as a rallying cry incited the Klansmen's and Nazis' violent response (Institute for Southern Studies, 14–15).

These misleading reports bred widespread confusion that was only compounded by the trials that followed. In the first criminal trial, six members of the KKK and American Nazi Party were charged with first-degree murder. In spite of ample evidence, including video provided by multiple news agencies, the all-white jury declared the defendants not guilty, because the jurors believed that the Klansmen and Nazis had acted in self-defense. In a federal criminal trial in 1984, another all-white jury found nine defendants not guilty because the jurors did not believe that the prosecutors had proven that racial hatred motivated the murders (Jovanovic, 13). Finally, in a civil suit, five of the shooters, a police informant, and two members of the Greensboro Police Department were found liable. Some considered this unprecedented decision to be a victory because it was the first instance in our nation's history in which the KKK, the American Nazi Party, and members of a local police force were found jointly liable in a wrongful death suit (Beloved Community Center Board of Directors, 2). However, none of the perpetrators paid reparations to the survivors and their families, and the city continued to deny any wrongdoing.

As the events of November 3 were being misconstrued and neglected in the media, survivors, grassroots activists, and artists came together to preserve the historical record and demand justice for those whose lives had been prematurely ended or irreparably altered. This process began with the trials, continued through the formation of the Beloved Community Center (which I discuss in the next section), and culminated in the work of over one thousand Greensboro citizens who came together to conduct the first Truth and Reconciliation Commission in the United States. Emily Mann wrote *Greensboro: A Requiem* in the midst of this process: after the legal system had failed the survivors but before the Truth and Reconciliation Commission had begun. Mann's play brings together the voices of the survivors, their legal representatives, city officials, and members of the KKK, including a key police informant, to retell the story of the massacre. They play's form allows Mann to simultaneously hold the perpetrators accountable while also scrutinizing the systems and ideologies that failed to incriminate them in the first place. Theater scholar Carol Martin, therefore, situates Mann's play within the tradition of documentary trial plays, which she suggests have "created a forum apart from the legal justice system in which to examine justice itself." She goes on to argue that "[t]he difficulty here is that the resulting theatre is not necessarily more truthful than what formal legal processes yield." While Martin makes an essential point, her use of a legal/ theatrical binary and "truthfulness" as an indicator of theatrical efficacy underestimates the political potential of documentary theater. Because theater and law are seen as two distinct entities, theater is afforded only a secondary role in the construction of culture, one in which it can, at best, serve as "a powerful critique of our system of justice" (Martin, 115). The process of collectively examining and critiquing the justice system, however, is not merely an intellectual exercise.

When artists, historians, community members, and audiences come together to engage in the type of critical analysis of history that plays like *Greensboro: A Requiem* facilitate, we are often asked to imagine alternative responses and outcomes to the issues at the play's core. When we acknowledge the work's potential to inspire this sort of collective envisioning, we can embrace a more capacious understanding of the ways documentary theater contributes to social change. Instead of reading performance as separate from, and perhaps secondary to, the process of shaping society and writing history, I would therefore argue, as Athol Fugard preemptively notes in his introduction to a collection of Mann's plays (Mann, xi) and Spoma Jovanovic highlights in her subsequent analysis of the Greensboro Truth and Reconciliation process (Jovanovich, xv), that Mann's play actively contributed to the memorialization and rectification of the Greensboro Massacre. In both the process of its creation and in its publication and national tour, *Greensboro: A Requiem* generated awareness about the events of November 3, 1979, held space for local and national dialogue, and countered mainstream narratives about the root causes of the massacre. In so doing, Mann's play advanced the work of countless activists and community organizers committed to redressing the harms caused by both the massacre and its aftermath. Together these activists and artists altered many of the narratives surrounding the massacre, resulting in better living circumstances for the survivors and victims' families.

In our study of Mann's play, the ensemble, Kelly O'Sullivan, and I were struck by Mann's ability to bring clarity to the many contradictory accounts of the massacre and its aftermath, but it was not until we learned of the profound effects that *Greensboro* had on her public partners that we were able to recommit to our faith in the political potentiality of the documentary form. Our mentor, PJ Paparelli, had been a documentary playwright himself, and we knew through his work that documentary theater can often make a lasting impact not only on its creators and audiences but also on the individuals whose stories it endeavors to tell. Following his death, however, we had lost sight of those potentialities, which often remain wholly invisible to audiences unless those public partners, like Mann's collaborators in Greensboro, make the work's impact known. We took these lessons with us as we prepared for our research trip, which not only confirmed that Mann's play had benefited the individuals with whom she created it but also introduced us to a collective of experienced activists who provided us with a new set of tools for remaining politically active in the face of hardship.

Active Citizenship: Embodying Change at the Beloved Community Center

> [The trip] was one of the first times I realized the significance of what we, the ensemble, were doing. It changed my perspective on the role of theatre. Now I see theater as a platform for furthering discussion, whether it be pleasant or painful, rather than something simply for entertainment. It became clear that putting the play together with the sole purpose of entertaining would be a huge disservice not only to the story we were sharing but also to the people [to whom] the story belonged.
>
> Matt Gomez-Hidaka

On a hot Sunday afternoon, just a few days after the Charleston shooting, the ensemble and our staff joined several survivors of the massacre in the gathering space of the Beloved Community Center (BCC) in Greensboro.[5] Upon our arrival, Reverend Nelson Johnson and Joyce Johnson, codirectors of BCC and former leaders of the Communist Workers' Party, were finishing their preparations for the first of several dialogues that they would facilitate between the ensemble, survivors of the massacre, and other local activists and leaders. They welcomed us into their space and encouraged us to use the time before our first conversation to look at the archival photos that line the walls of the BCC. Those photos chronicle nearly sixty years of civil rights activism by the center's members, many of whom are survivors of the massacre and characters in Mann's play. The ensemble delighted in seeing images of the individuals they would be portraying and marveled at the myriad forms of resistance that those photographs document. We knew from our prior research that, for a city of its size, Greensboro has a remarkably robust and consistent history of civil rights activism, but the BCC archives brought that history to life and drew our attention to the resilience of the many activists and community leaders we would meet during our trip.[6]

FIGURE 11.3 Ensemble members at the Beloved Community Center, Greensboro.

At this point in the process, we knew the story of the Greensboro Massacre well. In the weeks leading up to the trip, we had studied Mann's play and read dozens of articles about the tragedy closely, but we soon learned that those materials had provided us with an incomplete understanding of the massacre itself and the collective of activists who had been targeted by the violence. Over the course of four days, we spoke with over a dozen individuals, each of whom recounted their own version of the massacre and provided us with a richer understanding of its lasting effects. These conversations were held across Greensboro at the Beloved Community Center, in individuals' homes, and at relevant historical sites, including the abandoned textile mills where the Communist Workers' Party conducted their labor organizing, North Carolina A&T (where some of the survivors first engaged in activism), and the site of the massacre. While each of these conversations deepened our understanding of the play and the massacre, I want to focus here on our ongoing dialogue with Reverend Johnson, who is both a pivotal character in Mann's play and the person with whom we spent the most time. His story of persistence in the face of incredible personal and political hardship put the challenges we had experienced that year into perspective and dramatically altered our understanding of how social change comes into being.

In Mann's retelling of the massacre, Reverend Johnson is the most prominent figure in the Communist Workers' Party. While his story serves as one of the primary narrative arcs in the play, most of his lines provide the audience with factual information about how the massacre and its aftermath unfolded rather than personal details about the impact of these events on his life. In one of the final scenes in the play, Emily Mann's "interviewer" character addresses these gaps in the narrative by telling Nelson, "You know I realized there's a whole chapter that I missed and that's when you went from post-November 3rd and went into the ministry, what that thought process was" (322).[7] In response, Nelson speaks briefly about his faith and then describes some of the challenges he faced in the aftermath of the massacre: "In the early eighties, I really was so rejected around here that—I think I shared with you—once I went to get a job, and the guy went to call the police; I sat in the courtroom, everyone got up and moved to the other side of the court. I listened to radio talk shows when people said they wished I had been shot, and all this kind of stuff. And my children had to listen to it" (323). Over the next several pages of the play, Nelson tells us about the intimate relationship between his faith and his activism, but it is clear that a great deal has been left out about the twelve years between the massacre itself and his decision to cofound the Beloved Community Center in 1991.

Over the course of our trip, many of those gaps were filled by our conversations with Reverend Johnson and his wife, Joyce Johnson. Through their stories, we came to better understand both the persecution that most members of the Communist Workers' Party faced after the massacre and the particularly harsh treatment that Johnson and his family experienced as a result of his history as an outspoken advocate for racial and economic justice. Reverend Johnson told us that he was a few years younger than most of the ensemble members when he participated in his first sit-in with two friends in Littleton, North Carolina, at the age of fifteen. He remained politically engaged through his college years at North Carolina A&T, where he led the Greensboro Association of Poor People. During his time there, Johnson developed a reputation with the Greensboro Police Department as a "dangerous" political figure for his involvement in Dudley High and North Carolina A&T University disturbances in 1969.[8] Later, Johnson joined the Workers' Viewpoint Organization (the direct precursor to the Communist Workers' Party) after his studies of African liberation and Marxism alerted him to the intimate relationship between economic and racial injustice (Jovanovic, 23–24). Throughout the 1970s, he remained an outspoken presence in Greensboro and developed increasingly tense relationships with city leaders, including Mayor Jim Melvin, who used a misdemeanor charge from Johnson's civil rights organizing to label him "a dangerous man with a proven police record" (Waller, 274). Because of these existing tensions and Johnson's strident response to the violence on November 3, he and his family faced especially brutal harassment and mistreatment for years after the massacre. In the face of these challenges, Reverend Johnson and his wife eventually decided to leave Greensboro with their two young daughters and did not return until Johnson entered the seminary in 1989. While Johnson admits that these circumstances led him to reconsider his approach to advocating for social change, his commitment to the fight for racial and economic justice has not wavered.

I do not remember, or have a record, of anyone asking Reverend Johnson how he has sustained his activism in the face of these hardships. I imagine someone did and that I simply failed to note his response, but it is also possible that none of us asked because his approach to remaining engaged seemed so clear. In every moment that we spent with Reverend Johnson, he treated us, and everyone else with whom he interacted, as full members of the beloved community that he has committed his life to cultivating. In other words, he practiced what might be considered a "politics of prefiguration," which Rebecca Solnit describes as "the idea that if you embody what you aspire to, you have already succeeded. That is to say, if your activism is already democratic, peaceful, creative, then in one small corner of the world these things have triumphed. *Activism, in this model, is not only a toolbox to change things but a home in which to take up residence and live according to your beliefs, even if it's a temporary and local place"* (Solnit, 81, my emphasis). In a moment in which many members of our ensemble and staff were confronting a deep sense of uncertainty regarding the possibility of social change, Reverend Johnson and many of the other activists and community leaders we met in Greensboro provided us with a different means of assessing the success of our efforts. In a 2008 interview about this shift in his thinking, Johnson stated, "If we as a community can actually embrace a vision and set of principles to which we are faithful, then that is our victory in life" (Johnson Purpose Prize Winner). During our time in Greensboro, we learned that this shift in focus did not mean that Johnson or the other members of the Beloved Community Center had given up on a vision of radical change. Instead, they had altered their approach to fighting for that change in order to make their ongoing activism more sustainable. Of the many lessons that we took back with us to Chicago, this model for prolonging and nurturing one's activism by committing to living one's values and cultivating a community of like-minded people had the most profound impact on the ways in which ensemble members approached the rehearsal and performance process.

Reclaiming Agency through Research and Rehearsal

> At American Theater Company (ATC) we always go the extra mile. We dive deep into places that might lead us nowhere, but we'd rather know there's nothing there than wonder if we are missing a crucial part of our piece. The research that goes into our documentary plays [is] the foundation for our production. ATC creates an environment where people want to learn more about what was going on. . . . The research process is what keeps us informed and searching for more. It's what leads us to question ourselves and others.
>
> Madison Pullman

As Madison Pullman suggests in the epigraph above, the research process did not end with our trip to Greensboro. Instead, we asked the ensemble members to engage in two forms of intensive research throughout the rehearsal process. On the one hand, every ensemble member was responsible for developing a nuanced understanding of each of the individuals that they played in the production. For most, this meant delving into the lived experiences of at least three people from a wide range of ideological backgrounds and identifying corresponding physical and vocal choices that distinguished between those characters. On the other hand, our director, Kelly O'Sullivan, proposed that we begin each rehearsal with a conversation about the contemporary resonances of the play. Over the course of the rehearsal process, each ensemble member was therefore responsible for leading two or three discussions about compelling news items or contemporary works of art that they believed could contribute to or be elucidated by our production of *Greensboro: A Requiem*. This research was intended to inform the rehearsal process and production, but the daily practice of sharing and discussing this material ultimately enabled us to reclaim our sense of agency as members of and contributors to an informed public.

In the script of *Greensboro: A Requiem*, Mann frames the conflict between the Communist Workers' Party and the Ku Klux Klan, American Nazi Party, and various government agencies as a conflict between the multiracial—but predominantly black and white—members of the Communist Workers' Party and the white men of the KKK and American Nazi Party (Mann, 254–55). This depiction of events is mostly accurate and potentially necessary for the dramatic clarity of an otherwise complicated narrative, but it posed a particular casting challenge for the six actors in the ensemble who fell outside of that racial binary. This challenge was heightened by the sheer number of roles for white men in the play. The 2014–15 ensemble included no white men and only two white women, so moving forward with the production demanded that several members of the ensemble portray individuals whose views were not only opposed to their own but whose views were also intended to incite violence against people whose race, gender identity, and/or sexual orientation matched the performers'. Before deciding to produce the play, we therefore held a frank conversation about the implications and challenges of these particular casting decisions. The ensemble unanimously determined that the story was compelling enough to take on these challenges and move forward with the production. When it was decided that three young people of color—all of whom identify as either Asian American or Latinx—would play the majority of these roles and that the two white women in the ensemble would primarily portray women in the Communist Workers' Party, with one exception each, there was a general consensus regarding the dramatic expediency of this choice and awareness of the many political and social questions that it raised. Maintaining a consistent group of actors portraying members of the KKK, American Nazi Party, and antagonistic members of government agencies facilitated audience comprehension of a fast-paced, dense theatrical text. However, this casting choice placed an exceptional burden on that group of performers of color who would be required to develop intimacy with some of the most challenging content of the play.

In a series of interviews that I conducted two years after the production, I asked the members of the ensemble who had portrayed white supremacists about how researching, rehearsing, and performing those roles had affected them. In their responses, they consistently described the process of developing those characters as personally and politically transformative. Marcel Dizon told me that "delving into the psyches of Klansmen and American Nazis" had "stuck with [them] . . . and . . . driven [their] current political mind-set."[9] Similarly, Michael Sandoval stated, "The process had a huge impact on my life and shaped my thinking about racism in America." Liv Shine, a young white woman who played a character identified as a young "skinhead" in the play, compellingly articulated the value of taking on such a challenging role: "It was a great education for me to step into something that I wanted to ignore, that so many white people want to ignore because that's easy and comfortable. It was uncomfortable. I felt gross. I felt apologetic. But now, I always remember [that white supremacy is] in me. That's in my blood." In each of these comments, ensemble members clarify the connection between their artistic practices and their political engagement. By researching and embodying the white supremacists in Mann's play, these individuals were compelled to confront their own relationships with racial privilege. At the same time, they became intimately familiar with white supremacist ideologies and were able to use this expertise to refine their understandings of racial inequality in this country. Over the course of the rehearsal process, each of these ensemble members became more outspoken not only about this history of racism but also about the sociopolitical forces that continue to perpetuate racist ideologies today. Like Mann, they used thorough research into individuals' personal narratives and beliefs to elucidate broader sociopolitical issues. In so doing, these ensemble members refined their ability to make nuanced, evidence-based contributions to conversations about race in the United States and deepened their commitment to doing so.

Alongside this character-based research, the ensemble and our staff engaged in daily conversations about the contemporary resonances of the play. These conversations were sparked by a range of materials, from news reports to hip-hop tracks and clips of movies, all of which were used to illuminate some element of the work's urgency in our particular sociopolitical moment. On the surface, there was nothing spectacular about this daily practice. It was part of the culture of the ensemble and served largely as a means of maintaining our commitment to an artistically and personally demanding project. Over time, however, it became clear that these conversations were reaffirming the lessons we had learned from Reverend Johnson and the members of the Beloved Community Center. The ensemble, in a collectively written note to the audience, described those lessons as follows: "The survivors we interviewed taught us that the fight ends when we lose hope. Because we live in a world where information is at our fingertips, it is easy to become disillusioned by violence, fear, and injustice. [The members of the Beloved Community Center] have been fighting for 36 years and haven't stopped yet. . . . By committing to this show, we the Youth Ensemble are taking on the *responsibility of hope* . . . and are more than willing to bear the burden of continuing to fight for our communities."

Our daily conversations became one of the methods that we used to generate and sustain this sense of hope. By dedicating the first twenty minutes of our days to acknowledging and addressing the omnipresent realities of racial and economic injustice, we began to develop a daily practice of activism. Instead of thinking about activism solely in terms of large-scale movements, we created an environment that encouraged us to take action on a daily basis, in whatever ways that we could. Committing to those small steps undermined the overwhelming sense of despair and frustration that had characterized the early days of our process and allowed us to re-embrace the multitude of ways in which theatrical practice, in general, and documentary practice, in particular, can contribute to social change.

Months earlier, when I proposed *Greensboro: A Requiem* to the ensemble, I had convinced myself that the story of this often-forgotten moment in history would inspire our audiences to reexamine their attitudes toward race and class. It is possible that some members of the audience did exactly that, but in focusing on the impact of the final product, I lost sight of a truth that every theater practitioner knows. Theater, like most forms of activism, contributes to social change in subtle and unpredictable ways that are often invisible to those involved. More often than not, its most significant and tangible effects take place in the rehearsal room long before audiences arrive. In the case of this ensemble, that was undoubtedly true. The *Greensboro: A Requiem* production process contributed to enacting social change by creating the opportunity for each of us to show up day in and day out to be with one another, confronting our pasts, celebrating our differences, generating empathy, and seeking new ways to be in this world. Though it was never perfect, being in the rehearsal room with the ensemble always meant striving to change the world by striving to change ourselves. We worked to make the world a better place by modeling the possibility of a radically kinder, more inclusive, more thoughtful world than the one that existed outside of our rehearsal space. The most lasting effects of our production of *Greensboro*, then, were forged through the creative process and can be seen not in their effect on the audience but in the artistic and activist work that members of our ensemble and staff remain committed to today.[10]

Notes

1. On Wednesday, June 17, 2015, at Emmanuel African Methodist Church in Charleston, South Carolina, Cynthia Marie Graham Hurd, Susie Jackson, Ethel Lee Lance, Depayne Middleton-Doctor, Clementa C. Pinckey, Tywanza Sanders, Daniel Simmons, Sharonda Coleman-Singleton, and Myra Thompson were killed in the name of white supremacy by a white man who openly admitted to attempting to incite a "race war." Their murderer has since been convicted and sentenced to death. Jason Horowitz, Ashley Southall, and Nick Corsaniti, "Nine Killed in Shooting at Black Church in Charleston," *New York Times* June 17, 2015.

2. The term "documentary play" or "documentary theater" is generally used to reference theatrical works crafted largely, if not exclusively, from primary source materials, such as public records or personal interviews. For more on the form, see Attilo Favorini, ed., *Voicings: Ten Plays from the Documentary Theatre* (Hopewell, NJ: Ecco Press, 1995), 1–25; and Gary Fisher Dawson, *Documentary Theatre in the United States: An Historical Survey and Analysis of Its Content, Form, and Stagecraft*, Contributions in Drama and Theatre Studies, 89 (Westport, CT: Greenwood Press, 1999).

3. In the summer of 2014, Eric Garner and Michael Brown were both killed in controversial confrontations with police officers. National protests coordinated in part by Black Lives Matter, which had been cofounded by Alicia Garza, Opal Tometi, and Patrice Cullors a year earlier, drew national attention to the murders and spurred a national debate about the prevalence of anti-black racism and the regularity of extrajudicial killings by police officers in the United States. Between July 2014 and July 2015, the extrajudicial killings of Michael Brown Jr., Samuel DuBose, Ezell Ford, Eric Garner, Brendon Glenn, Freddie Gray, Laquan McDonald, Natasha McKenna, Tamir Rice, Walter Scott, and Christian Taylor, among others, resulted in public protest and in demands for greater accountability in policing and the criminal legal system. Daniel Funke and Tina Susman, "From Ferguson to Baton Rouge: Deaths of Black Men and Women at the Hands of the Police," *Los Angeles Times*, July 12, 2016.

4. Each summer the ensemble traveled to the site of the documentary play they were producing in order to re-interview the community members whose stories they would be telling through their theatrical performance. This unique practice was instituted by PJ Paparelli, a documentary playwright himself, who believed that seeing the physical sites of these plays and meeting the individuals represented is an essential ethical and pedagogical practice. Among other benefits, it encouraged the ensemble to confront the reality of the stories they were about to tell, pushed them to reevaluate any stereotypes they might have had about people whose views differed from their own, and reminded them of the inherent limitations of the documentary form—the people they portray are infinitely more complex and human than a play can ever capture. The cognitive dissonance created by this realization allowed the ensemble to create more fully developed, nuanced characters on stage and to speak to their audience about the ethical complexities of the documentary form.

5. The Beloved Community Center was formed in 1991 by two survivors of the Greensboro Massacre, Reverend Nelson Johnson and Joyce Johnson, and two local faith leaders, Reverend Barbara Dua and Reverend Z. Holler. A "community-based, grassroots oriented organization rooted in Dr. Martin Luther King, Jr.'s legacy of proactive struggles for racial and economic justice, democracy and beloved community," the center is "committed to grassroots empowerment, especially among minorities, within the context and spirit of forging a beloved community for all resident[s]." Beloved Community Center Board of Directors, "Beloved Community Center Tenth Anniversary Retrospective 1992–2002," Beloved Community Center archives, Greensboro, North Carolina.

6. For a concise overview of this history, see Joseph W. Groves, "Greensboro, NC Local Organizing around Forty Years of Struggle," Beloved Community Center archives, Greensboro, North Carolina.

7. Throughout this section I distinguish between our in-person conversations with Reverend Johnson and his character in the play by using his character name, "Nelson," to refer to the dramatic representation of him.

8. For a brief overview of these events, see Karen Hawkins, "Dudley High School/NC A&T University Disturbances, May 1969," Civil Rights Greensboro, University of North Carolina, Greensboro, Digital Collections, http://libcdm1.uncg.edu/cdm/essay1969/collection/CivilRights.

9. Marcel identifies as gender-nonconforming and uses "they" and "them" pronouns.

10. Kiah has lobbied for more diverse seasons and leadership in her university's BFA theater program by crafting a list of diverse directors and educators who would be suitable for the program and engaging in conversations with the administration about this issue. Eddie has bravely spoken out against horrific racial prejudice on his campus and contributed to organizing aimed at changing that culture. Liv has begun teaching spoken word poetry in the same schools that brought her to activism and art in the first place. Lawren and Tevion have each performed in multiple professional productions, each of which engaged with issues of gender and/or racial inequality. I could go on, listing a relevant accomplishment for each ensemble member, but I am less concerned about those individual accomplishments than I am in awe of the continued efforts of this ensemble. I don't doubt that this group of young people would be doing this work regardless of their experiences with American Theater Company and their interactions with the Beloved Community Center, but I do hope that both experiences contributed to deepening their understanding and intensifying their commitment, and I will always be grateful for all that they have taught me.

Works Cited

Beloved Community Center Board of Directors. "Beloved Community Center Tenth Anniversary Retrospective 1992–2002." Beloved Community Center archives, Greensboro, North Carolina.

Block, Melissa. "Dylann Roof Said He Wanted to Start a Race War, Friends Say." *All Things Considered*, June 19, 2015.

Dawson, Gary Fisher. *Documentary Theatre in the United States: An Historical Survey and Analysis of Its Content, Form, and Stagecraft.* Contributions in Drama and Theatre Studies, 89. Westport, CT: Greenwood Press, 1999.

Dizon, Marcel. Interview with author, April 6, 2017.

Garza, Alicia. "A HerStory of the #BlackLivesMatter Movement." http://www.blacklivesmatter.com/.

Gomez-Hidaka, Matt. Interview with author, April 8, 2017.

Institute for Southern Studies. "The Third of November." *Southern Exposure* 9 (1981): 55–67.

"Johnson Purpose Prize Winner." *Encore.org*, 2008. https://encore.org/purpose-prize/nelson-johnson.

Jovanovic, Spoma. *Democracy, Dialogue, and Community Action: Truth and Reconciliation in Greensboro.* Fayetteville: University of Arkansas Press, 2012.

Mann, Emily. *Testimonies: Four Plays.* New York: Theatre Communications Group, 1997.

Martin, Carol. "In Defense of Democracy: Celebrating Emily Mann." *Women and Performance: A Journal of Feminist Theory* 14, no. 2 (2005): 111–16.

Pullman, Madison. Interview with author, April 5, 2017.

Sandoval, Michael. Interview with author. April 10, 2017.

Shine, Liv. Personal Interview with author, April 7, 2017.

Solnit, Rebecca. *Hope in the Dark: Untold Histories, Wild Possibilities.* Chicago: Haymarket Books, 2016.

Waller, Signe. *Love and Revolution: A Political Memoir: People's History of the Greensboro Massacre, Its Setting and Aftermath.* Lanham, MD: Lowman and Littlefield, 2002.

CHAPTER 12

"From the Projects to the Pasture"

Navigating Food Justice, Race, and Food Localism

BOBBY J. SMITH II

Bobby J. Smith II is the great-grandson of share-croppers in Pitt County, North Carolina, and grew up listening to incredible stories about the importance of hard work, determination, and advancement. His family cultivated land that produced tobacco, cotton, potatoes, onions, cucumbers, tomatoes, and corn—yet their profit margin only yielded enough income to keep them comfortable, secure, and self-assured in a time when black farmers and sharecroppers could not guarantee their future from season to season. Nonetheless, their hardy spirit was passed down to him. At the time of his writing this chapter, Bobby was an activist in Black Lives Matter Ithaca and a PhD candidate in Cornell's Department of Development Sociology, where his work focused on historical and contemporary understandings of food justice. He is now an Assistant Professor in the Department of African American Studies at the University of Illinois at Urbana-Champaign, and his work continues to focus on the historical and contemporary relationships between race, food, agriculture, power, and inequality in black communities.

In 2015, he met a black farmer, Rafael Aponte, at an event in downtown Ithaca for people interested in working on local food issues and was introduced to the social justice side of food work and surprisingly stumbled upon the field of food justice. The story of Rafael's farm, the Rocky Acres Community Farm in Freeville, New York, helps Smith to understand how food justice rises in local food spaces. His chapter seeks to explore food justice in places where you would seemingly expect to not see it or need it. Even in a small city like Ithaca that has a vibrant local food scene—boasting five farmers' markets surrounded by a host of small-to-medium-scale farms that produce healthy, organic foods—farmers of color, low-income communities, and communities of color still struggle to access and produce healthy and organic foods for local consumption. It is the stories of black farmers, farmers of color, low-income communities, and communities of color engaging in food justice in places like Ithaca that this chapter is interested in understanding.

Introduction

In May 2017, black farmer and food justice activist Rafael "Rafa" Aponte participated on the opening panel of the first Farm-to-Plate Conference in Ithaca, New York. Speaking about the development of his ten-acre Rocky Acres Community Farm, Aponte challenged Ithaca and the greater Tompkins County area to center on the food and farming needs of black and brown communities throughout the region. For me, a sociologist who studied food justice in Ithaca and a former member of the inaugural Tompkins County Food Policy Council, this wasn't the first time I had heard Aponte speak about his work in the area. I had worked with him on several food projects before and interviewed him about his farm two years prior. However, this platform was radically different than any other Aponte had ever participated in. Alongside him on the panel were three other black food activists, Jamila Walida Simon of the Ithaca-based Giving Involves Virtually Everyone (GIVE) program, Karen Washington of Rise and Root Farm in Orange County, New York, which serves the South Bronx, and Malik Yakini of the Detroit Black Food Security Network (DBFSN). As each panelist discussed their work in the context of food justice, or "the struggle against racism, exploitation, and oppression taking place within the food system that addresses inequality's root causes both within and beyond the food chain" (Hislop, 24), I observed two intersecting types of food justice activism being articulated.

The first type of food justice activism was articulated by Karen Washington and Malik Yakini, situated in the context of urban areas that lack of access to local, fresh, and nutritious foods and the land to produce food, often referred to as *food deserts* by the US Department of Agriculture. The second type of food justice activism, articulated by Rafa and Jamila, is situated in the context of non-urban local food spaces with an abundance of local fresh foods, farmland to produce food, and community organizations dedicated to the production, consumption, or distribution of food locally. Yet the literature on food justice has focused almost exclusively on the movement in locations similar to where Karen and Malik operate (McEntee 2011; Alkon and Norgaard; Alkon; White). Consequently, there exists an "urban bias" in food justice scholarship (McEntee 2011) that has overlooked or erased how the movement is realized in non-urban food spaces. This could be due, in part, to the prevalence of explicit and highly visible instances of race- and class-based food insecurity in urban areas linked to practices of gentrification and redlining (McClintock). It could also be due to the fact that the social and political contexts of non-urban areas can be hard to penetrate as a researcher examining certain issues (McEntee, 2011). As a result, we know very little about how food justice is navigated in non-urban local food spaces, like Ithaca in Tompkins County.

Ranked among the top ten healthiest counties in New York and surrounded by over four hundred farms within forty miles, Tompkins County is known for its devotion to the production, consumption, and distribution of organic and healthy foods for local people.[1] This devotion is visible through a number of places in the county's largest city of Ithaca, home of the main campus of an Ivy League school, Cornell University. Places like the Ithaca Farmers Market, GreenStar Natural Foods Market, Groundswell Center for Local Food & Farming, Cornell Cooperative Extension-Tompkins County, and the Cornell Small Farms Program. Every weekend throughout the summer, farmers and vendors from within thirty miles of Ithaca drive to the Ithaca Farmers Market, alongside Cayuga Lake, to set up tables full of fresh foods, crafts, and other offspring of their hard work. Consumers from all over central New York rush to this market to access locally produced items to satisfy their demand for local food and display their support for small-to-medium-scale farmers. The Ithaca Farmers Market also offers over five additional weekly local food access points across the city.

According to the 2016 American Community Survey (ACS) Project, 70.8 percent of Ithacans identify as white, 6.1 percent identify as black, 16.5 identify Asian, and the remaining 6.6 percent report being Hispanic or of mixed race, in a population of 50,689. The 2014 ACS Project indicated that the median family income is $83,404, with 12.3 percent of Ithaca families and 30.1 percent of individuals living below the poverty level (US Census Bureau, 2016). Ithaca's predominantly white population and relative affluence, coupled with its strong devotion to local foods, illustrates many attributes of the mainstream local food movement. However, Ithaca is also a place where many low-income people and people of color have inadequate access to food, especially local food, associated with issues of hunger and poverty. These communities are often in the shadows of Ithaca's local food metropolis and rarely benefit from the current Ithaca local food system. While local programs have been initiated by Cooperative Extension and

GreenStar to address these issues in this community, they often miss the mark. In response, initiatives like GIVE and farms like Rocky Acres Community Farm in the area align themselves with the concept of food justice to develop programs that actually get local, nutritious food to the people. GIVE was begun in the fall of 2016 by Our Children's Future, a group of mothers at West Village Apartments, a mostly low-income community of color on Ithaca's West Hill. In response to the need for food access points and economic conditions of their community, "Our Children's Future" partnered with the local Lehman Alternative Community School on West Hill to design and develop the GIVE program. They partner with the Friendship Donations Network and other Tompkins County–based food organizations to recover fresh produce from area stores and farms to donate to communities in need and also use them to prepare various healthy "test" meals cooked with the rescued food. Their focus is threefold: mentoring, food justice, and strengthening the West Hill community through working to build the whole family.

The Rocky Acres Community Farm works with the Titus Towers senior complex in downtown Ithaca to address issues of food access among this population. Rafa noted that this population had a hard time accessing Ithaca's farmers' markets to obtain fresh foods and being able to purchase nutritious food due to the lack of income. "One of our main sites is the Titus Tower senior housing facility in Ithaca," Rafa told me. "They have some physical access problems . . . [and] the market does not cater to the elderly. It's very fast-paced; it's like a rock concert in there. People are bumping up against you." Even though the mayor of Ithaca, Svante Myrick, and president of the Southern Tier Food Bank, Natasha Thompson, have openly talked about senior citizen food access problems, arguing that these issues are "underreported" and that this population is "hard to reach," little is known about the food realities of senior citizens living here (Stein). In January 2017, the Tompkins County Office for the Aging released its action plan for the year, which included seven different local focus areas to address the needs of seniors. However, food access was not even mentioned. As far as I know, Rafa's Harvest Box model is one of the only programs attempting to address senior citizen access to local foods in Ithaca.

The food justice work of GIVE and Rocky Acres represent what McEntee (2010) has termed *traditional localism*. This framework is embedded in the conceptual framework of food localism, based on an actor's intent and motivations for obtaining local food, representing two types of localism: contemporary and traditional (McEntee 2010). Contemporary localism is characterized by the mainstream local food movement and is often associated with affluent and white supporters who are strongly interested in the well-being of the small farmer, the environment, and their community. Such individuals exercise their "food citizenship" rights by "voting" with their forks in support of a more localized, regionally based food system. In contrast, traditional localism is associated with individuals who are interested in obtaining local food that is nutritious and affordable. Most important to those who align with traditional localism is the ability to obtain food without having to spend all their income to ensure food security and/or the ability to produce their own food through community gardens or farms. Both localisms exist in the same physical but separate social space, with contemporary localism being more ideological while traditional localism is more associated with food access.

To verify his framework, McEntee used Grafton County, New Hampshire, as a case study and argued that rural food justice efforts should focus on those who identify with traditional localism to ensure adequate access to food for low-income communities. He also noted that he applied this framework to an area that is characterized by traditional localism. Most of the respondents in Grafton County, he mentioned, "chose not to buy local products frequently because of the perception of that prices were unaffordable," representing tenets of traditional localism. While his work illustrates how the traditional localism framework works in places characterized by traditional localism, how could this framework be used to study food justice efforts in places characterized by contemporary localism? In other words, how does food justice operate in a place characterized by the mainstream local food movement?

In this chapter, I examine the case of the Rocky Acres Community Farm to answer these questions. The presence of a strong, predominantly white, and affluent local food movement, food justice efforts, and inadequate food access make Ithaca an ideal research site to understand and illuminate how food justice is navigated in non-urban local food spaces. While building this case, I pay attention to how food justice is navigated in 1) the development of the Rocky Acres Community Farm, 2) Rafael Aponte's experience as a black farmer in the area, and 3) the local food scene in the Ithaca–Tompkins County area. I also briefly explore themes that emerge from this case. Such themes are not isolated: they push us to see how food justice is navigated in non-urban local food spaces within the context of McEntee's (2010) food localism framework. It is important for me to note here that this case study purposefully sidesteps the traditional lines of case study methodology in order to see what we can learn from the case.

The Rocky Acres Community Farm

Now approaching its eighth growing season in 2020, the ten-acre Rocky Acres Community Farm is located less than ten miles northeast of Ithaca, just south of New York Route 34B. The farm sprang up in response to the struggles of low-income people and people of color to access adequate food and to serve almost exclusively those communities marginalized by Ithaca's vibrant local food scene and system. These communities include Ithaca's historic black Southside neighborhood, West Village area, and independent senior living housing complexes downtown. The farm produces about a half an acre of vegetables, raises chickens and goats, and also does some programming around social justice issues. The farm uses food as an entry point to discuss issues of access linked to the experiences of those marginalized by the food system in the area. "Our farm is more than food production," Rafa explained when asked to describe Rocky Acres:

> It's really using agriculture as a way to get at justice issues—issues around food access: Who has it? Who does it belong to? Who has the ability to engage in it? By operating a farm, we kind of remove some of those barriers by simply just providing more healthy food to communities who don't have access to it. We strive to be a model, a different way that a farm could work to tackle social issues. To be a space where folks can learn not only about agriculture but about history. . . . For people of color, that history is full of exploitation or trauma. However, being able to see me as a farmer of color, who now owns the means of production myself, makes a huge difference. Instead of coming at agriculture or some of the social issues from a disempowered place, I'm the owner here. We're able to talk from a different space. It doesn't start from the trauma and exploitation.

The exploitation and trauma Rafa cite derive from instances of racial violence toward people of color, sanctioned by systems of domination organized around race, class, food, and agriculture. These systems of domination have penalized and disempowered black farmers (Green, Green, and Kleiner) and Native Americans (Norgaard, Reed, and Van Horn) in the United States and have impacted their respective relationships with land. For black farmers, land historically provided a sense of security that goes beyond farming as a means of food security to include economic security.

In the case of Native Americans, land is historically and culturally embedded in the sacred relationship between nature and humans, linked to food provision and land stewardship. By being an owner of his own farm, Rafa is exercising his right to land and using this right to empower marginalized communities through discussions on social issues around food. These discussions rely on a type of farm education that draws upon a structural interpretation of Ithaca's devotion to contemporary localism that "problematizes the influence of race and class on the production, distribution, and consumption of food' (Alkon and Agyeman, 5). This way of approaching local food production is linked to Rafa's journey to farming, which started back during his time as a community organizer in New York City.

Rafa's Journey to Farming

Rafa grew up in the South Bronx's Millbrook Projects in the 1980s, and he attributes his upbringing to his desire to work with communities:

> I was born in the eighties in the Bronx, New York, and, looking back at that period, it was tough. This was after "the Bronx is burning" phase. Everything had already been burned, and we were trying to reform. The Bronx was the epicenter for so many things . . . pollution, gentrification, blatant neglect on a structural level, or all kinds of failing infrastructure. . . . Both my parents are immigrants from Puerto Rico and met in the Bronx. They had a difficult time adjusting here, but family and community was very strong for them and for me, and they instilled that in me. I had some resilience, my family had some resilience, and we were doing okay. We wanted to help others out and overcome some of the barriers that we were facing. I wouldn't say they were too politically active. They were around during the eras of the Black Panthers and the Young Lords and things like that. That would remain in the memory—folks that got up and did something. . . . They really helped shape my dedication to helping people.

Relating farming to his urban community organizing work, he says:

> In regard to how I got to farming, I'd say it all started when I was in New York City. I was a community organizer working with nonprofits and after-school education. A lot of the issues that we were working on with the students came out organically, based on whatever they were going through at the moment in their communities. Food became a big one, and that one I didn't know too much about. I felt like I needed to get some training on this. I started by looking at different community gardens and tied myself to some folks and mentors that could teach

me about agricultural processes and the history of all that. I got tied into Farm School NYC, doing a two-year urban agriculture certificate program so that I could bring a lot of the information back to the students. That took me [in] a completely different direction. I was, like, this is actually my calling.

Discovering farming as his calling, Rafa got heavily involved in the New York City community gardening scene and urban agriculture movement, and, while looking for land of his own to farm, he got the opportunity to farm with a group of folks north of the city in Dutchess County, New York. He describes his first farming experience as "a farming *Real World*—it was like seven adults, one barn, sixty acres."

I didn't know what I was getting myself into. If this could be a livelihood, if this could be a viable business. I didn't know what it could be or what it entails. I needed to learn some more about it. I interned on a number of farms just to try and get some experience and see what each aspect is like—crop planting, looking at a business and some of the stuff you have to go through to do that, and making sure that this is something I wanted to do and something I was capable of doing. Through farming in Wassaic I was able to get hands-on experience and say, "All right, I think I'm ready to do this now." We lived there for a while and farmed communally for about a year, and then my partner, Nandi, got the call to work here at Cornell, which is like the mecca of agriculture. We decided to make the jump. We were like, "We're going to get it started as soon as we hit the ground in Tompkins County."

However, making the jump to farming in Tompkins County proved to be a struggle. When they first moved to Ithaca, Rafa and his partner had no support. They looked at about sixteen different properties and places around the area before landing in Freeville. This process took about three years, and because of Rafa's background in urban farming communities, it was difficult to navigate the local socio-agricultural landscape. "There has been a big back-to-land movement up here, and a lot of rural communities don't take folks from urban communities very seriously when it comes to farming," Rafa explains. "And there's so many hurdles to jump over, and it's even more difficult to navigate when you don't know the nuance of it in this particular community. Having that separate identity from what they're used to and doing something completely different. Folks sometimes don't know how to help you, and other times they don't want to help you because they don't want to see something like that grow."

For example, when describing to other small-to-medium-scale farmers in the area his vision for the types of programs he was interested in developing through his farm, they would say things like, "Oh, that's cute. You all want to farm. That's not what a farm looks like. A farm looks like this." But they misunderstood. "What this was for them was not what I was trying to do," Rafa says.

> I looked completely different. They treated me like an alien. I didn't have the same experiences that they had. I didn't have the same history, I didn't have the same background, and I definitely didn't have the same identity. They were like, who are these people, and why are they trying to do this here? . . . They had never seen an Afro-Caribbean person before. There was just no point of reference for them. They were just like, "Are you Black? What language do you speak? You want to do what? You want to grow goats?" It was just too much of a culture shock for many people. They would either be really curious and ask a whole bunch of questions or just be, like, *I want to stay away from this. I don't want to have nothing to do with it.*

Statements like "That's not what a farm looks like" and Rafa's feeling of being treated like an "alien" illustrate the "universalism" and "colorblindness" (Guthman) of the local food movement and traditional farmers. Conversations around these concepts draw attention to tensions around farming and race in local food systems. The farmers of the area assumed that Rafa had no prior knowledge of farming because he was black and wanted to farm a different way. As a result, Rafa needed to be "shown" what a farm looks like. Essentially, these farmers assumed that knowledge about farming was universal and that Rafa didn't know how to farm because of his approach to farming.

Ultimately, what Rafa was trying to do with his farm was empower those marginalized by local food experiences, through community education, while also creating a space for those marginalized to learn from each other and produce food to meet their needs. However, this way of farming counters the "Ithaca way" of farming. Rafa wanted a space that would allow those marginalized to take control of their situation and create their own food system. In a sense, Rafa was trying to build what the late Brazilian educator Paulo Freire called "conscientização" or critical consciousness, which "represents the *development* of the awakening of critical awareness" (Freire, 15).

For Freire, the food system would be an "unfinished" project plagued by the production of hunger, racism, and classism; and food justice would be used as education to radically liberate those marginalized from food system dominance at the nexus of culture, problematization, and critical consciousness (Freire, 10). We see this playing out in Rafa's desire for the farm to provide a space for low-income people and people of color to develop a critical awareness about the current food system and to imagine or create their own local food system. As Rafa stated about the other farmers, "What this was for them was not what I was trying to do." What he was trying to do was farm in a *radical* way, and because Rafa wanted to farm this way he had a harder time developing his farm in an area dominated by the mainstream local food movement. Thus, he had to prove himself and build trust, not based on his skills as a farmer but because he looked and wanted to farm differently than those in the area. "Our farm looks a lot different from other farms in the region," Rafa explains.

> We put people and education first. That's not to say that the farm isn't financially sustainable, because that's an important part of it. Most of the agricultural picture out here is driven by that—profitability, economies of scale, commodification of crops, and all kinds of things. We use education and really make sure people have access, putting that first and using that as a center and then working out from there. I see the farm as the perfect place for learning. There are so many other ways that you can use a farm. It shouldn't be just about growing food, it should be a place to address some barriers to food access and also be used as a place of education.

Rafa's focus on people and education first is aligned with food justice and against barriers to food access. By addressing these barriers and building a critical consciousness among those with the least access to food in Ithaca, the farm is engaging in food justice activism to build "community sovereignty" among those most left out of Ithaca's local food scene.

Food Justice as Community Sovereignty

Community sovereignty uses culture as a form of resistance to the oppressive characteristics of the US food system, situated in the "historical-cultural" dimension of communities of color (Freire, 110). This sovereignty allows communities to imagine and create their own local food systems through food-provisioning strategies like farmers' markets and community-supported agriculture (CSA) partnerships. These strategies are similar to market strategies of the local food movement. However, they are reimagined to benefit those left out of the local food movement or marginalized by issues of access at the intersection of agriculture, food, race, and class. This process of reimagining market strategies sheds light on how these strategies can be more inclusive and provides a more holistic picture of food systems. At the core of this process is understanding how Rafa defines food justice. When asked to define it, he responds:

> Food justice for me is looking at the whole picture of food. The food system, the labor that goes into it, the ethical and humane treatment of animals, life, and employees are part of that picture, and really justice, fairness, not equality. We're not all the same. Everybody needs something a little different but in the principle of justice and fairness, making sure that people get what they need. It's important to understand this and the power relationship that exists between these different places. Employer/employee, consumer/producer, and trying to right or direct that in a way that is fair and just. That's what food justice is to me. I think for me especially it's important to situate that within the spectrum of what food is or the way that we talk about it. That's what food justice is to me. I think for me especially it's important to situate that within the spectrum of what food is or the way that we talk about it. Food security, food justice, food sovereignty. Again, for the do-for-self people, if they're able to have their own tools and have everything that they need, they can make their own decisions for themselves without other interventions. That's more of the food sovereignty piece.

For Rafa, food justice also includes an understanding of food sovereignty, illustrated locally through the farm's food justice efforts that move beyond food toward community sovereignty. It also explicitly includes a need to understand power dynamics in social relations around food. Rafa says, "I feel like people should have access and ownership of their food system, what they're able to create, and what they don't want. To say 'I don't like that, I don't want that at all.'" This idea of people having ownership of their own food system shows Rafa's desire for people to define food access on their own terms and reminds me of McMichael and Morarji's notion of *emancipation* that "is not simply about access to resources, but also about the terms of access" (McMichael and Morarji, 240).

Food Justice as Food Provisioning Strategies

The *terms* of access are considered in the food justice movement discourse on food provisioning strategies and can be observed in Rafa's Harvest Box model. This model embodies the emancipatory character of the food justice movement and derives from what Rafa calls a "food justice ethos." The

Harvest Box model is "not quite a CSA," but it reimagines the local food movement's community-supported agriculture (CSA) model and makes it work for Ithaca's communities of color and low-income communities. The Harvest Box idea came about from conversations between Rafa and a farmer in New York City who was doing a similar program for communities there. Patrons of the Harvest Box pay twelve dollars a week for five to eight pounds of food, and they don't have to pay up front. "We want everyone to be able to pick the food that's appropriate for them," Rafa says.

> Some people, in part of their share, don't even get a whole bunch of vegetables, they just want herbs. They want herbs that they are familiar with, that they can cook with, that taste like home. [One] person's [whole] bag will be full of cilantro, basil, thyme, sage, and all these herbs that they can cook with, because that's what important to them, and they have the choice to do that, as opposed to being given an alien vegetable that they've never cooked with before. The main complaint was kohlrabi. They're like, "I don't even know how to pronounce that, I've never eaten that in my life, but it's in my CSA share week after week. Why is that there? I don't want that. I never cooked with that in my life." This model is about meeting people . . . where they're at, giving them control over something that they should have control over—their food system.

Specifically, in this model, Rafa grows some staple foods, but he also goes "exclusively" to marginalized people and asks patrons of the Harvest Box "what they want to eat," what they would like for him to grow, "so they get exactly what they want every week."

> One of our main sites is the Titus Tower senior housing facility in Ithaca. They have some physical access problems [in] getting into the farmers' markets here. You just can't take a walker over gravel. The market does not cater to the elderly. It's very fast-paced, it's like a rock concert in there. People are bumping up against you. People don't really want to do their grocery shopping there. At the south side it looks different because the Ithaca farmers' market is majority-white. There are some cultural barriers when a black consumer or people of color might come to try and buy something there. There's food that's not culturally appropriate for them, not stuff that they grew up eating. They're looking for stuff that is part of their culture.

Rafa's ability to provide what people want every week is extremely radical, however, it also made me wonder: How is he able to make this work? Are there any challenges to this model? During an interview, I inquired about this, and he responded, "[It's about] trying that and making sure that that works. Then figuring out and coming back and reassessing and tweaking things so they work better for both the consumer and you. I come at this from a place saying, 'Okay, I'm secure, and then managing my risk to engage in those activities and seeing that they work before we even put a seed in the ground or put any infrastructure up." He also says:

> It's a conflict [because] your traditional or conventional logic is say-
> ing, "As a farm you need to produce this, and you want to capture the
> highest price for that, that is the most beneficial to you as a farmer"—
> all else be damned. This is just throwing that on its head and saying,
> well, we need the community to eat better. We need the community to
> participate in their food system, all else be damned, and then looking
> at it from [a] model and still trying to tweak your numbers and make
> sure that you can provide that. You're not meeting [it] 100 percent, but
> that's the center that you work from. All the enterprises are able to be
> sustainable financially. I'm able to meet all the feed costs. I'm not pay-
> ing myself what I should be getting . . . as a farmer, but we're building
> up to that. There's growth there, and it's a long-term plan. Instead of
> investing so heavily in my business, I'm investing more in the commu-
> nity, and that's going to really uphold the business and the stuff that
> we're doing here.

For Rafa, the key is not meeting "100 percent" but engaging in an ongoing battle to gain food justice for all people.

Conclusion

One year before the Ithaca Farm-to-Plate Conference, the Tompkins County Food Policy Council held its inaugural meeting in downtown Ithaca. As inaugural members, Rafa and I were there, excited, and had met beforehand to talk about the work we were interested in doing on the coun-cil. During the meeting, we were asked to introduce ourselves and tell why we had been interested in joining. When it came time for Rafa to introduce himself, he stood up and said, "My name is Rafael Aponte, and I am a local farmer. I raise goats . . . and my journey to farming in Ithaca was from the projects to the pasture . . . and that is at the center of my work." At that very moment, Rafa made it very clear that he was coming to this "food work" from a very different place than most people in the room and across Ithaca's local farming and food scene. For Rafa, food policy was about how food is produced but also who food is distributed to and produced by in Tompkins County. While the Millbrook projects of the South Bronx are far from Rafa's farm, his experience there shaped his approach to farming. He understood there that food work is not just about providing food but also about providing empowerment and education for those with inadequate access to food.

This chapter has sought to explore how traditional localism looks in a place characterized by contemporary localism by examining how food justice is navigated in non-urban local food spaces. It has shown that the work of food justice is not only about exercising one's right to healthy foods or creating additional food access points but also about empowering communities to take control of their own food systems. This type of work, which contributes to the dismantling of unjust relations between race, class, agriculture, and food, will take many years to complete. Rafa's story and the case of the Rocky Acres Community Farm show that traditional localism in a place characterized by contemporary localism must go beyond the ideology of affordable food and engage in the power dynamics that influence the production, distribution, and consumption of food.

Note

1. County Health Rankings and Roadmaps, http://www.countyhealthran kings.org/.

Works Cited

Alkon, A. H. 2012. *Black, White, and Green: Farmers Markets, Race, and the Green Economy*. Geographies of Justice and Social Transformation 13. Athens: University of Georgia Press.

Alkon, A. H., and J. Agyeman. 2011. *Cultivating Food Justice: Race, Class, and Sustainability*. Cambridge: MIT Press.

Alkon, A. H., and K. M. Norgaard. 2009. "Breaking the Food Chains: An Investigation of Food Justice Activism." *Sociological Inquiry* 79, no. 3: 289–305.

Freire, P. 2005. *Education for Critical Consciousness*. 30th anniversary ed. New York: Continuum.

Green, J. J., E. Green, E., and A. M. Kleiner. 2011. "From the Past to the Present: Agricultural Development and Black Farmers in the American South." In Alkon and Agyeman, *Cultivating Food Justice: Race, Class, and Sustainability*, 45–64.

Guthman, J. 2011. "If They Only Knew: The Unbearable Whiteness of Alternative Food." In Alkon and Agyeman, *Cultivating Food Justice: Race, Class and Sustainability*, 263–81.

Hislop, R. 2014. "Reaping Equity: A Survey of Food Justice Organizations in the U.S.A." Master's thesis, Department of Plant Sciences, University of California, Davis.

McClintock, N. 2011. "From Industrial Garden to Food Desert: Demarcated Devaluation in the Flatlands of Oakland, California." In Alkon and Agyeman, *Cultivating Food Justice: Race, Class and Sustainability*, 89–120.

McEntee, J. C. 2010. "Contemporary and Traditional Localism: A Conceptualisation of Rural Local Food." *Local Environment* 15, nos. 9–10: 785–803.

McEntee, J. C. 2011. "Realizing Rural Food Justice." In Alkon and Agyeman, *Cultivating Food Justice: Race, Class and Sustainability*, 45–64.

McMichael, P., and K. Morarji. 2010. "Development and its Discontents." In *Contesting Development: Critical Struggles for Social Change*, edited by P. McMichael. New York: Routledge, 233–42.

Norgaard, K. M., R. Reed, and C. Van Horn. 2011. "A Continuing Legacy: Institutional Racism, Hunger, and Nutritional Justice on the Klamath." In Alkon and Agyeman, *Cultivating Food Justice: Race, Class and Sustainability*, 23–46.

Stein, J. 2014. "Hunger in Ithaca: Understand the 'New Normal' Facing the Southern Tier Food Bank." *Ithaca Voice*. https://ithacavoice.com/2014/09/hunger-ithaca-understand-new-normal-facing-southern-tier-food-bank.

US Census Bureau. 2016. *American Community Survey*. Washington, DC: US Census Bureau. https://www.census.gov/acs/www/data/data-tables-and-tools/data-profiles/2016.

White, M. M. 2011. "Environmental Reviews and Case Studies: D-Town Farm: African American Resistance to Food Insecurity and the Transformation of Detroit." *Environmental Practice* 13, no. 4: 406–17.

Chapter 13

"I Heard You Help People"

Grassroots Advocacy for Latina/os in Need

Debra A. Castillo and Carolina Osorio Gil

Debra A. Castillo and Carolina Osorio Gil have been working together since 1999, when Carolina was a psychology undergraduate at Cornell and began collaborating with the theater troupe Teatrotaller (which Debra advises). Carolina escaped Ithaca for a couple of years to do a graduate degree in early childhood education at Columbia University; when she returned, together and separately she and Debra worked on numerous after-school and summer theater and arts programs for area children. This work became the nucleus for CULTURA, the arts and advocacy project they discuss in this chapter.

Other collaborations include the international, multimedia, scientific, and performance art installation on our relationship to water, Aguakinesis, and a collaboration with the Chiapas-based Mexican NGO Cántaro Azul on leadership development for women in rural communities working on water-related issues.

Debra is a comparative literature professor, director of the Latina/o Studies Program at Cornell, advisor to students and organizations, and the author of numerous academic studies. Like many of the other contributors to this book—a coincidence we only realized months into our discussions—she is a first-generation college student. Carolina is an immigrant from Colombia, who arrived in the United States as a young child. After spending a decade as a community leader, co-owner of a small catering business called BiciCocina, and administrator at a small robot company startup, she is now a PhD student at Cornell's Department of Development Sociology where she studies transnational indigenous alliances across the Americas.

Early in spring 2016, a Salvadoran woman in her mid-sixties walked into the CULTURA office, a cubicle in the Tompkins County Workers' Center, on the second floor of Autumn Leaves Used Books on the Ithaca Commons. Carolina smiled because she had been expecting her.[1] Several months earlier, at the end of 2015, the woman's husband, Ernesto, had stopped in and said that she would come to get help filling out the paperwork to get her permanent residency, after over thirty years of living in the United States.[2] However, that day Francisca was there for a more urgent matter. Her Medicare had expired, and she was trying to figure out what to do about a medical bill that she had received for $200. She was very concerned about what might happen if she didn't pay on time. Carolina made a phone call to the medical center to see if they could give her some time on the bill while she sorted out her Medicare, and they were very understanding. She then called the county's Department of Social Services to make sure Francisca could make an appointment to renew her Medicare.

When Ernesto had come to the office at the end of the previous year, he needed help enrolling in low-cost health insurance through the Affordable Care Act (ObamaCare) and the New York State Department of Health. He didn't think he would qualify for anything affordable, and he was worried because he needed to go in for gallbladder tests because he was prediabetic and had already received a $350 bill for a preliminary radiograph he'd had done. He had gotten Carolina's phone number from the poster for a Spanish-language ACA informational session that CULTURA had organized in collaboration with the Ithaca Health Alliance, Tompkins County Human Services Coalition, and the state health department. Knowing that our main target audience, low-income and potentially undocumented Latinas and Latinos, would likely be unable to attend the workshop, she and her collaborators put together all of the information that someone would need to get help enrolling in affordable health insurance, and they were glad to see that their plan had apparently worked.

Carolina called one of the local "health navigators" who had helped organize the event, and, since Ernesto didn't speak English and she was translating, the navigator didn't even require him to come in. She signed him up over the phone for health insurance that would cost him twenty dollars per month. Ernesto had been fined on his taxes the past preceding years for not being covered, and he was extremely grateful to finally have the information to get it taken care of.

This isn't the story of two social service workers who finally found their non-English speaking clientele, satisfied that they can now do their work. It's a story about unintended consequences and bumbling through challenges with *rascuachi* solutions. It's about how the idea of collaborating with the local community to celebrate Latina/o culture ballooned and took us to unexpected places and taught us something unexpected.

While CULTURA was founded in 2008 as an arts and educational project, we (the cofounders) have been doing programming in the community since the 1990s. People started coming to the CULTURA office more regularly for individual advocacy and help around 2013. That summer, two young women showed up at the CULTURA office, having been referred by our longtime collaborator Ana Ortiz, the director of a small youth program called No Más Lágrimas / No More Tears. Although these two women in the CULTURA office that day had never met, they both found themselves in eerily similar situations. Both had run to Ithaca to escape domestic violence. The first, Yazmin, was a seventeen-year-old Dominican-heritage girl, born in the United States and raised in the Bronx. She had run away from home and claimed that her parents had been abusing her and that she had often been kept locked in her apartment. Leticia was significantly older, in her thirties, and she was escaping an abusive husband. She had lived most of her life in her native Puerto Rico but had moved to upstate New York with her husband, where she had found herself in an increasingly dangerous cycle of abuse. Leticia had already been to a local women's shelter, where she'd been turned away, and both women were on a waiting list at the homeless shelter.

When Carolina and Ana heard their stories of rejection from the women's shelter, they were surprised and angry. After an entire day negotiating with the Department of Social Services, one of the advocates at the women's shelter, and representatives from several other women's shelters in the region, Carolina had gotten nowhere, and she and Ana agreed to put up the women that night in their homes. Finally, the representative of the local shelter scheduled an appointment for Yazmin and Leticia (and Ana and Carolina) for the next morning. The next day, the director of the shelter greeted the group with coffee and cookies. Yazmin looked to Carolina in disbelief and whispered in her ear, "They didn't treat me nice like this when I was here. You must be special."

Between Yazmin and Leticia's visit and that of Ernesto and Francisca, Carolina has supported dozens of individuals in a similar way. In almost every case, they are referred through word of mouth. She typically answers the phone, and a person speaks to her in Spanish: "Ms. Carolina. I need help, and I heard you help people."

While both of these women happened to be US citizens, their backgrounds associate them with the most vulnerable and disadvantaged groups among Latinas/os in Ithaca and Tompkins County, the undocumented workers who perform the majority of the work in farms outside Ithaca and a good deal of service work in Ithaca. These workers reflect a national and global concern— international migration. Carlos Gutiérrez, a local workers' rights advocate and occupational safety and health trainer at the Tompkins County Workers' Center, says of his efforts with undocumented workers: "Part of my mission [is] to really educate that person so the person at some point, when they feel empowered, also feels safe that they are going to do an action that is protected [reporting poor working conditions to OSHA]" (personal interview). According to Gutiérrez, "Dairy farm workers and agricultural workers are the most vulnerable workers in the United States." He says there are two ways of tackling the problem of unjust treatment of undocumented workers: "One is organizing people on the ground, educating them and organizing them. And the other part also is to pressure basically the government and politicians to change the laws."

These two options are reminiscent of civil rights movement, when organizers worked on direct action and education projects but also voter registration. Our own freedom struggle today poses somewhat different challenges, though. In the view of Gutiérrez, "The workers are so vulnerable and fearful that it's difficult to educate them. You can train them and so on but to take them to the level from empowerment to action is very difficult." Gutiérrez presents a predicament. We would like to think that, as Paulo Freire says, "the important thing is to help [people] help themselves, to place them in consciously critical confrontation with their problems, to make them the agents of their own recuperation" (Freire, 13). What Gutiérrez reminds us is that this is not always possible. The systematic oppression of migrant workers who work under abusive conditions seemingly voluntarily is a daunting challenge to face.

Undocumented individuals are not the only ones marginalized and abused by "the system." According to journalist David Bacon: "Maintaining [the] distinction between legal and illegal status has become a code for preserving inequality, a tiered system dividing people into those with rights and those without. . . . Once established, growing inequality eventually affects all immigrants, including legal or permanent residents. . . . The effects of inequality spread beyond immigrants to citizens as well, especially in a society that has historically defined unequal status by skin color and sex" (Bacon, 250). Bacon's assertion demonstrates a need—indeed an urgency—for documented immigrants and US-born Latinas/os to support our undocumented counterparts, if only out of self-interest. The way that undocumented immigrants are treated reflects on the treatment of immigrants and Latina/os in general. One needs to look no further than the hateful rhetoric of US president Donald Trump to see how xenophobic views of undocumented individuals ("illegals," "rapists," and "criminals") can extend to entire groups of "legal" Latina/os (among other racial and ethnic groups). Indeed, the four individuals whose stories began this chapter are all in this country legally, yet the sort of experiences they had with systems of health, safety, and shelter in Ithaca were deplorable, and their initial fear and hopelessness seem incongruous with people who are residents and citizens. They, like many other people of color, are treated as foreigners in their own country.

Yazmin and Leticia were not admitted to the women's shelter, even after all the efforts made on their behalf, and they ended up spending a few nights in the homeless shelter. But those days spent with these vulnerable, desperate women and with people like Francisca and Ernesto highlighted crucial issues. First of all, this clearly pointed out some of the very tangible ways that we were (and are) treated differently based on our education, command of the English language, perceived ethnicity, and imagined legal and socioeconomic status, even in a small, presumably progressive town. And this led us to see some of the systematic changes that needed to occur in Ithaca, including appropriate translation and interpreting services and cultural competency training for all nonprofits and human service providers in the area. In this sense, Ithaca—which likes to think of itself as a liberal bubble in the midst of a sea of "deplorables" (to use Hilary Clinton's unfortunate term from her presidential campaign)—is no different than many other rural towns and shares some of the same infrastructure problems. This broader context is our real challenge, since it is from rural America that Donald Trump disproportionately and unexpectedly drew his support. Liberal USA was (and remains) puzzled, and the rural contexts in our country continue to be understudied.

Experiences like these inspired us to extend the mandate we originally set for CULTURA Ithaca from celebrations of Latina/o arts and culture to also designing events and programs around issues like financial education, food security, and health care. We also realized that CULTURA—as one of the few readily identifiable Spanish-speaking, Latina/o-serving community organizations—needed to do more one-on-one advocacy work, along with developing a greater awareness of these issues in our community. Thus, we intensified our collaborations with students from Cornell University and Ithaca College, and Carolina intentionally sought out and forged strong relationships with service providers interested in improving their relationships with Latina/o constituents, such as the Ithaca Health Alliance, the Tompkins County Health Department, and the Tompkins County Human Services Coalition.

Some History of Ithaca Latina/os

In his 2009 Cornell PhD dissertation, Sean Eversley Bradwell discusses the importance of maintaining a comprehensive record of the history of African

Americans in a transient college town like Ithaca: "According to [Blake] Gumprecht (2003), the seasonal, almost natural ebb and flow of college towns keeps them youthful, unconventional, and cosmopolitan. What Gumprecht does not mention is that this transience—the frequent flow of people into and out of a community—easily disrupts the collective/community memory" (Bradwell, 206). Bradwell is speaking here about the racial rallies and protests that occurred in the fall of 2007 around issues of race, but the same disruption of collective and community memory contributes to the lack of organizing around Latina/o issues too. Thus, one of our challenges is that, in order to help new community members understand their community's history and continuing networks of activism, they need constant reminders of the legacy of the town-gown collaboration. As examples we point to Ithaca's participation in the Underground Railroad in the 1850s, collaborative organizing around African American issues in the 1969 Willard Straight Hall takeover, the participation of Ithaca in the 1980s sanctuary movement to protect Central American refugees, and the 1993 student occupation of Day Hall to protest the vandalism of a site-specific Latino art.[3]

Ithaca, like much of the rest of the rural United States, is largely white. According to 2015 census information, the city's population of 30,788 was 70 percent white, 17.6 percent foreign-born, 16.2 percent Asian, 6.9 percent Latina/o, 6.6 percent African American, and 4.3 percent two or more races.[4] When the census information is broken down, about 20 percent of the Latinas/os are of Mexican background, 25 percent are Puerto Rican, and the rest are listed as "other," which we know anecdotally includes substantial numbers of people of Chilean, Cuban, and Peruvian origin, as well as a smattering of folks from practically every Latin American country. More than 22 percent of Ithacans speak a language other than English at home, and while 64.3 percent of Ithacans have earned a bachelor's degree or higher, 45.5 percent are formally "persons in poverty," and 5.5 percent have no health insurance. These last few numbers point to a troubling divide.

In 1997, Parents of African Latino/a Students (PALS) addressed the new principal of Ithaca High School: "At this time, Ithaca High School is 9.4% African American, and 1.6% Hispanic. Only 2% of all African American and Hispanic students are in AP or Honors classes. Conversely, we are 23.6% of the Special Ed department. How can we turn this around? What can you or are you planning to do different to ensure the success and high academic achievement of our students?" (Bradwell, 223). In 2006, the Village at Ithaca and Ithaca City School District publishing an annual Equity Report Card. Since then, according to Bradwell, "The equity report card has become the baseline measurement of equity work" more generally in our area (247).

At this writing, the most current information on Latina/o students in the Ithaca City School District is available from the tenth Equity Report Card, published in 2017. The report counts 655 students of Asian descent in our K–12 system (12.1 percent), 470 African Americans (8.7 percent), 316 Latinas/os (5.8 percent), 440 non-Latina/o mixed-race students (8.1 percent), and 3,522 whites (65 percent). In this report, the district is happy to point out the excellence of our school system, including its high graduation rate and high level of participation in AP classes, arts, and athletics, and less happy to recall the class differences that make for stark divides between more privileged and less economically advantaged families.[5] These class differences are signaled in the rough listing of FRPL (eligible for free or reduced price lunch) and non-FRPL students. According to this division, while whites and Latinas/os have approximately the same percentage enrollment in special education courses among the economically challenged group (17.2 percent of Latinas and 25.8 percent of Latinos; 15.7 percent of white girls and 24.5 percent of white boys), 92.9 percent overall of the more economically privileged students graduate successfully, as contrasted with an 87 percent rate for students in the less privileged economic situation. If we compare the Latina/o rates with those of white students, 93.7 percent of the more privileged white kids graduate in four years, compared to 80 percent of Latinas/os in the same category.

These figures have fluctuated in the ten years the report card has been published, but the numbers remain very worrisome. Latina and Latino students overall are improving slowly and show steady improvement in such markers as at-grade reading (78.8 percent for non-FRPL Latinos/as and 58.1 for FRPL Latinos/as, up from 78.7 percent and 41 percent two years earlier), but they still lag behind whites in the same categories (86.6 percent and 59.8 percent). Latinas/os have more chronic absences, are less likely to participate in co-curricular arts and sports activities, and are less likely to enroll in AP and honors courses than their white classmates. Despite twenty years of efforts, students of color from less economically privileged backgrounds (except for Asian students, who are categorized on their own due to their significantly different achievement patterns) are systematically disadvantaged in our school system, a concern that continues to be part of many Latina/o families' daily lives.

When we turn to the tertiary education institutions that have such an enormous effect on the local community (keeping it "youthful, unconventional, and cosmopolitan") and double the city's population during the academic year, there are approximately 1,630 Latina/o undergraduate students at Cornell—about 11.4 percent of the student body—and about 500 Latina/o

Ithaca College students, 7.5 percent of the student body (Forbes), few of them from local backgrounds.[6] In 2014, at a "Latinos at Cornell" panel, community members reflected on Latino demographics at Cornell: "Cornell's incoming Latino student population has grown in recent years, from 10.1% of the Class of 2014 to 12.7% of the Class of 2018. While they have had an official home on campus for 20 years, students, faculty, and administrators in the Latina/o community say progress can still be made." At that same meeting, Sofia Villenas, Latina/o Studies Program director at the time, said: "Latinos may be 12% of the population, but our Latino faculty is still about 3.3%" (Aloi). Villenas's comment reminds us that in our tertiary institutions not only is the population skewed young and highly transient, there is also a dearth of permanently resident adults to serve as teachers, mentors, and community elders.

When asked by a student at the "Latinos at Cornell" panel how students could contribute to the university, Law School dean (and Cornell alum) Eduardo Peñalver deflected the question and suggested contributing to the larger community by joining the Cornell Farmworker Program. He said, "You're empowered here . . . but you're also empowered as citizens. . . . There are Latinos all around us in Upstate New York—they're not visible, they're isolated, and they need your support" (Aloi). Thus, he reminds us that the "Ithaca bubble" is surrounded by rural areas with a mostly Mexican and Guatemalan farmworker population of fifty thousand to seventy thousand (Cornell Farmworker Program), whose needs are not met because they live in isolation on farms.

Peñalver reminds us that while Ithaca is a college town, its colleges, however influential, are not all there is to the community or the surrounding rural upstate communities. Likewise, in a 2005 interview, professor Hector Vélez, who has taught at Ithaca College and currently teaches a highly popular Latina/o sociology course at Cornell, pointed to the importance of his involvement in the larger surrounding community when he stated: "One of the things I am most proud of is that I am one of the founders of the Latino Civic Association of Tompkins County, which serves as a vehicle for the social, cultural, educational, and civic expression of the Latino community of the county" (Berry). Sadly, although the history of Latinas/os at Cornell has been at least modestly documented in Héctor Vélez's annual reports on their status, such is not the case with the general and much longer history of Latinas/os in the city of Ithaca.[7] This undertaking, tracing and documenting the history of Latinas/os in Ithaca and Tompkins County, is now a collaborative endeavor that CULTURA began to explore with Rod Howe, director of the History Center in Tompkins County, as well as through collaboration with historian and Cornell professor María Cristina García. As we worked to get at this history through multiple lenses, we also developed an oral history art show under the mentorship of La Casita in Syracuse in the fall of 2017, called *Balcón criollo* (after the La Casita program's successful lead and with artist Pepón Osorio's inspiration).

In addition, to get a better grasp of the most pressing contemporary concerns for the community, CULTURA developed a survey of Latinas/os in Tompkins County that measures individuals' experiences with various social services, including transportation, education, health care, and employment. Called "El Pueblo" ("The Village" or "The People"), the survey also asks participants about challenges they have faced and about resources they most use. The goal of the survey, which has been distributed at numerous events and is available online, is to assess the needs that Latinas/os in the county have, where there are gaps, and how local service providers with Latina/o clients can improve to better meet their needs.

What We Know, and Some Big Questions

Donald Trump's 2016 election as president, after running an exceptionally divisive, anti-immigrant campaign that spoke largely to validating the fears of whites in smaller communities and rural residents of the US heartland, reminds us that we need to take a closer look at the changing demographics of our country and how small cities and rural areas have been impacted. If the terms of the so-called immigration debate have helped bring many Latinas/os together in an incipient social movement, they have also had the perhaps unintended consequence of heightening violence and discrimination in many rural communities. As many of us have been telling ourselves in the wake of November 2016, Trump's election has served as a wake-up call. Among scholars and activists, we realize that we know very little about these rural locations where his support is concentrated, since they have seldom been significant sites of research.

What we do know following the election is that there is no "sleeping giant" (the term obsessively used in the press to characterize a presumed Latina/o voting block). Indeed, as Cristina Beltrán reminds us, this contentious assumption only obscures the agency of a diverse body of subjects (Beltrán, 9) while making them responsible for larger electoral failures. At the same time, we also know that there has been a tremendous growth of Latina/o populations in nonmetro areas during the new millennium, giving context, if never justification, to the background story about heartland white voter unrest about the new diversity in their midst. Currently, emerging locations for immigrant settlement outpace traditional locations of arrival by a factor of 2.6 (Hall and Stringfield, 6). Cromartie adds: "While the overall nonmetro population grew 4.5 percent in the 2000s, the nonmetro Hispanic population increased 45 percent" (Cromartie).

One effect of Latina/o populations on new destinations is, paradoxically, that traditional white and African American communities become less segregated, while Latina/os are highly segregated (Hall and Stringfield, 2). It has long been known that whites are reluctant to share neighborhoods with even modest-sized populations of people of color. What these new demographics tell us is that, when Latinas/os arrive, whites become somewhat more willing to share space with African Americans but work very hard to keep Latinas/os out of their neighborhoods (Hall and Stringfield, 4).

Yet "Latino" itself is often an insufficient category of analysis, as Beltrán, among others, reminds us. Other scholars have argued that "researchers relying on a homogenous pan-ethnic construct have ignored, for the most part, the differences that exist within the Latino category. These differences include, but, of course, are not limited to identity, culture, language, and citizenship status" (Sandoval and Ruiz 295). Studies of traditional Latina/o populations in larger metro areas demonstrate that, when given a choice, Latinas/os prefer to live in concentrations of other people of their heritage background, such that "as the proportion of Latinos increased in the neighborhood, Latino neighborhood diversity declined." This trend can be reversed; the researchers also learned that diversity increased when the community experienced a confluence of positive economic indicators (Sandoval and Ruiz, 308). In this sense, one of our greatest challenges is that studies show there is only mixed support for any kind of a pan-Latina/o consciousness or group solidarity of the type we hope to achieve in Ithaca, especially among people in the more vulnerable economic categories.

Research has shown that rural Latinas/os in these emerging destinations are a younger, disproportionately male population, that they "have relatively low education levels, weak English proficiency, and undocumented status," and that "this recent settlement has increased the visibility of Hispanics in many new regions of rural America whose population has long been dominated by non-Hispanic Whites" (Kandel and Cromartie 1). These scholars also confirm Hall and Stringfield's findings: "within smaller geographic areas, the level of residential separation between them increased" (Hall and Stringfield, 1). Put together, these studies draw a picture of a highly segregated rural environment, where, at the same time, pan-ethnic Latina diversity can be very high, given small numbers. While as a rural college town, Ithaca has its own peculiarities, this combination of segregation and diversity is more or less the case, as our preliminary El Pueblo survey findings are helping us to understand.[8]

Challenges come to us from the most basic levels. From our El Pueblo study, as well as anecdotal evidence gleaned from many conversations with community members over the years, we know that there are food deserts even in our small town and food insecurity in the countryside, among the very people who produce our food. We know from stories like those that started this chapter that there are service gaps in this small liberal town that prides itself on the excellence of its public services. We know that many Latinas/os feel isolated and that their cultures are disrespected or ignored. We know that many progressive "allies" find it hard to see the micro-inequities they practice daily.

The handful of published studies on rural communities reminds us that research questions are often framed by unconscious assumptions about diversity and space that may not apply to other nonmetro populations and could distract us from important observations. In this sense, as Cristina Beltrán notes, the history of Chicanos in California and Puerto Ricans in New York in the 1960s are often used as a template for all Latina/o heritage groups even today, and most of the research done on Latinas/os focuses on traditional populations in large metropolitan areas like those of New York, Miami, Los Angeles, and Chicago (Beltrán, 11–12). Likewise, in another problematic move, scholars who study social justice organizations have largely extrapolated their research questions from a historical focus on African American organizations, using mostly conventional participation and mostly quantitative analysis tools (Martínez, 575). Large cities like New York City have a long history of heterogeneity, but, conversely, social justice organizations in metro areas are likely to be very homogeneous. Thus, most research done on organizations in urban settings focuses on Latina/o subgroups or national origin groups as the grounding for their work (e.g., Chicano, Dominican, Puerto Rican).

In small cities like Ithaca, Latinas/os are heterogeneous in both national origin background and economic status, but the city itself, with its 70 percent white population, is seen as homogeneous (the reverse of how we imagine an urban setting). Because Ithaca is a college town, we also face the challenge of incorporating into our work a large transient (student) population with little, if any, exposure to the community's historical memory or even a sense of belonging to the community. One of our first tasks for our student collaborators is to walk downtown, and we continue to be amazed by how challenging students find this twenty-minute walk, how fearful they are at the beginning of the semester, and how exhilarated they find their new spatial awareness by the end. This lack of connection to community has serious implications for how we imagine our work or understand it in a larger context. We need to build coalitions among many often disconnected groups, including groups of students, but, as Walker and Stepick remind us, coalitions in general are fragile forms of organization, acceptable to many but exciting to few (Walker and Stepick, 960).

Similarly, social movement research tells us that heterogeneous groups will work together as long as they share a similar structural position (Martínez, 562), but that shared structural position is seldom true in small communities like ours, where class divides are significant between our most vulnerable and most privileged members. How do we frame questions and find practical recommendations related to a partially heterogeneous, rural community where there is very little extant research? How do we understand Latina/o identities in contemporary life in small communities and support our constituencies? How does CULTURA as an organization deal with the special challenges of an intersecting group of communities that are largely defined as transitory and have little continuous sense of its history? How do we balance seeking out and listening respectfully to the voices of the most disadvantaged and vulnerable members of our community while making sure not to alienate our Latina/o middle-class base?

CULTURA, or *Bregando*

Puerto Rican Spanish has a great verb: *bregar*. It combines the senses of *to argue, to struggle, to fight, to chip away at something, to persevere*. Spanish etymological dictionaries tell us it is also used to describe a certain way of kneading bread. Since the work or struggle is never done, *bregamos*, always in the present tense, can be used to describe kneading together community members. The kneading metaphor is helpful in another way. We have noticed that not only do women comprise most of the community organizers we work with most closely, we ourselves also engage in what is often called a "woman-centered style" of community organizing, featuring considerable tending of individual relationships and ties and working collectively and horizontally rather than hierarchically. In their study of organizing practices, Walker and Stepick find that this kind of organizational model tends to be more modest in scale than organizing done in the "male centered style," while creating deeper gains (Walker and Stepick, 965).[9] That is to say, with this intense work we get great, long-lasting results, but they are not very scalable and don't fit well in the kinds of frameworks we are asked to provide for the funders we rely on for our lifeblood.

CULTURA's original mission was to provide free and low-cost arts and educational activities by and about Latina/o and Latin American cultures for the community. Despite the challenges, we have been fortunate in getting both community support and modest funding to sponsor a wide variety of activities in the community (up to sixty-five events and programs per year). We have become highly visible with our Latino/a Heritage Month activities, from September 15 to October 15, which for several years have included a major film festival (primarily hosted at the local independent cinema, with additional events in other theaters) and a well-attended Latina/o art exhibition. Nevertheless, day in, day out, our signature programming is our "series" format, in which we run four to six linked events weekly, generally with guest facilitators for individual dates. In this way, we offer a coherent and visible set of events, while the individual commitment of the guest facilitator is modest—a couple of hours on a single day. This is also clearly an asset-based approach, where we see our collaborators as people with important knowledge to share. Everyone has something to contribute; everyone has social capital, whether or not they have economic capital. We help with the bridging.

These programs are geared for people of different ages: thus, for example, our Cuentacuentos (storytelling) program is aimed at small children and involves guest storytellers and related art activities in the public library. Our Antojitos series brings together guest chefs who cook favorite dishes with the participants, mostly adults and teens. We have also done series like Música (with local musicians), Baile (dance), Arte (handicrafts), and Teatro (plays). Other series include Buen Vivir (with speakers who give tips on living well, Latino-style) and Tu Dinero (financial advice from local experts).

We also sponsor large events that draw two hundred to three hundred people, like our dessert competition FLANdango, our Latina/o Heritage Month kickoff party, our annual art show opening reception, and our Día de Muertos and Cinco de Mayo events. These events are always open to the entire community, and it is heartening to see the diverse mix in the audience, people who appreciate that we are offering a wholesome, positive introduction to Latino cultures.

As our relationships with the community deepened, we realized that we wanted and needed to have more input from local community members about their concerns and needs so as to better guide us in our work. The El Pueblo needs assessment survey has been an important part of this learning curve. It consists of three distinct phases and a combination of qualitative and quantitative methods. During the first phase, Carolina worked in collaboration with three undergraduate students in Ithaca College professor

Elan Shapiro's Topics in Sustainability course. In this phase we employed unstructured story-based interviews with a sample of twelve local Latina/o individuals to identify concerns, aspirations, and goals which could then inform the questions for the survey. During the second phase, we worked with these same students, as well as with a second group of four undergraduates and two graduate students in the Cornell University course Cultures and Communities that Debra and Carolina co-teach, to create relevant questions for the survey. Students investigated good practices for asking survey questions and developing effective platforms for administering the questions and collecting the data.

After creation of the survey, the third and current phase has been distribution of the survey, which thus far has been completed by twenty-three Latina/os in Tompkins County. An additional ninety individuals participated in the El Pueblo game we developed for quick quantitative measurement. Current results of these two instruments demonstrate that areas of most concern for Latinas/os in Tompkins County are employment, education, transportation, and language barriers to accessing resources. Our goal is to administer the survey to 4 percent of the Latina/o population

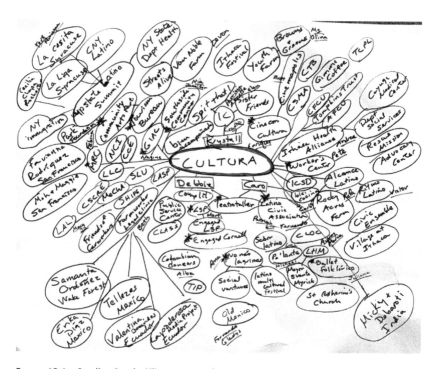

FIGURE 13.1   Carolina Osorio Gil's attempt to draw a network map.

of Tompkins County—two hundred individuals. We have already shared the intermediate results with relevant local service providers, both formally and informally, including a formal report to the Latino Civic Association of Tompkins County.

It was in this context that we knew we needed to expand our programming to more directly address social justice issues, including the kind of work we did in hosting specific events on financial and health care information or developing our "Browns and Greens" event to highlight the efforts of brown people doing green activities and participating in sustainable practices. In general, our work in community organizing has opened up collaborations with numerous local organizations in Ithaca to develop strategies, events, programs, and actions around topics like racial justice and sustainability, food security, entrepreneurship development, indigenous land rights, LGBT+ issues, and dismantling institutional racism.

Carolina also significantly amplified her one-on-one advocacy efforts, and—as noted in the anecdotes in the opening of this paper—has provided support for homeless individuals, victims of domestic violence, undocumented and documented low-wage workers, migrant farmworkers, runaway teens, and families with young children to gain access to much-needed services, including food stamps, emergency housing, health care, health insurance, and financial assistance.

We began in the arts, and the arts and humanities remain central to the kinds of work we do and the programs we develop. Unfortunately, political scientists, sociologists, and movement scholars often overlook the role of the arts, poetry, history, performance, and cultural studies in the broadest sense in community organizing and social justice work. (This is something that scholars like Beltrán and Guarnaccia and other have also underlined; see Beltrán, 10–13, Guarnaccia et al., 3). In our experience, we can confidently say that personal narrative is the most powerful tool for building bridges across diverse participants and creating real, profound collaborations. When people have the opportunity to hear each other's stories, whether through theater, shared cooking, gardening together, decorating an altar, or informal conversations, they are more quickly and more successfully able to work together toward a common goal. Storytelling has become an integral part of our approach to community building and teaching.

CULTURA happened upon this model fortuitously, more through trial and error than studied practice. Yet there are important precedents that can guide us. Early in this discussion we mentioned Brazilian thinker Paulo Freire, whose pedagogy of the oppressed has been enormously influential in movements ranging from liberation theology and Augusto Boal's practices of theater of the oppressed to concrete organizing practices successfully deployed by the world's largest and longest-lived social movement, the Brazilian Landless Workers Movement (or MST, its Portuguese acronym). The MST is a movement of poor people, with limited resources, yet it has over one and a half million members and has inspired organizations throughout Latin America and the world. The organization is flexible, versatile, and innovative, using dynamic, multidimensional networks to achieve its goals of creating opportunities for landless peasants to settle and work underused land. Decision-making in the MST is collective (Carter, 119–20, 400; Tarlau 4, 14). Their motto is "Everyone coordinates and everyone is coordinated" (Tarlau 15). Officially founded in 1984, as of 2012 it had successfully created two thousand settlements, meeting its primary goal. Along the way it also established 161 cooperatives, four credit unions, and eighteen hundred schools, as well as a national university in Brazil (Carter 8–10). The movement's pedagogical practice is directly inherited from Freire (along with core ideas derived from liberation theology, and inspiration from key Brazilian figures such as Zumbi dos Palmares), and MST's educational goal is to help people think critically and act strategically. Thus, their schools teach critical thinking while emphasizing the importance of cultivating organic ties with their base communities.

While much organizational scholarship in the United States stresses that populations need incentives, resources, and leadership to organize successfully (see, e.g., Martínez, 562, for a summary of this position), the MST has historically had very few of these things. Instead, the MST promotes an asset-based methodology grounded in reframing problems and courses of action; it emphasizes collective, not individual, identity, and actively promotes broad participation (Karriem and Benjamin, 29–32). It has been more successful than almost any organization we can think of, including ones that US scholars celebrate.

More important for us, the MST highlights the important role of cultural practice and the arts in all its organizing work. All major actions begin with and are framed by what they call a *mística*, or performance, which MST sees as an essential component of organizing and a way to embody history. Tarlau notes that the mística "can include dance, music, theater, videos, or other cultural expressions that reflect on past and current political struggles." Likewise, in the MST schools, "at the start of every school day, before meetings, and during social events, MST students organize these cultural performances" (Tarlau 19). In our own case, we know that even well-meaning people often find it hard to reach a shared understanding. Bringing cultural and humanistic values back into community organizing, as the MST does—front and center—through their cultural projects, is educational and entertaining; it bridges divides and creates opportunities for networking on other issues.

Conclusion

We are proud of CULTURA's success in helping to creating space for Latinas/os and bringing them together, in providing support and advocacy, in making the general community more aware of Latina/o issues, and giving all of us reasons to celebrate and join in the promotion of the really beautiful and rich variety of Latina/o cultures. But this is not a celebratory essay.

One of the common concerns among those of us working around Latina/o issues in Ithaca and Tompkins County is that a significant portion of our constituency does not feel safe to be engaged in the community, something that came very much to the fore in the spring of 2017, when ICE agents, without informing city authorities, staked out a street corner in Ithaca to detain one of our local residents. The subsequent well-attended protest held on the Ithaca Commons, as well as discussions among many activist groups, reminded us that Ithaca and Tompkins County's "sanctuary" status has limited legal weight when the federal government decides to target us. Since we are a small rural community, one appeal we can make to each other is to watch out for our neighbors in a way that folks in larger cities cannot do. At the same time, precisely because we are a progressive community surrounded by a much more conservative rural environment (the places where many of our most vulnerable community members live and work), the immigration raid was a wake-up call to all of us. In some ways, more densely populated urban areas can also be more protected, and vulnerable members of our population in the metro areas have more places of refuge.

Another challenge is that local organizations are often working insularly because there is no central Latina/o space to meet. For many years, the Latino Civic Association of Tompkins County as well as other individuals locally have talked about wanting a cultural center. That would be a massive organizational and financial undertaking requiring not only time but also resources, which are currently very slim. With the exception of the Cornell Farmworker Program, which has a half-time paid director, all the other local Latina/o organizations depend solely on volunteers and minimal programming funds attained through individual donations along with small city and county grants.

Given the diverse ethnic, racial, and socioeconomic disparities among Latinas/os in Ithaca and Tompkins County, the only way to have any significant presence is to unite across these boundaries and the challenges Latinas/os face individually and organizationally. If we find ways to create unity among

Latinas/os, we will be able to strategically overcome the injustices that the most vulnerable among us face, and we will also have spaces to preserve and celebrate our cultures. That unity will not be possible until the most vulnerable among us are able to come to the table—have enough food to eat, a safe place to live, a living wage, and no fear of the consequences of participating in society. And since those are key goals for the Latino Civic Association, CULTURA, and the Cornell Farmworker Program, among other organizations, one step we can take is for those groups to come together and share strategies and information to help our brothers and sisters most in need.

Another key is to develop leadership among the individuals we serve, while recognizing that working with the diverse Latina/o communities presents special challenges. If we take as our point of departure community organizer Saul Alinsky's much-repeated line, "Never do for others what they can do for themselves" (Rogers), in our case undocumented workers and other vulnerable Latinas/os are limited in their ability and often unable to "do for themselves"—out of fear of losing their jobs, being incarcerated, or deported. However, Carlos Gutiérrez, who works directly with undocumented and documented workers, offers a keen insight into this great challenge: "The workers are so vulnerable and fearful that it's difficult to educate them. You can train them and so on, but to take them to the level from empowerment to action is very difficult. Basically because that's the system. They're working to pay their bills and send money to their families. And they take what they are taking because there's no other way. . . . I cannot pass judgment on that and say, 'These people don't want to organize and do it themselves.' But that's the way it is." These people have very little space to breathe or to claim their rights. For us, as organizers, it is very sobering.

On the other end of the spectrum we have privileged, educated Latinas and Latinos, including professionals, business owners, and educators, and their participation in this process of organizing is also key. In a city whose population doubles when Cornell and Ithaca College are in session, Latina/o faculty, administrators, and students have an interest in supporting the Latina/o communities of this area—at least for nine months of the year. That seasonality and inevitable turnover is both a cause for celebration and part of the problem. CULTURA's collaborations with the Latina/o Studies Program at Cornell and with faculty at Ithaca College's Center for the Study of Culture, Race, and Ethnicity have provided opportunities for dozens of students, most of them Latina/o themselves, who want to work with "the community"—and learn from other Latina/os. Furthermore, these students often come from larger cities and areas of the country where there are much higher and more ethnically homogenous Latina/o populations. They long to feel that sense of community that they had back home and gravitate to our heterogeneous populations, opening themselves to new cultural experiences.[10] So far, our local community members have been very open to working with them, though it is exhausting to constantly have to reorient enthusiastic new collaborators.

Another large challenge we face is that both undocumented and documented migrant workers and university students are transient groups, and added together they are considerably larger numbers than the Latina/o permanent resident population. However, the issues remain the same. We need to involve those transient individuals, but also those of us who remain here need to make sure that we don't lose the cultural and community consciousness. It is only in the slippery negotiations of working with these heterogeneous and shifting populations that we can make real change happen for justice for all Latinas and Latinos in Ithaca and Tompkins County. We hope to create unity despite the many challenges we face.

We have no illusions about our expertise in most of the areas in which we have become advocates. At the same time, we are wary of the posturing and paralyzing false humility of limiting one's action to a narrow field of "expertise." Given the need we see around us, we are unwilling and unable to wait for experts and are instead committed to continuing the work, in whatever way we can, with all our stumbles and uncertainty and messiness, learning in the midst of doing.

Finally, we worry constantly about how we will continue to serve our communities effectively and meet their now higher expectations. When we started CULTURA, we had no money and were, paradoxically, free to do as little or as much as we wanted, whenever we wanted. Now we worry about burnout—our own and that of our allies—and know that our programming is fragile, dependent on our success in raising funding through a series of small grants. Our uncertain edifice could crash at any moment, leaving our collaborators worse than they started, in a sense, since they would then have the bitterness of lost expectations.

Debra is still up the hill at Cornell, teaching and administering the Latina/o Studies Program. After a run for county legislature in 2017, Carolina is now a PhD student at Cornell in the Department of Development Sociology. The work goes on.

Notes

1. The term *Latino* is a 1990s product of the reaction against the earlier agglutinating word *Hispanic*, rejected for its connection with the Iberian peninsula

and even more for its official use on the US Census. Since the 1990s, tussles with Spanish grammar in the service of greater inclusivity have given us *Latina/o, Latin@*, and *Latinx*, but there is no one style universally accepted in the English context. We choose to use *Latina/o* since it is the most familiar general term in our constituency.

2. All names in these stories are presented as first name only (and some details have been changed) to protect the anonymity of the individuals.

3. "In the fall of 1993, students occupied Day Hall for four days in protest of the underrepresentation and underserving of Latinos at Cornell. As a result of the demonstration, the Latino Studies Program (LSP) was expanded and the Latino Living Center (LLC) was created. The protest was sparked by the vandalism of a site-specific installation by artist Daniel J. Martínez entitled 'The Castle is Burning'. . . . Students used the blank walls for self-expression and political messages, but the panels were defaced by messages of 'vandalism expressing class bias and racial hatred,' including 'Cesar Chavez is dead,' 'kill the illegals' and 'white pride.'" Sascha Hernández, "Recalling the '93 Day Hall Takeover by Latino Students," *Cornell Chronicle*, October 30, 2014.

4. Because many Latinas/os do not have formal documentation status, they are understandably reluctant to participate in the census, and in Ithaca—as everywhere in the country—population counts are approximate at best.

5. "Equity," Village at Ithaca, http://www.villageatithaca.org/equity/.

6. Cognate with its goal of serving the local community, Tompkins Cortland Community College has 7 percent Latinas/os among its fifty-five hundred students, a ratio similar to Tompkins County census numbers. Tompkins Cortland Community College, *US News and World Report*, http://www.usnews.com/education/community-colleges/tompkins-cortland-community-college-CC08688.

7. For instance, Ithacan Latina/o history still has nothing approximating the elegant timeline of African American history in Ithaca constructed in the appendix of Bradwell's dissertation.

8. One of these ongoing conflicts is the amount of tax-exempt land held by the two colleges, especially Cornell, in the city, seriously affecting the tax burden in the community. The mayor, Svante Myrick, who has been attempting to get Cornell to pay a larger sum for city services, is himself a 2009 graduate of the university. Kelsey O'Connor and John R. Roby. "Taxed off" (four-part special report on "Town-Gown Conflict"), *Ithaca Journal*, October 2016.

9. One question this finding raises is whether scaling itself might not be a masculinist concept. The exploration of this topic, however, is outside the scope of this chapter.

10. Personal conversations and final reflection papers written by students for the Cultures and Communities course at Cornell, taught by Debra A. Castillo and Carolina Osorio Gil every semester since spring 2014.

Works Cited

Aloi, Daniel. 2014. "Panel Reflects on Latino Experience at Cornell." *Cornell Chronicle*, September 10, 2014.

Bacon, David. 2008. *Illegal People: How Globalization Creates Migration and Criminalizes Immigrants*. Boston: Beacon Press.

Beltrán, Cristina. 2010. *The Trouble with Unity: Latino Politics and the Creation of Identity.* Oxford: Oxford University Press.

Berry, Lorraine. 2005. "Bridging Campuses—and Cultures: An Innovative Sociology Professor Brings a Latin American Perspective to Students on Both Hills." *Ithaca College Quarterly* 2.

Bradwell, Sean Eversley. 2009. "Always Room at the Top: Black Students and Educational Policy in Ithaca, NY." PhD diss., Cornell University.

Carter, Miguel. 2012. *Challenging Social Inequality.* Durham: Duke University Press.

Connecting with Cornell: News from the Office of the Vice Provost for Research, Summer 2002.

Cromartie, John. 2011. "Hispanics Contribute to Increasing Diversity in Rural America." *Amber Waves.* https://www.ers.usda.gov/amber-waves/2011/december/hispanics-contribute-to-increasing-diversity.

Forbes. 2016. "America's Top Colleges." 2016 ranking. *Forbes.* http://www.forbes.com/colleges/ithaca-college; and http://www.forbes.com/colleges/cornell-university.

Freire, Paulo. 1974. *Education for Critical Consciousness.* London: Bloomsbury Academic.

Guarnaccia, Peter J., et al. 2007. "Assessing Diversity among Latinos: Results from the NLAAS." *Hispanic Journal of Behavioral Sciences* 29, no. 4: 510–34.

Hall, Matthew, and Jonathan Stringfield. 2014. "Undocumented Migration and the Residential Segregation of Mexicans in New Destinations." *Social Science Research* 47: 61–78.

Kandel, William, and John Cromartie. 2004. "New Patterns of Hispanic Settlement in Rural America." Rural Development Research Report 99. US Department of Agriculture. https://www.ers.usda.gov/.

Karriem, Abdulrazak, and Lehn M. Benjamin. 2016. "How Civil Society Organizations Foster Insurgent Citizenship: Lessons from the Brazilian Landless Movement." *Voluntas* 27: 19–36.

Long, Taylor, 2012. "Rhythmic Roots." *Ithacan*, April 29, 2012.

Martínez, Lisa. 2008. "Flowers from the Same Soil: Latino Solidarity in the Wake of the 2006 Immigrant Mobilizations." *American Behavioral Scientist* 52, no. 4: 557–79.

"Quick Facts: Ithaca, NY." 2015. US Census Bureau. http://www.census.gov/quickfacts/table/PST045215/3638077.

Rogers, Mary Beth. 1990. *Cold Anger: A Story of Faith and Power Politics.* Denton: University of North Texas Press.

Sandoval, J. S. Onésimo, and Bienvenido Ruiz. 2011. "Pan-Latino Neighborhoods: Contemporary Myth or Reality?" *Sociological Focus* 44: 295–313.

Tarlau, Rebecca. 2015. "How Do New Critical Pedagogies Develop? Educational Innovation, Social Change, and Landless Workers in Brazil." *Teacher's College Record* 117, no. 11.

Walker, Edward, and Lina M. Stepick. 2014. "Strength in Diversity? Group Heterogeneity in the Mobilization of Grass Roots Organizations." *Sociology Compass* 8, no. 7: 959–75.

Afterword
The Prophetic Aspiration of the Scholar as Human

SCOTT J. PETERS

Scott J. Peters, the youngest child of working-class, Depression era parents, grew up in a small town nestled in the corn and soybean deserts of the Midwest. He fell in love with stories and storytelling as a child. And music, which he pursued first with trumpet, baritone, and tuba, and then with a Fender Stratocaster. After graduating from the University of Illinois at Urbana-Champaign, he recorded his first album with his band Crayon Rubbings at a recording studio in a converted packinghouse in Denver. He then left the glamorous world of rock and roll for a decade of equally glamorous work as a political activist in Illinois and Minnesota. Troubling questions about higher education's roles in supporting or hindering democracy led him to pursue a PhD in history and political theory with Harry Boyte at the University of Minnesota, which then led him to his faculty position at Cornell University in 1999.

Soon after he began his work at Cornell, Scott's childhood love for stories and storytelling was revived, thanks to his colleague, mentor, and friend John Forester. As a professor in Cornell's Department of Global Development, Scott now uses a range of narrative methods—including oral history—to co-construct and interpret stories about people's life and work experiences. For five years (2012–2017) he served as faculty codirector of Imagining America: Artists and Scholars in Public Life.

In line with the scholar-as-human project, he is most interested in exploring the humanizing power of stories and storytelling. Situating his work in the transdisciplinary field of civic studies, he focuses on the social, cultural, and political dimensions of what is often referred to as development.

When I was just beginning my doctoral work at the University of Minnesota in the early 1990s, my advisor, Harry Boyte, told me the following story:

> A professor of political science asked one of his students to write a list of all the political issues and problems about which she was personally concerned. When she was finished, she brought it to him. "Now," the professor said, "you should pick something that's *not* on this list for your dissertation research."

We laughed at what we took to be the absurdity of the professor's advice. But as I would later discover, both in my research as a historian of American higher education and my experience as a professor, for many, such advice isn't absurd at all. It's wise. And correct. What makes it so is its alignment with a particular way of understanding how trustworthy knowledge and theory are discovered, produced, and developed—a way that's usually described as being "scientific," "disinterested," and "objective." In dogmatic versions of this way of knowing, we are required to bracket or dismiss our concerns and interests, our opinions and convictions, our standpoints and worldviews, our beliefs and values, our emotions and feelings. To be provocative, I would say that we are required to bracket our humanity—to *dehumanize* the inquiry process. In support of this requirement, dogmatic advocates of this way of knowing have succeeded in establishing (and reproducing, as we see in my advisor's story) a norm in the academy that encourages—even celebrates—a sharp separation of the identities of *scholar* and *human*. For those who embrace this separation, the theme of the Mellon Diversity Seminar at Cornell University that led to this book—the scholar as human—doesn't represent an enticing possibility to be embraced. It represents a corrupting danger to be avoided.

In my view, efforts to (re)humanize the academy and academic work by taking up the task of (re)connecting and (re)integrating our identities as scholar *and* human do involve dangers that we must learn to see and avoid. But I also know that there are many things of value to be gained by such efforts. I say *know* rather than *think* or *argue* because I have been engaged in them my entire academic career. The same advisor who told me the story I related above invited me to connect and integrate my identity and work as a civic agent (a more inclusive way of saying *citizen*) with my identity and work as a scholar. I took up his invitation. It opened a life path that has been deeply satisfying to travel. But it's also been deeply difficult—at times almost painfully so—due to critical pushback I've encountered and the challenge of navigating the many dangers, dilemmas, and tradeoffs it has involved.

In this afterword, I'd like to pose and briefly take up a set of key questions about the idea—or, perhaps better put, *aspiration*—of the scholar as human. My questions emerge from the view, shared by the organizers of the Cornell seminar, that the way things are with respect to this aspiration is not the way things should be. And that the vision and pursuit of what should be is, or in powerful ways can be, prophetic.

Here are the questions:

- What's the situation we're in?
- What's the story about how we got there?
- What's the argument about why it's problematic?
- What's the vision of a better place to be?
- What's the theory of change about how we might narrow or bridge the gap between where we would like to be and where we are?

Because the scholar-as-human aspiration is to a significant degree personal, these questions must be taken up by individuals in ways that are grounded in their particular locations, desires, interests, standpoints, worldviews, and convictions. But there are collective dimensions to the aspiration as well, and they call on us to take up the questions together. In doing so, we will need to invite and fruitfully engage differences of many kinds, including perspective and experience. That means that in addition to developing answers to questions posed in singular terms (e.g., "the" situation, "the" story, "the" vision), we will also need to pose and answer them in plural terms: What are the situations we're in? What are the stories about how we got there? What are the arguments about why the situations are problematic (or are not problematic)? What are the visions of better places to be? What are the theories of change about how we might narrow or bridge gaps between where we would like to be and where we are?

The scholar-as-human aspiration isn't new. Named in different ways, it has been a topic of concern, conversation, and debate throughout the history of American higher education. As I was making notes for this afterword, I searched my memory for examples. While I wasn't immediately sure why, what came to mind first was a book I had long ago discovered in my research—*Higher Education and Society: A Symposium*. It was published by the University of Oklahoma Press in 1936. It contains a collection of addresses that were delivered at the Southwestern Conference on Higher Education, held in November 1935 at the University of Oklahoma. A professor of philosophy from the University of Oklahoma named Charles M. Perry wrote the introduction.

After pulling it down from my bookshelves and blowing off the considerable amount of dust that had covered it, I began to read Perry's introduction and the rest of the book. As I read I felt as though I had found a time capsule that was meant to be opened exactly when I had opened it. During a time of great economic, political, and cultural upheaval that in some ways resembles our own, here was a group of scholars and administrators discussing the nature and value of the academy and academic work, arguing as they did so about the changes they thought should or shouldn't be made. Most notably, Perry's introduction sounded an alarm about developments and trends in higher education that are closely related to the aspiration of the scholar as human. Before I take up the questions I posed above in relation to our own historical moment, let's take a look at how Perry implicitly took them up in his.

"To Eliminate the Personal Equation"

Perry opened his introduction by noting that democracy, which he described as the "golden mean between anarchy and dictatorship," depends on education. But, in his view, education in the United States had proved to be a disappointment. It had misled people and failed to prevent them from becoming "dupes of propaganda." Not only the public schools, but colleges and universities of all types, he argued, had "failed to make as large a contribution to the success of democracy as might be expected." He spent the rest of his introduction telling a story about misguided change and reform in American higher education, from the colonial period to the mid-1930s, and laying out what needed to be done, from his vantage point, to open a path for reform.[1]

Perry's story began with a critique of American higher education's focus during colonial years and the early decades of the Republic. In that period, he wrote, colleges and universities "stressed character at the expense of content." They focused on "why" over "what." He argued that this began to change during the mid-nineteenth century, and not for the better. According to him, things began to flip to the opposite position around 1840, when institutions of higher learning "began to stress content at the expense of all other considerations," turning their focus to "what" over "why." Things devolved, Perry claimed, to a "sole recognition of content"—of "what"—through three distinct stages. The first stage featured an emphasis on "practicality," which emerged from worries about declining enrollments, a rising industrial economy, and other forces. The second stage featured a focus on science and what he called the "methodology of investigation." The third stage, which Perry characterized as "unexpected," featured the emergence of uncertainty, skepticism, and relativism in theories of knowledge. This was particularly threatening and dangerous, he noted, as it not only disappeared the "why" but also the "what." "The moral and esthetic experience at this point," he wrote, "has the consistency of very thin air."[2]

It is in Perry's characterization and critique of the second stage that we connect most directly with a prophetic view of the aspiration of the scholar as human. "The research worker in every field," he wrote, "rightly attempts to eliminate the personal equation. That which exists is thus utterly disso-ciated from anything subjective. He comes thus to think of all that is con-cerned with his person as suspect and of that which is impersonal as the true and the real."[3]

Interestingly, there's an essay in *Higher Education and Society* that exempli-fies Perry's characterization of this second stage. While he didn't name it, he likely had it in mind when he wrote the passage I just quoted. The essay is by Isaac Lippincott, a Harvard-trained economist who was a professor at Washington University in St. Louis. Titled "Training the Economist of the Future," it's included in a section of the book headed "Higher Education and the Training of the Social Technician." Lippincott wrote it in a collective voice, using the word "our" to speak for the whole of the scholarly commu-nity. "In our capacity as discoverers," he claimed, "it is our duty to discharge that function without prejudice or bias, without an injection of likes and dislikes, and without an eye on tradition. Our likes and dislikes have nothing to do with the case."[4]

Here is Lippincott's conclusion:

> Summarizing, I may conclude: first, our function is to promote the spirit of discovery; second, to sharpen the powers of observation; third, to develop analytical powers; fourth, to encourage accuracy of work; fifth, to learn to check theories with data; and finally to develop a spirit of scholarly neutrality. On the other hand, we must train our students to avoid snap judgment, to repress bias and prejudice, to abandon the vicious ideal-forming habit while in the process of investigations, and to avoid in all our researches the intrusion of personal attitudes. These latter are the attitudes of social reformers. They must be shunned by the man who is imbued with the spirit of true discovery.[5]

It's possible, of course, to give Lippincott's essay a sympathetic reading by noting his commitment to accuracy and his concern about "snap judgment," bias, and prejudice. But it's also possible to give it a sharply critical reading. Perry's introduction offers several key points we might include in such a reading. Let's return to it. After Perry described what the "research worker in every field rightly attempts" to do—"to eliminate the personal equation"— he offered a stinging critique of some of the assumptions behind that action, and a sobering account of its results in and implications for higher education and society. In Perry's view, the assumption researchers make that there is "no teleological principle operating in the material studied" disallows "the objective world to have any values even for itself." This effectively disappears values "from the universe." Working on this and other assumptions, the researcher "becomes the indifferent observer of the passing objective show," he argued. "Being trained not to care what happens, he is beyond good and evil." "It would seem," he went on, "that methodological assumptions could be held strictly subordinate to human interests or if extended to speculation could be disregarded, but so great is the power of habit that, when students are subjected to these requirements years on end, they come to apply them not only to research problems but to their friendships and all other human concerns."[6] Perry proclaimed that the "social effect of this development has been disastrous." In summing up the situation as he saw it in the late nineteenth and early twentieth centuries, he offered a bleak portrait of higher education's failings:

> In society at large during the time in question, mass production and the piling up of profits were being made the main objective. Quantity of material goods and the amount of income were being exalted over the quality of life. Personality, the arts, and social loyalty were being discredited. During this time the higher institutions of learning, paralyzed by uncertainty, weakened by compromises, more than half committed to materialistic standards, deserted the proper interests of mankind. Students were either left to drift whithersoever they would or were encouraged to use the knowledge and skill acquired in colleges and professional schools to serve anti-social interests. In this way democracy has been betrayed by her most trusted helper.[7]

According to Perry, the way out of this situation required the restoration of three abandoned principles. First, despite limitations and inescapable subjectivity, "it is possible," he asserted, "to get dependable knowledge about the world we live in." Second, there are not just things in the universe but values and meaning as well (in his terms, both "what" and "why"). Third, and most important, "the greater values" such as freedom and creative activity "must not be ignored in favor of the lesser." A focus on the "lesser" value of making a living was, in Perry's view, insufficient. "Man is not able to subsist on bread alone," he wrote.[8] People's lives "must be encompassed by beauty and truth and justice. These additional spiritual elements which are so necessary for the complete and happy life involve a utilization of all the social interests as well as an attempt to procure a balanced development of the individual."[9]

With respect to professional training, Perry warned that it was becoming so "practical" that "all social ends" were being "sacrificed to personal ambition." Is it possible, he asked, "to make use of this powerful motivation and at the same time impart a sense of the part which the profession serves in society as a whole?" Noting that, while the planning committee for the Southwestern Conference on Higher Education was meeting, "dust storms had been raging for weeks," he asked if students could be "initiated into a sense of some immediate social need and enlisted in meeting it." Research, in this context, was not to be abandoned, he wrote, but "co-ordinated with human needs."[10]

Perry called for reforms that would embrace and enact a commitment for academic institutions and professionals to attend to "the whole of experience, in a word, to the normal, healthy interests." With vital principles "restored to their proper perspectives," he wrote, "educational reform can be considered intelligently. It is not enough merely to continue with the amassing of a vast compilation of unenlivened facts. It is not enough to develop practical talents alone. Something more is demanded than the gaining of credits. The primary objective of all education must be the cultivation of the student as a human being."[11]

Charles M. Perry: The Scholar As Human?

I've spent a long time reflecting on what Perry wrote in his introduction to *Higher Education and Society*. I see much that I admire and agree with in it, including moments I would characterize as being prophetic. Most notably for this essay, I see a thread that runs through it that connects remarkably well with the singular version of the questions I posed above. I see a sobering perspective on the situation in American higher education during the mid-1930s; a story about how it got there; an argument about how and why it was problematic; and a brief vision of a better place to be. However, beyond the vague move of restoring "vital principles" to their "proper" perspective, I don't see a credible theory of change for how to get to the better place Perry envisioned—or, more modestly, how to narrow the gap between what was and what in his view should be. I also don't see something else: I don't see the word "I" anywhere in his introduction. He didn't say anything about his personal experiences, his personal values and commitments. He wrote in the disembodied voice of the humanities scholar, performing the important role of social or cultural critic without implicating himself in what he was writing.

When I recognized this, I did an internet search to see what I could find out about Perry. The only thing of substance I turned up was a biographical entry in the 2005 edition of *The Dictionary of Modern American Philosophers*. Beyond the usual things that are included in such biographies—when he was born (1876) and when he died (1942), where he was from (Union Township, Michigan), and where he got his degrees (BA from Albion College in 1900, PhD in philosophy from the University of Michigan in 1911)—the entry includes the following interesting facts. He "devoted several years to religious and social service, first as a Unitarian minister in Iowa City during 1914–19, and later as a social service worker in Minnesota during 1919–23." While he was a professor at the University of Oklahoma, he "was equally active in his university and community." He served as state chairman of the American Civil Liberties Union in Oklahoma in 1938 and 39. He was a member of the Norman, Oklahoma, Chamber of Commerce. And finally, to me the most humanizing detail in the entry: "he was an enthusiastic member, and at one time President (1934–5), of the faculty club, where he was an avid member of the square dance group."[12]

Learning these personal details, I went back and reread Perry's introduction, looking for hints of the Unitarian minister, the social service worker, the ACLU activist, the chamber of commerce member, and most of all, the avid member of the square dance group. Did he purposely bracket all these parts of his identity out of his essay, and the knowledge he undoubtedly gained from all his rich and varied life experiences? Or are all these things there in his introduction nonetheless, between or behind the lines, animating, informing, and guiding his scholarship and his voice and vision? And what about other details of his life and personality we don't learn from the biographical entry? Was he struggling to hold on to hope, to prevent himself from sliding into despair and cynicism? Was he at times confused and doubtful about his convictions, his expertise, his talents, his colleagues, his university, his community, his country? And what about the nature and consistency of his character? Did he practice what he preached? Or was his behavior at odds with his ethical convictions?

We don't know. But surely, like all of us, he had weaknesses as well as strengths; flaws and shortcomings; quirks and contradictions. Surely, in other words, he was human. If he was one of my colleagues, and he had asked me for feedback on his essay, I would have advised him to revise it by putting himself in it. In doing so, he might have been able to enhance its trustworthiness and power by making it more real. More *human*.

Putting Myself In

In order to answer the singular version of the questions I posed earlier, in relation now to our historical moment instead of Perry's, I'll follow my own advice and put myself in this essay even more deeply than I already have. As an agitating provocation, I'll use two sentences from an essay that was recently published in the *Chronicle of Higher Education*: "There Is No Case for the Humanities," by Justin Stover, a fellow at All Souls College, University of Oxford.

In his essay, Stover defends a narrow conception of what a university is and should be that aligns remarkably well with the one that Abraham Flexner laid out in 1930 in his book *Universities: American, English, German*. Like Flexner, Stover wants to keep many things out of universities, and out of the work that academic professionals who are employed by them are expected (and allowed) to perform. Among the things he wants to keep out are professional schools (except medicine and law) and most forms of "applied" research, public service, and engagement. Like Flexner did, Stover bemoans cultural and political forces that have led to the inclusion of these things and many others. "What has happened relatively rapidly," he complains, "is the absorption of all areas of human endeavor into the university. One of the premises behind the land-grant universities dotting the American landscape is precisely that they could foster progress and innovation in agricultural science. That may well have been a fine idea, but there is no particular reason that you need a university to improve yields and reduce livestock mortality."[13]

When I first encountered these sentences, I had to stop and reread them. I did so because I couldn't believe what I was seeing. I've spent nearly twenty-five years studying the history of land-grant universities, including the "premises behind" their establishment. What Stover does with these two sentences effectively erases the very thing I find most important and inspiring in land-grant history: *women and men who took up and pursued the scholar-as-human aspiration in prophetic ways that are aligned with the project of building and sustaining a democratic culture.*[14] His sentences accomplish this erasure by removing all considerations of ethics, politics, culture, and power from the "area of human endeavor" he refers to as "progress and innovation in agricultural science." By implying that the nature, meaning, and significance of "progress and innovation" include only material, economic, and technical dimensions (and perhaps also environmental), he strips "agricultural science" of all its cultural and political aspects, including—beyond improving yields and reducing livestock mortality—its human purposes and ends.

There are profound implications here for how we are supposed—and not supposed—to understand the mission, purposes, practices, and identities of scientists and scholars who are employed by land-grant colleges and universities as academic professionals in the agricultural sciences. In short, Stover's sentences render such scholars and scientists as instrumental technicians who perform technical work for measurable material and economic ends (e.g., improving yields and reducing livestock mortality). There are also profound implications for how we are to understand agriculture. In short, we are to understand it as a business with only technical and financial aspects. The "culture" part of the word "agriculture" is to be ignored.[15]

With all this in mind, we can see how Stover is able to claim that there is "no particular reason that you need a university to improve yields and reduce livestock mortality." But here's the catch. If we understand the meaning and significance of the premise of fostering "progress and innovation in agricultural science" as *including* rather than dismissing considerations of ethics, politics, culture, and power, as well as the critical issue of which ends scientists and scholars should and should not be pursuing, then there are many "particular" reasons why we need a university. Such reasons have to do with the things we would include in a vastly expanded and highly complex understanding of what "progress and innovation in agricultural science" not only involves but also requires, particularly when it is taken up and pursued in societies that aspire to be democratic in ways that reach beyond periodic elections to the realm of everyday life and work: namely, a set of nontechnical matters that are normative in nature, including decisions about both the ends and means of agricultural science in land-grant colleges of agriculture. Embodiments of the scholar-as-human identity that are shaped by and aligned with the project of building and sustaining a democratic way of life are in my view prophetic. Those who aspire to this identity would (and in my view should) welcome deliberative and reflective attention to nontechnical matters of cultural purpose and significance as components of their professional work. Those who aspire only to a limited identity of the scholar as technician do not.

Here's an example of a moment from land-grant history when an aspiring scholar as human spoke up—with a critical and prophetic voice—in defense of the larger vision of purpose and work I'm referring to. In an address she delivered at the annual conference of the Association of Land-Grant Colleges and Universities in 1937, a home economics leader from Illinois named Kathryn Van Aken Burns directed a stinging criticism to the men in the audience. She noted that her Illinois colleague Isabel Bevier had recently told her that the development of home economics had given land-grant colleges "an idealism and a cultural element not always recognized, as well as a new measuring stick. Heretofore, results had been largely in terms of livestock or crops; hereafter, the measure of successful agriculture was the kind of life produced." Burns went on to argue, however, that "in spite of much fulsome oratory" about extension's larger cultural elements and purposes, they were "pretty much lost sight of in carrying out the immediate objectives for improved agricultural practices."[16]

Stover's sentences by implication erase such moments or render them illegitimate. The "cultural element" tied to "the kind of life produced" has no place in the narrative his sentences reflect and reproduce about how and why land-grant institutions were founded, what their purposes and work have been and are supposed to be (and not be), and what they have accomplished. The narrative his sentences reflect and reproduce, whether he's conscious of it or not (I expect not), is consistent with a deeply problematic master narrative or meta-narrative that many people have told and reproduced for more than a century. This master narrative obscures historical and contemporary debates and disagreements about three key issues: (1) what the "premises behind the land-grant universities dotting the American landscape" were; (2) what is to be included in—and left out of—their public purposes; and (3) judgments about not only the results but also the *nature* of their work, including its cultural and political meaning and significance.[17]

Knowledge about what is obscured by the master narrative constitutes what Michel Foucault referred to as "subjugated knowledge."[18] In my work as a scholar I seek to unearth and examine such knowledge, using historical and narrative methods. While I never put it this way until I was invited to write this afterword, what I have discovered and examined in my research is in essence a hidden history in the land-grant system of the embodiment of the scholar-as-human aspiration that is closely (and always everywhere, imperfectly) aligned with the prophetic project of building and sustaining a democratic way of life. Importantly, this isn't a historical phenomenon that is finished. It continues in our time in many places, including my own institution: Cornell University.

Sufficiently provoked and agitated, I can now offer brief answers to the first set of questions I posed above: What's the situation we're in? What's the story about how we got there? What's the argument about why it's problematic? What's the vision of a better place to be? What's the theory of change about how we might narrow or bridge the gap between where we would like to be and where we are? I answer these questions from the vantage point of a particular "we": those of us who are employed as academic professionals in land-grant colleges of agriculture.

The situation we're in is, in several important ways, positive and inspiring. But it's also deeply troubled and troubling. I'll briefly elaborate, drawing on oral histories of faculty members' life and work experiences that I have co-produced with many colleagues and students.[19]

The situation we're in is one in which many scholars and scientists are establishing relationships with others—in and beyond their fields, and in and out of the academy—in pursuit of projects and purposes that offer them a deep sense of significance and meaning (or that they interpret in ways that provide them with a deep sense of significance and meaning), including but not limited to the project of building and sustaining a democratic culture and way of life. They are taking part in community life not only as scholars and scientists but also as interested rather than disinterested human beings, motivated and propelled by human emotions, passions, commitments, hopes, and fears. In different ways and combinations that fit their own distinctive likes and dislikes, they are reveling in the joy of connection, of communion, of collaborative public work, of larger social or cultural purpose, of discovery, of the freedom to follow their curiosity. They are mentoring and supporting each other and their students and nonacademic colleagues and partners as human beings with lives that are larger and more complicated than the positions they occupy and the roles they are assigned and expected to play. And they are doing all these things imperfectly and unevenly—sometimes successfully and sometimes not; sometimes with admirable humility, generosity, and gratitude, and sometimes not; and sometimes in ways that are connected to and consistent with their interpretations of what "the land-grant mission" obligates them to care about and be, and sometimes not.

In other words, despite their failings and imperfections, land-grant colleges of agriculture comprise an institution in which the scholar-as-human aspiration already exists. *This is a key aspect of the situation we're in.* I know this not only from my research but also from my personal experience. I embrace and pursue the aspiration myself, with many colleagues. It adds meaning and significance to my work and life.

As I've noted, the situation we're in isn't all good. In many ways it's troubled, and troubling. Those who embrace and pursue the scholar-as-human aspiration in land-grant colleges of agriculture (and elsewhere) often find themselves up against counterforces that not only discourage but also disrespect, discredit, marginalize, and even undermine them. These counterforces, which come both from within and outside of academic institutions and fields, include and involve the enforcement of the separation of scholar and human identities as the "correct" way of being and working. Enforcement is enacted through such things as tenure and promotion decisions, review processes for publication and funding, graduate program selection and training, and much more. As a result, the scholar-as-human aspiration is difficult to pursue and sustain. I think it's fair to say that those who do manage to pursue it against its many counterforces are an endangered species. And part of what is troubling about that is the relative lack of attention it is receiving as an issue or problem.

It's a long story, how we got to the situation we're in. It's not a story of the loss of a golden age. It's a complex, ongoing drama with tragic and prophetic qualities. It goes something like this: From the very beginning, some women and men who were hired as academic professionals in land-grant colleges of agriculture pursued their hunger to be whole persons in ways that aligned with the scholar-as-human aspiration. Some of them did and said remarkable things. Some of what they did and said was prophetic, in that it revealed ways that unfulfilled possibilities and commitments might be achieved—especially those tied to the project of building and sustaining a democratic culture and way of life, in everyday places that included farms and small rural communities. Struggling with and against all kinds of counterforces, and their own weaknesses and faults (e.g., their racism, sexism, selfishness, greed, laziness, and antidemocratic tendencies), many of them fell short or were co-opted or fired. But many also persevered in at least partially admirable ways. In doing so they made an imprint into the culture of land-grant colleges of agriculture that continues to this day, just as counterforces made enduring imprints as well. In essence, the story of how we got to the situation we're in today with respect to the scholar-as-human aspiration is a story of tensions and battles between competing forces and visions. Importantly, the story isn't finished. It hasn't yet become *only* a tragedy. It still has prophetic qualities.

Good prophetic stories don't just offer visions of what can and should one day be. They also offer critiques of what is. And they illuminate paths for moving from what is to what can and should be. Paths that can be understood as theories of change.

To all-too-briefly finish the line of questions I posed above, writing now as a member of a larger "we" that includes scholars from many fields and disciplines working for many different kinds of colleges and universities, below are some of the things I would include in a prophetic story about the scholar as human.

First, here's a brief critique of what's problematic about the situation we're in with respect to the aspiration of the scholar as human. In short, the forces and realities that make up the situation we're in—which we all too often collaborate with or surrender to—are restraining the range of possibilities for our work. And they're doing so in ways that diminish and sometimes even damage its value, its impact, its meaning and significance (including its personal satisfaction), and its trustworthiness. *Our* value, impact, significance, and trustworthiness. To borrow from Charles M. Perry, the forces that are combining to create the situation we're in are diminishing and damaging our ability to pursue the primary objective of "the cultivation of the student as a human being." Of the *scholar* as a human being, since scholars are by definition students. They are also combining, as they were in Perry's time, to elevate lesser over greater values and to betray what, I think we should say more modestly than Perry, has never actually been democracy's "most trusted helper" but rather one of its most important resources.

Second is a vision of what can and should one day be. Here I need to address a flaw in this essay. I've left too much to readers' imaginations, putting me at risk of being misunderstood. Readers may suspect that my vision of what should be is the scholar as political protester, activist, or advocate. The scholar who abandons objectivity and science and functions as a sloppy relativist or a propagandist.[20] The scholar who abandons her laboratory, library, or studio and takes to the streets. But these things are not what I have in mind. My vision of what should be is the scholar and scholarly work—scholarship, the methods and purposes of scholarly inquiry, and our institutional cultures—freed from the restrictive shackles of dogmatic, either-or, zero-sum thinking. Thinking that is at its core dehumanizing because it dishonors and disrespects difference and dismembers not only our identities but also our very beings. My vision of what should be dissolves damaging either-or thinking and opens up rather than shuts down difference, enabling, for example, scientists to be both in the lab and in off-campus communities if they wish to be, without being punished for it. But my vision is also of a robust and rigorous culture of debate and discourse and the pursuit of high standards of quality and responsibility. The scholar-as-human role, as I envision it, is fruitful, responsible, and satisfying, all at once. But it isn't inherently or automatically so. It requires practice and support. It requires us to broaden our understandings of what counts as fruitful and productive, responsible and satisfying. And it requires us to promote and defend these things against many forces that seek to squash them.

Third, a path for closing or narrowing the gap between what is and what should be. As I have stated, my view of the situation we're in includes the inspiring and hopeful truth that the prophetic aspiration of the scholar as human isn't merely a dream. It's a living, breathing reality, already here among us. And not just in land-grant colleges of agriculture. Therefore, a critical element in a theory of change that can narrow the gap between what is and what should be is to find ways to learn from and with the prophets who are already among us. To support them and join with them in our own distinctive ways. The most powerful practice we can engage in for operationalizing this element is the practice of storytelling, using rigorous methods of inviting, hearing, constructing, and interpreting stories from our life and work experiences to illuminate breakthroughs as well as barriers, successes as well as failures, dangers and dilemmas as well as possibilities and epiphanies.

This is both an individual and collective practice. I'm convinced that it's indispensable for the development and testing of effective theories of change. I'm also convinced that our theories of change must always be contextually and situationally sensitive. There can never be a single theory of change that works for all people in all places, for all disciplines and fields, at all times. The helpfulness of stories is not that they tell us "how to do it," then, but rather that they can open our imaginations to possibilities as well as perils, in ways that enhance our sensitivity to the many social, cultural, and political dimensions of our work and experiences. In other words, to its *human* dimensions. Above all, then, the scholar as human is a storyteller, a story listener, and a story interpreter, strong in her conviction that despite their many shortcomings, and despite their dangers, stories are valuable and indispensable. We desire them, tell them, and use them to give our lives and work meaning. And the more we live our lives in virtual reality bubbles, the more we long to tell and hear them in person, face-to-face. As professional storyteller Dan Yashinsky has eloquently observed: "People have a new desire to reconnect to their own voices, memories and stories. We've come to realize that we can't double-click on wisdom. You must spend time listening, and what you must listen to are stories told by word of mouth. The human race has never found a better way to convey its cumulative wisdom, dreams and sense of community than through the art and activity of storytelling."[21]

As a move or practice, storytelling may sound like a weak and ineffective ingredient in a theory of change, especially considering what we are up against. If it's the only thing we do, it *will* be weak and ineffective. But I can report with conviction that it holds tremendous power and value. I know because I've both facilitated and participated in it with my colleagues and students here at Cornell and in many other places during my five-year term (2012–17) as faculty codirector of Imagining America: Artists and Scholars in Public Life. But I have yet to succeed in developing and testing a full theory of change that moves beyond storytelling and interpretation. That's not something I or anyone else can do alone. It's an organizing project, with both intellectual and political dimensions.[22] I'm hopeful that we're entering a time when such work can be taken up. And I'm eager to join it.

Spiritual Elements and Values

To conclude, I want to flag an element in the scholar-as-human theme that is particularly important to me—spirituality—knowing, as I do so, that many will likely be troubled by it. Using a problematic gendered voice, Charles M. Perry noted it in his introduction to *Higher Education and Society*. "Man is not able to subsist on bread alone," he wrote. Our lives must be "encompassed by beauty and truth and justice." These and other "spiritual elements" were in his view "necessary for the complete and happy life," because such a life involves "a utilization of all the social interests as well as an attempt to procure a balanced development of the individual."[23] When I read these passages from Perry's introduction while I was working on this essay, I immediately thought of my favorite passage from Ruby Green Smith's history of Cornell University's extension work, published in 1949 under the evocative title *The People's Colleges*: "Extension workers need to have faith in spiritual values and to recognize the human relationships that contribute to what the ancient Greeks called 'the good life.' They should believe that in the kind of homes, farms, and industries which are the goals of Extension service 'man cannot live by bread alone'; that it is not enough for people to have food, shelter, and clothing—that they aspire also to find appreciation, respect for individuality and human dignity, affection, ideals, and opportunities. These are the satisfactions that belong to democratic living."[24] I carry this passage from Smith's book with me every day. I see it as a core teaching from an unfinished script with a prophetic storyline. I love how it humanizes the people that land-grant institutions like Cornell are supposed to work for and with. And I love how, when we implicate ourselves in it as academic professionals, it can inspire and humanize us. In the end, I think most people who join the academic profession long to experience and support the satisfactions Smith wrote about in 1949, though for too many they have not been awakened and affirmed. Unfortunately, all too many are still being discouraged by professors who ask their students to pick topics to work on that are not on lists of issues and problems about which they are personally concerned. In other words, lists of things they care about.

I'm blessed to have had an advisor who didn't do that to me. And I'm blessed to have many colleagues at Cornell and elsewhere who serve as exemplars of the prophetic aspiration of the scholar as human, imperfect as they all may be. Colleagues in such disparate fields as plant breeding and philosophy, engineering and the humanities, horticulture and law, who take up work on things they care deeply about, boldly, responsibly, and productively, with humility and pleasure, on and off their campuses. They all have stories to tell. We need to make space and time for listening, and in response, for developing and testing a theory of change for narrowing the gap between the world as it is and the world as we would like it to be.

Notes

1. Charles M. Perry, introduction to *Higher Education and Society: A Symposium* (Norman: University of Oklahoma Press, 1936), 1.

2. Ibid., 1, 2, 3. There are, of course, plenty of reasons to critique Perry's characterization of (and story about) American higher education in colonial and early Republic years. For some of them, see Roger L. Geiger, ed., *The American College in the Nineteenth Century* (Nashville: Vanderbilt University Press, 2000).

3. Ibid., 2.

4. Isaac Lippincott, "Training the Economist of the Future," in Perry, *Higher Education and Society*, 177. For a book-length elaboration of Lippincott's positivist and narrowly technocratic view of the social sciences, see George A. Lundberg, *Can Science Save Us?* (New York: David McKay, 1947).

5. Lippincott, "Training the Economist of the Future," 179–80.

6. Perry, introduction to *Higher Education and Society*, 2.

7. Ibid., 3.

8. We can, of course, read Perry's paraphrasing of the biblical passage from Mathew 4:4 critically, as a collaboration with and reproduction of oppressive power dynamics that turn people's attention away from economic injustice and material depravation. In my judgment, such a reading isn't warranted here.

9. Ibid., 4, 5.

10. Ibid., 6, 8.

11. Ibid., 8, 5.

12. John J. Tilley, "Perry, Charles Milton," in *The Dictionary of Modern American Philosophers* ed. John R. Shook and Richard T. Hull (Bristol: Thoemmes Continuum, 2005), 1911–12.

13. Justin Stover, "There Is No Case for the Humanities," in *Chronicle of Higher Education*, March 23, 2018.

14. It is critically important for us to avoid both romanticizing and demonizing land-grant institutions, and the people who have worked as academic professionals in them. One tragic dimension of land-grant history—the original theft of indigenous land—has recently been highlighted through a project that located the acres that were stolen and distributed. See Robert Lee and Tristan Ahtone, "Land-grab Universities," *High Country News*, March 30, 2020, https://www.hcn.org/issues/52.4/indigenous-affairs-education-land-grab-universities.

15. The word *agribusiness*, which was allegedly coined in 1957 by two Harvard economists, captures this erasure. See https://en.wikipedia.org/wiki/Agribusiness.

16. Kathryn Van Aken Burns, "The Contribution of Home Economics to the Agricultural Program." In *Proceedings, Fifty-First Annual Convention, Association of Land-Grant Colleges and Universities* (New Haven, CT: Quinnipiack Press, 1937), 51.

17. For a discussion of the land grant master narrative and two of its counter-narratives, see Scott J. Peters, "Storying and Restorying the Land-Grant Mission," in *The Land-Grant Colleges and the Reshaping of American Higher Education*, ed. Roger L. Geiger and Nathan M. Sorber, Perspectives on the History of Higher Education, vVol. 30 (New Brunswick, NJ: Transaction Publishers, 2013), 335–53.

18. See Michel Foucault, "Two Lectures," in *Power/Knowledge: Selected Interviews and Other Writings, 1972–1977* (New York: Pantheon, 1980), 78–108.

19. As examples, see Scott J. Peters, *Democracy and Higher Education: Traditions and Stories of Civic Engagement* (East Lansing: Michigan State University Press, 2010); and Scott J. Peters, Theodore R. Alter, and Timothy J. Shaffer, eds., *Jumping into Civic Life: Stories of Public Work from Extension Professionals* (Dayton, OH: Kettering Foundation Press, 2018).

20. Sandra Harding's work has been especially helpful to me in developing a new way to understand the nature and meaning of objectivity in research. See especially Sandra Harding, *Whose Science? Whose Knowledge? Thinking from Women's Lives* (Ithaca, NY: Cornell University Press, 1991), and Sandra Harding, "Should Philosophies of Science Encode Democratic Ideals?", in *Science, Technology, and Democracy*, ed. Daniel Lee Kleinman (Albany: State University of New York Press, 2000). On the closely related theme of trustworthiness, see Naomi Scheman, "Epistemology Resuscitated: Objectivity as Trustworthiness," in *Engendering Rationalities*, ed. Nancy Tuana and Sandra Morgen (Albany: SUNY Press, 2001).

21. Dan Yashinsky, *Suddenly They Heard Footsteps: Storytelling for the Twenty-first Century* (Jackson: University Press of Mississippi, 2004), 4.

22. The theory and practice of broad-based relational organizing is particularly useful in higher education. See Maria Avila, *Transformative Civic Engagement through Community Organizing* (Sterling, VA: Stylus Publishing, 2018).

23. Perry, introduction to *Higher Education and Society*, 4–5.

24. Ruby Green Smith, *The People's Colleges* (Ithaca, NY: Cornell University Press, 1949), 544.